Educator's Guide
To Personalized
Reading Instruction

EDUCATOR'S GUIDE

TO PERSONALIZED

READING INSTRUCTION

by

WALTER B. BARBE

Professor and Head of
Special Education Department
Kent State University

Englewood Cliffs, N.J.
PRENTICE-HALL, INC.

Thirteenth Printing .. December, 1971

PRINTED IN THE UNITED STATES OF AMERICA

B&P

DEDICATION

Believing that the best education for children comes from community-school co-operation, the author dedicates this book to an outstanding group which has given continuing encouragement and support to the improvement of reading instruction:

THE JUNIOR LEAGUE OF CHATTANOOGA, TENNESSEE

Preface

The purpose of this book is to provide classroom teachers with an introduction to a new method of teaching reading. The author sincerely believes that no one method of teaching reading will be successful with all children, but that the resourceful teacher who uses a variety of methods to teach reading will have the most success. The author does not intend to imply that this is the only method by which reading should be taught to all children, for flexibility in methodology is a most important characteristic of a good teacher.

The material in the book is not intended to present only information which would be helpful to teachers using the personalized method of teaching reading. Included is information intended to be helpful to all teachers, regardless of whether or not they incorporate the personalized reading program into their everyday instruction. The sections on determining the reading levels of children, selecting reading material for children and the skills check lists, it is hoped, will be helpful to all elementary school classroom teachers.

The author's long association with the Junior League Reading Center of the University of Chattanooga accounts for the dedication of the book. In addition to the support of this group, however, the teachers with whom he worked, and who worked particularly on the skills checklists with him, deserve special thanks. Mrs. Jewell Rudicil, Mrs. Dorothy Nichols, Mrs. Jane Still, Mrs. Mildred Chapman, Mrs. Evelyn Orr, Mr. Jack Carr and others contributed advice, ideas and encouragement. The public schools of Hamilton County, Tennessee provided the classrooms, inspired teachers and willing children who aided the author in developing the ideas expressed in this book.

Credit for the name "personalized reading" goes to Dr. Eric Thurston of Northwestern Louisiana College, Natchitoches, Louisiana, and making clear the need for such a book as this goes to the School of Education of the University of Kansas City, for whom the author has conducted workshops.

Much more than just a secretary, Mrs. Louise Tone probably made this book possible by finding for me the time to write, keeping the goal before me, and being a friend. My son, Freddy, gave me both the determination to put my ideas into book form and the confidence that I would have at least one uncritical reader.

In the final days of preparing this manuscript, the author moved from Tennessee to Ohio. To the entire staff of the Special Education Department of Kent State University, the author expresses his thanks for the patience which they displayed, making his beginning months so pleasant. No amount of appreciation is sufficient for Miss Mary Lou Englehart who typed the final draft in the form that made it acceptable to the publisher.

Table of Contents

Educator's Guide

To Personalized

Reading Instruction

Chapter One

Introduction

The teaching of reading is recognized by all classroom teachers as the most important task of the elementary school. The child who learns to read well will very likely encounter little difficulty in all academic subjects. While it is true that the poor reader is frequently said to be good in arithmetic, this is only in comparison with his reading ability. Careful checking of these poor readers who are good in arithmetic clearly indicates that they are usually also deficient in arithmetic, but not quite so severely.

Many teachers interested in improving their ability to teach reading are turning to a different approach known as Personalized Reading Instruction (P.R.I.). Variations of this method or procedure have been labeled "individualized reading," "self-selection," "reading by invitation" and "free-choice," but they are all essentially similar in one particular respect—basal readers are *not* used, except in an incidental or supplementary manner in order to present a particular skill. In the Personalized Reading Instruction program, no child moves from story to story in a basal reader, and then from reader to reader. He learns to read from material of his own choice, with the teacher supplying individual and group skill instruction as it is needed to progress to more difficult reading material.

One might ask why there is a need for a new method of teaching reading. Has the basal reading program failed to do

1

what it set out to do; to teach large numbers of children of widely varying abilities to read? An emphatic answer of "No!" must be given to this. The basal reader approach has been highly effective for many years, and will undoubtedly continue to be successful for many years to come. The proponents of the personalized or individualized method of teaching reading who have developed the attitude that the basal reader program has failed and must be done away with are endangering the chances of personalized reading being given a fair trial.

The extreme position that any one method has failed completely, and therefore must be done away with, presupposes that another method has been found which will completely eliminate the bad features of the earlier program. In such a complex process as learning to read, it is not likely that any one method will ever be found which will be effective with all children. Just as children themselves are different, so must the methods of teaching reading be different. Personalized reading is merely another method of teaching. It is new in that it breaks away from some of the previously held convictions that every child should be taught by the basal reader approach.

The major goal of the Personalized Reading Program, and the reason for its developing as a method of teaching reading, is not that children are failing to learn to read. Even though children are learning to read, in too many instances they are not developing the love of reading which is essential if they are to continue through life using the skills which they have learned. There is certainly reason to question if children are developing the love of reading through the basal reader approach, plus the independent reading periods.

The extent to which children read comic books indicates that there is no lack of interest in reading. One can only question the type of material which children are choosing. The argument that children look at comic books, rather than read them, is actually not true. The pictures do, of course, carry the children along when certain words are too difficult, but careful checking of children's comprehension of their reading of comic books clearly indicates that they are truly reading them.

The enthusiasm with which children enter the first grade,

eager to learn how to read, is too often lost. Maintaining this enthusiasm for school and interest in reading must be a major goal of instruction. It is important that the methods by which we teach children encourage interest and enthusiasm, rather than in any way discourage it.

Teaching methods must not become static, unbending procedures which are above criticism. Individual differences within schools, within classes and indeed within teachers themselves demand different procedures. For any method to become so routine that a teacher dares not try a newer approach is a guarantee of the very thing which we are at last coming to recognize in education as a great danger—conformity, merely for the sake of being like others.

If we recognize that individual differences exist, both in innate ability to learn and in environmental factors which contribute to the desire to learn to read, then it is unlikely that any one type of approach or reading material will appeal to all children. Even though basal readers have attempted to incorporate many different methods of teaching, they nevertheless inherently require that each child read the same type of story. Great care has been taken in the manuals to avoid directing the teacher in such a way that she will teach every child in the same way. When this has been done successfully in some instances, the manuals have been criticized as not providing the teacher with enough guidance. On the other hand, when the teacher has been provided with a program which follows a step-by-step procedure, the manual has been criticized for being too rigid and allowing no flexibility.

Willard C. Olson[1] has established the concepts upon which the Personalized Reading Program is based. These concepts of seeking, self-selection and pacing become very important when applied to the learning to read process. With respect to seeking, Olson states: "The healthy child is naturally active and he is engaged almost continually while awake in an active exploration of his environment. He seeks from that environment those experiences that are consistent with his maturity and his needs." Olson applies this concept to the development of readiness for reading. Discussing self-selection, Olson states: "Throughout

nature there is a strong tendency for life to be sustained by the
self-selection of an environment appropriate to the needs of the
plant, animal, or human being." Pacing, Olson states, "refers to
the acts on the part of the teacher which ensure that each child
is provided with the materials upon which he can thrive and
also to the attitude which expects from the child only that which
he can yield at his stage of maturity."

The application of these concepts to the Personalized Reading Program, or to individualized reading instruction, is obvious. The seeking desire has been expressed in the development
of more and more reading materials of interest to the child.
The cry for high-interest, low ability level reading materials has
actually been only a plea for more interesting material which
children can read. Essentially, it meant that the materials which
were being prepared for children were less concerned about
their interests than their reading ability. Since it is a well accepted fact that children can read at a higher level from materials that interest them, than they can from materials which are
of little interest to them, the question arises as to why such
materials were not developed much earlier, such as the I CAN
READ ALL BY MYSELF SERIES (Random House), *The Cat in the
Hat; The Cat in the Hat Comes Back; One Fish, Two Fish,
Three Fish, Blue Fish; A Ball of String; A Fly Went By; You
Will Go to the Moon;* and many others; I CAN READ SERIES
(Harpers) *Sammy the Seal; Seeds, More Seeds; No Fighting, No
Biting; Danny the Dinosaur; Little Bear; Father Bear Comes
Home;* and still more; BEGINNING TO READ SERIES (Follett)
Nobody Listens to Andrew; Miss Hattie and the Monkey; and
others; TRUE BOOK SERIES (Children's Press) and the I WANT
TO BE SERIES (Children's Press).

Olson's self-selection concept is self-explanatory. Applied to
the reading program, it is little wonder that the program has
been referred to as "self-selection." It assumes that children
have within themselves the ability to select those reading materials which, sometimes for very apparent reasons and other
times not so apparent reasons, meet his particular interests and
needs.

The pacing concept deals with the development of skills and

interest at the rate of the child rather than at some predetermined rate which is applied either to the entire class or to some artificial grouping. Applied to personalized reading, it is essentially the plea for more attention to the development of each individual at his own rate.

Perhaps the greatest danger in trying to describe the Personalized Reading Program is that it will be confused with the highly successful procedure, but not method for teaching reading skills, commonly referred to as independent reading or free reading. In the independent reading period, children are allowed to select their own materials and read. There may be some occasional checking of the children's comprehension, but the goal is primarily one of developing interest in reading. Such a practice is highly commendable; its value lies primarily in its flexibility. In such a practice, however, there is no systematic program of skill presentation, nor should there be. This is the distinguishing characteristic between it and the Personalized Reading Program. Whatever method the teacher uses, either the personalized program or the basal reader program, the independent reading period should be incorporated into it. This will necessarily be a part of the individualized program, but in the basal reader program the independent reading period is highly successful in developing the desire to read. There is a great difference between personalized reading and the independent reading periods which are highly successful for their purpose but can hardly be called reading instruction. Independent reading periods must not be made to take the place of the reading program. This distinction is of the utmost importance, and if it is not clearly understood, will be a major deterrent to the development of the personalized method of teaching reading.

Essentially independent reading means providing a period when children select material which they want to read and are allowed class time to read. They may then report on them orally, or in written form. This is not reading instruction. It does meet the self-selection need described by Olson, but is not a method by which the teacher can instruct the child in reading skills. It is not uncommon to hear classroom teachers respond that they have "been doing personalized or individualized reading for years," when they actually mean that they have been providing their children with a free reading period. The difference between the independent reading period and Personalized Reading Instruction is that in Personalized Reading Instruction the child is given formal instruction in reading skills, careful record is kept of both his progress and the material on which he is working, and he individually spends time with the teacher at scheduled periods to check on his progress.

It is a strange but very real fact that all new programs in reading seem to be successful. Started with careful planning and based upon an understanding of the goals to be accomplished, every report in the literature of different methods reports more success with the new procedure than with the old. Almost amusing is the fact that those trying one method report better success, while others, rejecting that method but trying the different method, report better success. Is this not perhaps the best indication that like everything else, too much doing of the same thing makes it become routine and often sterile? And when teaching becomes routine, it is both more difficult for the teacher and less effective for the children. In discussing one particular program, Olson observed that "change in itself appeared to be beneficial." And so, perhaps a plea for flexibility, if not for change itself, is in order.

One research study, rather surprising in its results, was reported in *The Reading Teacher* by Safford[2] and is well worth thorough examination by those concerned with personalized or individualized reading. In this study, seven 3rd, 4th, 5th, and 6th grade classes, with a total of 183 children, were studied after the teaching was done so that there could have been no influence of being an "observed" group. The conclusions of this study point out the real danger of a new method being adopted without adequately evaluating its effectiveness or determining the procedures which should be followed.

Safford concluded that:

It may tentatively be suggested that: (1) For the majority of the individual pupils in the seven classes, the use of individualized [personalized] reading techniques resulted in lower gains in reading achievement over a period of one calendar year, when contrasted with the results of other methods of reading instruction that are currently being used in this district and throughout the nation. (2) The use of self-selective reading methods achieved no significantly different results with the superior students than with average students. (3) The use of individualized [personalized] techniques resulted in no significant difference in growth between reading vocabulary and reading comprehension.[3]

Only by thoroughly understanding why Safford found such evidence against the personalized method of teaching reading can others assure themselves that they will obtain different results with the personalized method. Essentially, the lack of skill instruction was undoubtedly the major factor in the children's not making so much progress as with the basal reader approach. Carefully following the sequence of skill presentation found in Chapters 7 and 8 would have given the teacher a guide for the presentation of skills. Along with this, the obvious lack of any adequate measure to determine interest in reading means that personalized reading must be evaluated on the basis of skill learning alone, without consideration for level of interest in reading. This is, of course, measuring a method using an inadequate measuring instrument.

The goal of personalized reading instruction is to develop greater and more lasting interest in reading. No claim is made that children will immediately score higher on traditional standardized reading tests, but they must do at least as well. In the long range picture it is believed that even on standardized tests the children will score higher, mainly because of the influence of having read more. But if skill instruction alone is the goal, it is hoped that in the personalized program the same high level of success obtained by the basal reader approach can be achieved.

Development of Personalized Reading

It has long been recognized that the most effective method of teaching a child usually is to teach him individually. This is a sound procedure from both a psychological and an educational point of view. There is no threat to the child's ego by his failure to learn so he does not hesitate to ask questions; instruction can be at the child's level without making any particular issue about whether he is ahead of where he should be or below it; responses can be praised immediately if they are correct or changed if they are incorrect so that there is immediate reinforcement; and the rate at which the material is presented can be determined by the teacher as the child progresses.

One may ask, "Why then did education ever develop into a mass situation?" The most obvious answer is that individual instruction is prohibitively expensive. Even in the state where the expenditure per child is the lowest, assuming that there are thirty in a classroom, the annual cost of educating a class runs something over five thousand dollars. To say that this amount will now have to be spent on each individual child is definitely not likely to happen soon, nor is our economy such that it ever will happen.

But there are reasons other than financial ones which prompted the development of mass education. The limited supply of good teachers must also be a factor, for even in the group situation many localities are finding it impossible to locate enough teachers. But a more important reason for the development of group education is that there are certain kinds of group learning that take place which cannot be taught to an individual separated from all others. The child in a classroom develops desirable attitudes and interests which an individual situation could not possibly provide. Part of a child's learning must be discovering how to get along with others, and if this does not come in his educational setup, then it must be provided in some other way. Then there are certain areas such as social studies which many feel can best be taught to groups, not individuals.

The idea of personalized or individualized instruction is certainly not a new one in American education. The earliest instruction was individual. The monitorial system in eighteenth century England was an attempt to individualize group instruction by the use of monitors. Washburn advocated individual instruction in the Winnetka plan in the 1920's.

An examination of the literature in an attempt to determine the beginning of the current increased interest in the personalized reading program labels it as a product of the 1950's. Certain isolated publications appeared earlier which described or referred to individualized instruction, such as Ray B. Dean's[4] "A Plan for Individual Reading in the Intermediate Grades," in a 1938 issue of *National Elementary Principal* and Daisy M. Jones'[5] "An Experiment in Adaption to Individual Differences," which appeared in a 1948 issue of the *Journal of Educational Psychology.*

As early as 1946 Emmett Betts made a plea for differentiated instruction in a chapter entitled, "Levels of Differentiation," in his definitive book on reading, *Foundations òf Reading Instruction.*[6] He identified eleven levels of teacher competency. Zero level is basically the traditional "complete regimentation" in which there is no grouping of children, variation in materials or instruction, based on the belief that all children of the same chronological age should learn the same material at the same rate. The highest level, Level Ten, Betts labels the "unified language-experience approach." He describes this as a continuation of the all-out unit approach, with "attractive library table with books for browsing; a variety of trade books supplementary to curriculum experiences; encouragement of home library and recreational reading; *basal textbooks in all school subjects used primarily as references* (italics my own); basal workbooks used to meet specific needs of pupils; handbooks of style used as references; curriculum experiences organized in large areas."

The Maury School Staff of Richmond, Virginia, *Teaching Reading in the Elementary School,*[7] and Willard Olson's[8] discussion of growth patterns of children in 1948 in *Child Development* contributed to this new interest. The 1940's was perhaps a period of some discussion about individualization of reading instruction. As David H. Russell and Etta E. Karp[9] wrote in 1950, "During the last ten years reading programs have increasingly given attention to individualized methods of instruction and a wide variety of reading activities leading to well-rounded reading abilities and interests."

So if the 1940's saw the beginnings of interest and experimentation in individualized reading instruction, the 1950's saw the full development of the idea. Starting slowly in the early 1950's, the professional literature has given more attention to the personalized or individualized method of teaching reading until now there is hardly an issue of a journal in elementary education which does not carry accounts of another program of personalized or individualized reading instruction.

In *Teaching Children in the Middle Grades,* Burrows[10] states that "the question is no longer whether but how to individualize instruction." Her discussion of a classroom situation is perhaps the first reference to the individualized method in a book for teachers. Included in Burrows' discussion is a five-day account of procedures in an individualized reading program which should be of much help to the teacher just beginning such a program.

The Association of Childhood Education gave considerable attention to the individualized method of teaching reading in a 1956 publication entitled *Reading*[11] and reprinted some of this with additional material in 1959 in a pamphlet entitled *More About Reading.*[12] The appearance of a publication entitled *Individualizing Reading Practices*[13] in the Practical Suggestions for Teaching series of Teachers College, Columbia University, in 1959 has added momentum to this movement.

A film on an individualized reading program, prepared by Teachers College, Columbia University, is an excellent introduction to this new procedure. The providing of reprints and unprinted mimeograph accounts of individualized reading programs by the Language Education Division of Pennsylvania State University has also spurred this movement forward.

The first book on individualized reading instruction as a method for teaching reading, written by a pioneer in this field, Jeannette Veatch, [14] is *Individualizing Your Reading Program.* Jacobs states in the preface that the book is helpful both to teachers who are already using the personalized or individualized reading practices, as well as to those who want to learn more about this "promising practice."

Veatch's book is divided into two, actually three, parts. Part

One deals with the description, direction, and philosophy. This part essentially describes what this new method of teaching reading is and was written by Veatch herself. Part Two is a series of some eighteen articles written by various people in the field either describing programs or philosophy of the programs. Another section of the book, although not labeled as Part Three, is the appendix. This is particularly valuable because it includes such things as a sample of teacher's record, and a sample profile chart.

Any teacher beginning a program of personalized reading would do well to examine thoroughly Veatch's book. Careful distinction is made between the recreational library and the personalized program itself. Veatch points out that in using an individualized approach, there is a daily period of instruction, continual instruction, a concern for skill development and frequent opportunities to read orally.

The April 1960 issue of *The Reading Teacher* devotes much attention to the personalized or the individualized method of teaching reading. In addition to a report of an experiment, and an evaluation of a reading program, a very complete bibliography is presented by Sartain.[15] In addition to thirty-eight references, Sartain includes an additional thirty-six on descriptions of individualized procedures. Rather than just a listing of publications, which in itself is valuable, Sartain relates them most effectively. Under a section entitled "Opinions Differ," Sartain discusses the fact that there are differences of opinion as to how personalized reading should be used. The essential difference seems to be whether the vocabulary should be carefully controlled, as it is in the basal reader, or whether personalized or individualized reading might be a better means of developing interest. He points out that although the individualized or personalized program "does not presuppose a laissez-faire attitude; however, several descriptions of programs of infrequent brief conferences cause one to wonder about the thoroughness of skills work." Another heading entitled "The Research Is Meager" points out that there has been little actual research which clearly demonstrates the effectiveness of one program over the other. As Sartain suggests "confronted with these inconsistent views and findings, the teacher should weigh carefully the evidence already in and be alert to note new evidence, especially of an experimental and unbiased nature."

In an article by Staiger,[16] entitled "Some Aspects of Individualized Reading," a plea is made to make use of the best ideas for teaching reading wherever possible. He points out that the problems in this new method are (1) the need for a quantity of books and (2) the need for "a teacher who is competent to deal with the diverse needs of the children that are in her group." While these problems may be somewhat greater in this new method, they are also problems which exist in any reading program, and this solution depends upon a resourceful, skilled teacher.

SUMMARY

Personalized Reading Instruction is a new method of teaching reading which does not follow the traditional plan set up in the basal reading series. Based upon Olson's concepts of "seeking, self-selecting and pacing," this new method allows children to select their own reading materials, but then offers them skill instruction in flexible groups using a wide variety of reading material.

The need for a new method does not mean that the old method has failed. It merely means that as flexible teachers, seeking to help every child in the learning to read process, we must be ever alert to new developments. Whether the teacher changes over to the personalized method entirely, whether she adapts it to her particular situation, or even if she does no more than learn more about it, she should nevertheless be informed about the first really major development in reading methodology in at least twenty-five years.

References

1. OLSON, WILLARD C., "Seeking, Self-Selection and Pacing in the Use of Books by Children," *Packet,* (Spring, 1952). Boston: D. C. Heath and Co., pp. 3-10.

2. SWAFFORD, ALTON L., "Evaluation of an Individualized Reading Program," *The Reading Teacher,* Vol. 13, No. 4 (April, 1960), pp. 266-270.

3. *Ibid.,* p. 269.

4. DEAN, RAY B., "A Plan for Individual Reading in the Intermediate Grades," *National Elementary Principal,* 17:557-63, July, 1938.

5. JONES, DAISY M., "An Experiment in Adaption to Individual Differences," *Journal of Educational Psychology,* Vol. 39, (March, 1948), 257-272.

6. BETT, EMMETT A., *Foundations of Reading Instruction.* American Book Company, 1954.

7. THE MAURY SCHOOL STAFF, Richmond, Virginia, *Teaching Reading in the Elementary School.* Richmond, Virginia: Hinds, Hayden, and Eldridge, Inc. Copyright, 1941, by the American Education Fellowship, 42 pp.

8. RUSSELL, DAVID AND KARP, ETTA E., *Reading Aids Through the Grades.* New York: Bureau of Publications, Teachers College, Columbia University, 1951, p. 4.

9. BURROWS, ALVINA TRUETT, *Teaching Children in the Middle Grades.* Boston: D. C. Heath, 1952, pp. 165-201.

10. "Reading," 1956-57 Membership Service Bulletin No. 98, Association for Childhood Education International, 1956, 32 pp.

11. "More About Reading," 1959-60 Reprint Service Bulletin No. 29, Margaret Rasmussen, Editor, Association for Childhood Education International, 1959, p. 32.

12. MEIL, ALICE (editor), "Individualizing Reading Practices," No. 14, *Practical Suggestions for Teaching.* New York: Bureau of Publications, Teachers College, Columbia University, 1959.

13. VEATCH, JEANNETTE, *Individualizing Your Reading Program.* New York: G. P. Putnam's Sons, 1959, 242 pp.

14. SARTAIN, HARRY W., "A Bibliography on Individualized Reading," *The Reading Teacher,* Vol. 12, No. 4 (April, 1960), 1960, pp. 262-265, 270.

15. STAIGER, RALPH, "Some Aspects of Individualized Reading," *Education,* Vol. 88, No. 9 (May, 1960), p. 528.

Chapter Two

What Is Personalized Reading Instruction?

The choice of the name Personalized Reading Instruction, rather than "individualized," "self selection," "free choice," or any other, is decidedly intentional. The purpose is to provide a descriptive word which explains, rather than adds another word to educational "jargon."

Personalized implies that the reading program is, for each child, adjusted in such a way as to promote the maximum amount of growth. The word "personalized" is not in any way intended to imply that the children never work together in groups, or are somehow always taught by the teacher in a one-to-one relationship. Instead, it indicates that the program is adjusted to the child, which means it may sometimes be individual in a one-to-one relationship between the child and the teacher, or it may be in a group, sometimes including every child in the class. It indicates that the individual make-up of the child is considered, without requiring him either to adjust to the interest and rate of other children in the group or to exclude the possibility that there will be children at various times who can benefit from working together and sharing both the instruction of the teacher and one another's interest.

The term personalized is different enough from the term independent to avoid confusion. In the Personalized Reading Program, formal instruction is an essential part. In independent reading, formal instruction is most often not present.

14

Use of other terms, such as "individualized," does not make this distinction clear.

Labels, in themselves, have little meaning. Their goal should be to clarify rather than to confuse. Unfortunately, the term "individualized" has been given widespread recognition. But, as one author has pointed out, individualized reading is not a method. It may well be that this will distinguish the Personalized Reading Program, which is a distinct method, from the less specialized term "individualized".

As the title implies, personalized or individualized reading instruction is essentially a program which teaches the child how to read on an individual basis. As Jeannette Veatch[1] states: "Briefly, this new reading program . . . is based upon the idea that children can and do read better, more widely, and with vastly increased interest, when allowed to choose their own reading materials. . . . The self-selection principle discards the well-known idea of planned, sequential development of level of difficulty programs of basal readers."

It is a well known fact, for example, that bright and gifted elementary school children enjoy biographies. This is obviously explained by the fact that they like to identify themselves with successful people. Children of less innate ability, and often less actual reading ability, until a later age tend to prefer adventure stories. Poor readers usually prefer fast moving, action-filled stories. They usually like a single main character, without the use of too many descriptive adjectives, and they want a fast build-up to the conclusion. In addition to these rather distinctive characteristics and reading preferences of children of various mental levels, the various economic levels from which children come must also be considered. Children from lower economic levels understandably are often impatient with the well dressed, over-indulged child found in many basal readers. Also, the child from a higher economic level often finds the stories, supposedly about his type of child, quite unlike reality.

Since it is not possible for any book to incorporate in the stories all the different types of children who will be reading the material, and meet all the particular reading needs found in any one classroom, the personalized method of reading allows the child to select those materials which do meet his needs and interests.

In essence then the program offered by the personalized reading proponents is one in which each child is allowed to select, from a wide range of materials, those books to read which he is able to read and which he wants to read. The teacher then instructs the child individually using this reading material of his own choice in necessary skills of word attack, comprehension, etc., without use of the traditional fairly static reading groups within the regular classroom.

Veatch[2] states that individualized or personalized reading is the following:

> It is a method devised to meet individual differences.
> Its major feature is that children themselves select their own reading materials.
> It allows children to read at their own rate.
> It permits teachers to work almost entirely with individuals.
> It combines the best elements of recreational reading and one-to-one skill teaching.
> It does away with groups based upon ability. When groups are organized, they are only temporary, with a single specific purpose.

Leland Jacobs[3] makes this clear by stating what the personalized or individualized reading program is not. He states, "in the first place, 'individualized reading' is not a single method, with predetermined steps in procedure to be followed." The very idea of its individual approach makes this apparent, although it is likely that even though Jacobs says that it is not a single method, it is nevertheless emerging as a broad, somewhat freely defined plan of teaching reading.

This particular point will undoubtedly be controversial in education for some time. Just exactly what "method" actually is has long been debated among teachers' groups. The traditional "methods" courses in the teacher-training program have been severely criticized because they failed to teach both "what" and "how" in preference for teaching "why." Although it must be recognized that the "why" is, of course, the basis upon which instruction must be built, both "what" and "how" do have a place in the teacher-training methods course. Whether or not the personalized program is described as a method is actually immaterial. It does meet the qualifications under the "why" heading, and is developing both the "what" and "how" aspects. Undoubtedly the next few years will see even further refinement of these aspects of the program.

"In the second place," Jacobs states, " 'individualized reading' is not a guarantee of the alleviation, for either the child or the teacher, of all the problems and pressures involved in reading instruction." Jacobs' warning is important for individualized reading instruction is no panacea, or even an easier method for the teacher who found the basal reader approach too time-consuming or tedious. It is not unlikely that those teachers who did the best job with the basal reader approach are the ones who may do a still better job with the personalized approach. A new procedure is always threatened by its appeal to those who want change because of their own shortcomings. The personalized approach does not offer this kind of a change.

Beginning any new program is time-consuming and, in its initial stages, requires more effort than the older method which already has been established. No method, the personalized method least of all, is going to take the place of the good teacher. The very characteristics of flexibility, wide interest and teaching skills, and deep understanding of children are even more important in personalized reading than in the traditional basal reading program.

Jacobs also points out that personalized or individualized reading "does not eliminate group reading." It does eliminate the traditional reading circle, or three group plan advocated by the basal reader approach, but establishes in its place groupings either for the purpose of teaching particular skills needed at a particular time or to meet interest needs, with these groups being only temporary for the purpose of solving the immediate problem or need.

For many years the classroom teacher has been told that she should have many different groups for many different purposes. The conscientious teacher, frequently in trying to do this, discovers that by grouping her class she soon has as many different groups as she has children. The idea of flexible grouping, while it is certainly sound philosophy, has not been widely practiced for very obvious reasons. In many situations, experienced classroom teachers have said they could keep up with no more than three groups. When they went beyond this they either forgot what the other groups were doing, or failed to provide true learning situations for one or more of the extra groups. Also, the problem of discipline becomes greater when too many groups are operating at the same time within the classroom.

The Personalized Reading Program offers an opportunity for grouping, for instruction, interest building, skill development, broadening interests, or any other of a variety of purposes. It eliminates the necessity of ever labeling a group "bluebirds" or "airplanes" or any other such term. When children are placed in such groups they often seek the level of this group, and are provided little opportunity for ever rising to a higher group. Only when motivation comes from outside the reading group itself does this change occur. The teacher, by the very organization of the three group system, essentially attempts to keep each child at the level of the group. In personalized reading, such grouping on anything more than a very temporary basis never takes place.

Most important of Jacobs' statements is that individualized reading "does not support a laissez-faire attitude toward instruction, in which the child merely does what he wants to do because he wants to do it." The biggest danger in the individualized program is that it will be confused with the independent reading period, in which the child chooses freely from a wide selection of books those he wants to read and then is allowed time to pursue this interest with perhaps incidental assistance from the teacher. The individualized program is as much a formal program of instruction as any other, but the formal instruction is individualized most of the time.

The personalized reading program is as much a skills program as any other, and the teacher to be effective must have as clearly defined a program of skill instruction as a teacher in the basal program. The teacher must be able to impart the techniques of using these skills to the child in order to help him read material of his own selection. To the extent that she is successful in doing this, her students will progress.

The greatest criticism of the Personalized Reading Program is that it does not allow for a systematic presentation of the skills. This is not necessarily so. It depends, of course, upon the individual teacher's ability both to present the skills and to teach the children how to use them effectively. Chapters 7 and 8 of this book itemize the specific skills which need to be presented at each level. The teacher who is following the personalized method of teaching reading needs some type of guide in order that there will be a sequential development of reading skills. This guide may well come from her own experience of teaching reading, and knowledge of the skills which are essential. In order that certain skills will not be omitted, however, it is recommended that the teacher frequently refer to such a chart as is developed in Chapters 7 and 8. The beginning teacher will, of course, have to depend upon the more formal type of sequential development of skills until she has learned these skills adequately and can develop them on her own.

As with any type of teaching-learning situation, far more than the method itself is the teacher. As Jacobs[4] has effectively said, "Individualized reading starts not with procedures but with a creative, perceptive teacher—one who believes that children want to learn; who thinks with children rather than for them; who basically respects the individual behavior of every youngster; who works with children in orderly but not rigid ways."

Distinguishing Characteristics

The Personalized Reading Program has certain distinguishing characteristics by which it can be identified. In spite of some attempt to prevent it from becoming a distinct method, it is most likely that the next decade will see its development as a separate method. More experimentation with the procedures will perhaps indicate which techniques are more successful, but essentially the real value of the Personalized Reading Program is its flexibility. It is therefore hoped that this method can remain somewhat undefined, or at best not a rigid step-by-step type of program. But to begin a program, it is necessary to do preplanning, and with this idea in mind, the distinguishing characteristics of the personalized program are discussed.

As was mentioned earlier the name "individualized reading" is misleading in that it implies that no group work will take place. This is not true, for many of the activities will involve groups. The term "personalized" seems to describe the program better. The individualized part of the program from which it has taken its name is the establishing of a definite period of time when there is a one-to-one working relationship between the teacher and the pupil. This is perhaps the outstanding value of the Personalized Reading Program, and is certainly a distinguishing feature of it.

Self-selection of material to be read is another characteristic of the program. Each student, sometimes with a form of guidance from the teacher, but often entirely on his own, or using his own discretion and the direction decided upon by the class as to the level of difficulty which the student can expect to enjoy, selects his own material from which he wishes to read and be taught skills. Because this is so definitely a characteristic of the program, the program has been called "self-selection."

From the negative approach, therefore, a basal text is not a part of the Personalized Program. It is not likely that a student would choose a basal text as the book he would most like to read, but if he did so, it would be because of his own particular needs and interests and his work in it would be personalized.

Progress is at the child's own rate, and as has been stated, is in material of his own choosing. Because of the individualized nature of the program, there is no difficulty in teaching the child at his own rate and at the same time trying to keep him up with the rest of the class, or back with the slower students. This is essentially a part of the individualized nature of the program, but is a distinguishing characteristic perhaps because it is so much more easily accomplished in the personalized program than in any other.

Skill instruction, so very important to all children regardless of actual comprehension level, is provided as in any reading program, but is provided at the level at which the child is reading rather than in materials carefully graded, which may be below his interest level. Anyone believing that the Personalized Program is a way out of teaching skills is misinformed, for Personalized Reading Programs teach just as many skills as the basal program. This is the distinguishing characteristic between the Personalized Program and the independent reading period, for in the independent reading period, the goal is reading for pleasure and not necessarily growth in reading habits and formal skills.

The difference in the skills program in the Personalized Program and the basal program is that in the Personalized Program skill instruction is less formalized as to when it is presented. Mainly, in the Personalized Program, skill instruction occurs when the child needs the particular skill, although it is necessary for the teacher to be well enough versed in the different reading skills and the levels at which the need for them will probably develop so that she will not fail to teach specific skills when the pupils need them.

Grouping is a part of the Personalized Program, although not in the traditional three-level pattern. Groups are established for a wide variety of purposes, only one of these being skill instruction. The skill groups are only temporary and will exist only until a particular skill which all of the group needed help on is mastered. Interest groups, for the purpose of discussing a book which has been read by several of the same students, or for the purpose of developing interest in a specific book would probably be very common. The label "personalized" must not be interpreted to mean the non-existence of groups, for group work is a very real part of the Personalized Reading Program.

SUMMARY

In an article entitled, "Another Way to Meet Individual Differences," Miriam Wilt[5] points out the differences and some of the distinguishing characteristics of the personalized or individualized reading program. She states: "Learning to read *is individualized* only to the extent that the child makes his own selection of reading material, with teacher guidance when necessary; he starts where he is, progresses at his own rate, has instruction according to his developmental and remedial needs; and is involved with the teacher in the evaluation of his own progress."

A second major difference, Wilt states, involves materials.

The third major difference concerns the activities of both the teacher and the children during the time allotted in the program to teaching reading.

Jeanette Veatch[6] prepared the following chart to distinguish between the personalized or individualized and the traditional basal approach:

INDIVIDUALIZED READING

vs

ABILITY-GROUPED READING

Individualized Reading	*Ability-Grouped Reading*
Children choose what they read.	Teachers choose what children read.
Wide variety and great numbers of books needed.	One basal text plus supplementary readers needed.
Reading occurs at exact ability level of child.	Reading occurs at ability level of group, hence not so exact.
Slow readers' choices of books unnoticed because of variety of books chosen.	Slow readers stigmatized publicly by assignment of easy books.
No child need hold up whole group.	Whole group must wait for one child.
Reading occurs at the child's own rate.	Reading occurs at rate of child reading orally.
Enthusiasm marked and frequent.	Enthusiasm tepid and infrequent.
Audience situation for oral reading genuine.	Audience situation for oral reading artificial.
Skills taught on an individual basis.	Skills taught on a group basis.
Spontaneous need to "plug" for favorite books is felt.	As material is chosen for child, he has no need to convince anyone else of its worth or value to him.
Reading has purpose recognized and originated by child as intrinsically valuable.	Reading apt to take on teachers' purposes, and give rise to reading for marks, grades, stars, or other extrinsic rewards.
Child reads what he likes, admires, and needs.	Child may read material which he may or may not like, admire, and need.

REFERENCES

1. VEATCH, JEANNETTE, "Children's Interests and Individual Reading," *The Reading Teacher*, Vol. 10, No. 3 (February, 1957), p. 160.
2. VEATCH, JEANNETTE, "Individualized Reading—For Success in the Classroom," No. 654. *The Educational Trend*. New London, Conn.: Arthur C. Croft Publisher, 1954, p. 2.
3. MEIL, ALICE (editor), "Individualizing Reading Practices," No. 14, *Practical Suggestions for Teaching*. New York: Bureau of Publications, Teachers College, Columbia University, 1959, p. 10.
4. *Ibid.*, p. 17.
5. WILT, MIRIAM, "Another Way To Meet Individual Difficulties," *Elementary English*, Vol. 35 (January, 1958), pp. 26-28.
6. VEATCH, "Individualized Reading . . . ," *Op. Cit.*, p. 10.

Chapter Three

The Personalized Reading Program— How Does It Work?

The question many teachers ask when they first hear of the personalized reading program is, "How does it work?". It is important to remember that the personalized program is indeed an individual type of procedure, and each teacher and school must make those adaptations which will best suit his particular situation. Any suggestions as to how to begin, which imply that the personalized reading program is a definite list of procedures to be followed, would be very misleading. Recognizing these limitations, however, certain procedures can be identified as being the way in which a personalized or individualized program was successfully operated in some situations.

> Organizing the classroom
> Collecting reading materials
> Keeping records
> Planning independent activities, group
>   activities and follow-up activities
> The individual interview or conference

Organizing the Classroom

The program of personalized reading for children above the first grade level involves changing over from the basal reader, three-group method, into a type of procedure that is quite different. Even for children in the first grade, it is different from what they have been led to expect from their brothers and sisters or friends who have been in the first grade before them. It is even different from the Sunday School experiences that many of them have had. Veatch[1] suggests that it may be better to shift over one group at a time to the new program, but she apparently feels that the change-over can be "in one fell swoop without the slightest difficulty." For the one-group-at-a-time change-over, she suggests decreasing the amount of oral reading and encouraging children to read on ahead, giving praise and encouragement. Skill instruction is saved until the end of the period and then is offered only as it is needed. As children finish the book, or get ahead of one another, or become bored with the basal reader, she suggests that they be given encouragement to select a book in which they are interested. Gradually the pupils are led into an individualized situation in which they discuss wth the teacher what they have read, or turn to the teacher for help.

Crossley and Kniley[2] reported that before they began their new program, each child went through the basal reader first. This is perhaps one way of preparing the child in case he either left the school in which the personalized program was being practiced, or if the next grade level teacher was on the basal reader program. It has some values, but indicates what will probably be characteristic of most teachers, some reluctance to change over too quickly to a new method without at least going through the basal reader.

The whole-class change-over should be preceded by an explanation of the new type of reading program which is to be followed. Veatch[3] suggests "role playing" as a technique for introducing the new procedures. The student actually goes through the process of selecting a book he likes, reads for a while, then comes up to the teacher to discuss the material and receive any needed skill instruction and then returns to his seat either to read further or to do certain types of follow-up activities which he and the teacher may have decided upon.

"Role-playing" is a highly effective method of introducing any new type of classroom or all-school organizational pattern. It is used at all grade levels, although it is not even recognized as "role-playing." Fire drills, so familiar to the elementary school pattern, are actually the best example of going through a procedure artificially so that students will know what to do when this type of behavior is called for.

Role-playing has been used effectively in aiding children to understand the problems of others. Classrooms where children are responsible for the discipline of their classmates is a type of role-playing. Children themselves are acting the role of the teacher, and in so doing better understand the problems which the teacher faces. This usually results in better behavior on the part of the children.

Role-playing has been particularly successful at the elementary school level. This may be partly due to the advantages found in a self-contained classroom. The periods can be longer, without the always present awareness that a bell will soon terminate the activity, the action can take place with other children with whom those who participate in the role-playing are already very familiar, and the children are usually less self-conscious.

In the personalized reading program, role-playing would be of great benefit in aiding the children to understand what is expected of them. It begins with each child selecting a book which he thinks he might like to read. The teacher then gives assignments to three or four different groups, indicating to one group that they discuss the story, to another that they read silently with the help of a leader, to another group to prepare actual illustrations of stories which they have read and reports which they will then present to the class and to still another group which had supposedly all read the same book a discussion of the most interesting parts of the book, the techniques which the authors used in writing the book, and the like. Other children in the room might be reading individually. The teacher lists the names of the children on the board who are to come to her and places herself in the particular spot in the room where the individual conferences are to be held. One chair is set aside where the next child to come up will wait. The children come up one at a time as they are scheduled to, the teacher discusses with them briefly the types of things she will do with each one of them during the conference, the groups continue and the children are encouraged to behave as they think they might in such a situation. Some of the children, to enter into the situation to the full extent, will immediately begin saying that they don't like the book which they have selected. They are told that they may select another book. As groups finish their activities the children then go back to individual reading, or join in an already preplanned type of group for another type of activity.

The advantage of going through the personalized reading program in the role-playing situation is that the teacher is then free to call out to the entire group directions for doing different types of things. The newness of the plan for the children provides it with an initial boost. The fact that children are not restricted to any one particular seat or spot can be another advantage, for children like to move about. Following the step-by-step procedure in the role-playing situation accustoms each child to the type of thing which he will be expected to do when the program actually begins. The program itself may actually begin immediately after it has been run through in a role-playing situation.

The time spent each day in the reading program will vary from about an hour to an hour and a half. There is no reason to change the time that is usually devoted to reading, although it may be necessary to extend the time slightly if less than an hour has been spent daily.

Sperber's[4] time schedule includes one hour and a half per day for reading. The first ten minutes of the day he explains the seat work to the children. He then interviews ten children a day during the reading period. The remaining twenty minutes, he helps children in their seats. Children are seated in "families" with at least one good reader in each. At the end of each day he checks to see what book each child is going to read the next day.

The reading books are placed either in the shelves or on a table at some point in the room where the children can move to and from with the least amount of disturbance. Some type of grouping of books either by subject or even by level may be used, but is apparently not in widespread usage in operating programs.

Determining the reading level of the child so that books may be available which he can read is one of the tasks of the teacher. This is not so difficult, or indeed even so important as it is in the usual basal reader programs, however. In the process of self-selection of their own reading materials most pupils tend to select those books which they can read without too much difficulty. Generally, it is a practice to prepare the pupils for the degree of ability expected in reading by indicating that for them to be able to read and comprehend they should encounter no more than three or four new words per page. This is sometimes explained in terms of errors and the same number, three or four per page, is considered the maximum number.

Initially it may be necessary for the teacher to provide some guidance in assisting students in making the right selection, but once the pupil becomes accustomed to the procedure, little if any such help is necessary. If a pupil chooses books too hard or too easy, the teacher suggests that he choose other books which will be better for him. It is not absolutely necessary that he always read material at any exact level. When the other pupils have read books which they particularly liked, it is to be expected and desired that he will want to read them, even though they may be below his reading level. On the other hand, books along the line of a pupil's special interest will probably not be too difficult for him even if they are somewhat above his usual reading level.

Children are encouraged to read those books that they are able to read and that they want to read. This is absolutely essential in the personalized program if it is to have any advantage over the basal approach. Some suggestions from either the teacher or other children may be helpful, but are not absolutely necessary if the child feels free enough to try out as many books as he wants until he finds one that he can read and in which he is particularly interested. The child must be allowed to move freely to and from the spot where the books are collected so that he may exchange for another book any book he has finished at anytime.

When the personalized program is first beginning, the teacher should encourage each child to select the type of book which he wants to read and which he feels that he can read. She should then make use of all the information which she has about the child, and his reading ability to determine if his selection of a book is in line with his ability to read and his interest. If it is not, the teacher should discuss with the child individually why this book was selected. It may be that the child can justify his selection. If he cannot, or if it appears as though he has merely picked a book because of an attractive cover or because someone else thrust it upon him, then the teacher should individually help him choose the right book.

Learning to choose the right book will necessarily take some time. It is nevertheless a skill which all children need to develop early. If it is learned well, then the periods which the children spend in the library will not be wasted. Learning to choose intelligently books to be read is a major feature of the personalized program. Although it cannot be measured in terms of any standardized tests, it is nevertheless a valuable and often overlooked skill.

Maintaining order in the classroom during the personalized reading period is, of course, vitally important. It is not meant to imply that chaos exists to any degree, for neither the individual conferences in which the teacher is engaged nor the children who are working individually or in groups will meet with any degree of success if there are disturbances throughout the room. For this reason, it is wise for the classroom teacher to prepare, with the help of the students, a list of rules governing behavior during the personalized reading period.

In the Cleveland, Ohio, Major Work classes, the students show how effectively such rules can be drawn up. The children, by making the rules themselves, are much more willing to obey and to enforce them. The rules will, of course, vary depending upon the size of the room itself, the number of children in the class, and many factors.

Children in the Major Work program in Cleveland form into reading clubs. The rules which they enforce during this period, which they have made themselves, usually include the number of children who can be up at the table selecting new books. Certainly it would not be sensible to have twenty-five children gathered around the table all trying to select books at the same time. A sensible limit would probably be anywhere from three to five children at the library table at any one time. It would also be necessary to place some time limit, so that students will not spend too long a period of time selecting books. The real advantage of the personalized reading program is that the child is actually encouraged to take a book which he thinks he will like, but then may return it at any time if he find that he does not care to read it.

If, within a particular classroom, there is actually a problem controlling the number of children selecting books at the same time, the teacher might have cards numbered from one to five at the table to be picked up by a child who wants to select a book but who must wait until some child leaves the table and then go in order. Assigning a student monitor is another technique. Such artificial devices should not be necessary for any great length of time, however, for the children should develop enough responsibility to understand that when there is already the allowed number of children at the table they must wait their turn.

Obviously, the table or corner in which the books are placed which are to be selected should be either toward the rear or at the side of the room. This would facilitate the children's going to and from the table without interrupting all the other children. It is most likely that such a collection should be as far from the point where the teacher is having her individual conferences as is possible. If the children have difficulty in selecting books, as very young children might have in the early stages of the new type of reading program, the teacher can assign one or two children who are good readers to act as librarians and to aid other children in selecting books which would interest them. This could be a good technique to encourage wide reading on the part of any number of children, so that they will better be able to assist other children in selecting good books.

Up to this point, the personalized program is no different from the free reading period or independent reading which the student already knows, with the exception perhaps that more materials are available to him within his own classroom. The difference comes in that the teacher must now be available for children to come to for skill instruction, checking on progress, comprehension checks or for sharing of the material read. The teacher usually places herself off to one part of the room away from other children with a seat for the child nearby. She may either be at a desk or at a table.

With children in the primary grades the teacher will most likely want to sit with the children either at a table or in a chair their size so that the relationship will not be one across a formal desk. Even with upper elementary grade children, this same procedure is often advisable. In no instances would it be wise to seat the child across the desk if this meant that the child was so far removed from the teacher that he had to speak loudly. Such loud speaking would not only interrupt other children but also tend to embarrass the child if he made mistakes.

The conference should be as nearly as possible a very individual thing, without anyone overhearing. It is likely that the children could hear if they wanted to, but the goal would be to have them so busily engaged in their own activities that they would not care to listen.

There is some disagreement as to whether this period which the child spends with the teacher individually is an assigned, planned thing, or whether it should be entirely voluntary. Some believe that "conferences must be voluntary," but numerous reports on programs in operation describe procedures in which the child is scheduled for his conference with the teacher. The length of the period which the child spends with the teacher individually will undoubtedly vary depending upon many things, but such conferences are usually scheduled for anywhere from five to fifteen minutes. From six to ten children are seen daily, and it is apparently agreed upon that every child should see the teacher individually once every three or four days.

Whether or not the teacher actually schedules the conferences, it seems likely that when personalized reading instruction is first started it would be wise for the teacher to list on the blackboard the names of those children whom she wanted to see on that particular day. Once the pattern is set, then it may be possible for the teacher to become more flexible and allow the children to come perhaps once every three days, choosing the exact time at their convenience. It would, of course, be most desirable to have the children only come when they want to, but this laissez-faire type of procedure could lead into less systematic type skill instruction than is desirable.

The length of time which a child spends with a teacher, varying somewhere from five to fifteen minutes, can be regulated by a rather systematic procedure of what is to happen at this time. The teacher and the class might decide that perhaps three major areas would be covered such as (1) checking new words and word attack skills (2) comprehension checks on materials read, and (3) a brief evaluation of the child's progress. As soon as these three things have been covered the conference is understood to be over. This would make it possible for the conferences to move more rapidly and yet also not lose their effectiveness by seeming to be rushed.

In order that there will be a minimum amount of time wasted between conferences, a seat somewhere nearby, but still at a great enough distance so that the conference is not interfered with, is occupied by the child who will see the teacher next. This seat, sometimes referred to as the "next at bat" or "on deck" chair, is filled either by a volunteer in some situations or the child assigned for the next conference. In the volunteer situation, the teacher must keep careful track so that every three or four days every child is seen, and if a particular child does not volunteer, then the teacher will request that he come up for a conference. While waiting the child continues his reading so that the waiting period is not an unproductive "as soon as the teacher is through, she will be to me" period.

During the time the teacher is having conferences with individual children, those children at their seats are reading silently, doing seat work or discussing in groups the material which they have read. Some teachers assign reading helpers to answer questions which may arise while the teacher is working with a child individually and which cannot wait until the child's conference time.

Collecting Reading Materials

Since the very basis of the personalized reading program is self-selection of materials which the pupil both wants to read and can read, a large supply of books covering many areas of interest and many different reading levels is absolutely essential. The teacher cannot hope to accumulate the many books necessary shortly before the program is to begin, for last-minute substitutions will mean books of less interest and therefore a less effective program.

The teacher beginning the personalized program may ask how many books should be available. It seems that three books per child is a "rule of thumb" which is predominating the thinking of those who are operating successful personalized programs. This would mean a minimum of something over one hundred books within the classroom at all times, and some of these one hundred books will need to be rotating so that at the end of the year there will have been far more than just one hundred titles in the room.

These one hundred or more books will need to be in a wide variety of areas. One program described by Crossley and Kniley[5] tells of marking by color the field which each book specifically covered. Red meant that the book was general literature, while blue meant it was a basic book. Green meant it was science and black meant social studies.

The number of copies of each book will perhaps vary. Apparently three copies of some titles are recommended in the primary grades. Teachers working in personalized programs in the upper elementary grades seem to suggest five or six copies of some books.

It is thought necessary by some teachers to mark the grade level of each book on the outside cover so that students can be guided to their approximate level. This seems to destroy some of the advantage of the self-selection process, however, for this is once again labeling reading levels as much as being in the slow, average or fast group does. If this is necessary, placement of books on specific shelves or tables according to level of difficulty will accomplish the same purpose. It must also be recognized that many of the books will actually be very hard to classify as to the exact grade level because the vocabulary is not strictly controlled.

The range of level of difficulty will necessarily be great. At the higher grade level, the range will have to increase. The teacher will have to judge the range depending somewhat upon her group, but it might be expected that the first grade would include materials from the pre-primer level up to the fourth grade level. Early in the year, the majority of materials should be as low a level as possible, but as the children develop reading ability the teacher will need to collect more books from the first and second grade level. The second grade program will have to go up to the fifth or sixth grade level and by the sixth grade level the range will probably be from first grade level all the way up through adult level books, with emphasis on the books at about sixth grade level.

How can a teacher possibly afford to buy all of the books that will be necessary in such a program? The answer is that in the first place there is no need to buy all of the books that will be needed, although there is certainly an advantage in having as many books as possible that actually stay in a particular classroom. Some books may be borrowed from children or checked out of the library.

The expense involved must be thought of in terms of the amount of money used to buy a single text for each child in the traditional program, plus the partial supplementary books which would probably number at least two or three per child. This money cannot be shifted over to purchasing library type books immediately, but certainly over a period of time, it can be without any additional expense to the school system.

At first thought the teacher might feel that accumulating such a variety of books would be an almost impossible task. Sperber,[8] in discussing a personalized reading program in the third grade, makes this sound much easier when he mentions where his books came from. Each of his students joined the public library and was encouraged to bring books from there. Books were checked out from the traveling state education department library, children brought books from their home libraries on loan for one year, an extra supply of the school library books was checked out, in addition to those checked out on the weekly trip of the entire class to the school library, the school collection of textbooks, supplementary readers and basal readers, books from the college library and second-hand books purchased from the Salvation Army.

In order for the personalized reading program to be successful, books which will interest children must be made available. For this reason classroom teachers must know a great deal about children's literature. Children's literature has long been one of the most popular courses offered in the teacher training program. Those teachers who have not had such a course should either take it from a nearby university, or can actually take the course by correspondence from almost any state university. If the teacher does not possess a wide knowledge of children's literature herself, there is little likelihood that she will inspire her students to love reading and books.

The role of the librarian in a school which is operating a personalized reading program is far more important than in the basal reader type program. If a librarian is available, she can aid the teacher in selecting the right type of books for a particular classroom, as well as books which might interest each individual child. Librarians have long felt that they deserved a more important place in the learning-to-read program than has been afforded in the past. The personalized reading program offers the librarian a real opportunity to be of great service to the classroom teacher.

Keeping Records

It has always been important to keep records of the material which each child has read, the difficulties he has encountered and the success he has had in overcoming these difficulties, the level at which he is reading at various times during the year and his attitude toward reading. In the basal reader program this record, which would have been so helpful to the logical development of the child's skill instruction and development of interest in reading, has been substituted with usually no more than the name of a basal reader and occasionally the page on which the student was reading. For the average child, making average progress, and the above average child who was not allowed to make more than average progress, it was assumed that he completed the reader and the skills at the grade level of the past year and is now ready for the basal reader of the next grade. This may or may not have been the case, but the teacher nevertheless assumed that it was and began with most children at the basal reader of that particular grade level.

In the personalized program, however, there is no such material so that the next teacher will know where to start unless the teacher from the year before has kept careful records, and passes these along with the children, showing materials read and skills upon which the child has worked. In the personalized program, the teacher must be able to remember not only what each of the groups is doing but must now keep careful record of what each child is doing. Only by careful record-keeping can she be sure that the child is making the expected progress, is reading a wide variety of materials, and is benefiting from the instruction itself. The importance of efficient record keeping practices cannot be over-emphasized. This is an absolute essential in the personalized program. Even though the child may keep his own record of materials read, the teacher must keep a careful record of the individual conference and what is accomplished.

The time to keep these records is not after the child has returned to his seat, but at the time he is with the teacher. It is impossible to later recall with any degree of certainty what was done with each child. Unless this is done, it is a certainty that the personalized program will deteriorate into nothing more than an independent reading period.

Folders for each child may be one way in which this information is kept, although this may become unwieldy. An advantage of folders is that they may easily be passed from grade to grade. Vite[6] describes the methods which she uses to keep records and has several such pages reproduced in *Individualized Reading Practices*. Anyone beginning a program should definitely study these pages both to obtain ideas about record-keeping and to understand better the types of activities which are carried on during this period.

Essentially, the information which must be included will be the date of the conference, so that no child will miss having a conference at least once every three or four days. The name of the book which the child is reading and the page on which he is reading should be recorded. The questions he has or the difficulties he has encountered should be noted and any suggestions made to him either to do immediately, or to do after the conference at his seat, should be noted. A comprehension check rating is probably essential at each conference. Notes should be made of any skill instruction which he needs, but which the teacher feels can just as well be supplied later to a small group.

In some situations the teacher has forms with children's names and blank space already prepared. With the child's name at the left of the page, and a place for the date, the skills which the teacher feels are necessary at that particular grade level are listed across the top of the page. (See Chapters 7 and 8.) In this way the teacher is reminded to check each child on these skills and provide practice and instruction in those skills with which the child needs additional help.

As the children are doing their individual reading, they keep a record of the book which they have read either on a card or in their notebook. The pattern which these children are to follow should have been set up before time. The title of the book should be stated with the author's name, the publisher, the date of publication, length of book, general reaction to the book should be stated. As words are encountered with which the child has difficulty either reading or understanding, he lists them. At the time of the individual conference he brings to the teacher his notebook which contains this information, or the cards, so that the teacher may quickly check on the amount of reading that he has done, his selection of materials, the words he has been having difficulty with, and his general attitude toward reading.

The advantage of keeping this information in a notebook is that it is less easily lost. The advantage of having the material on cards is that it may then be filed. As the child reads more books, the cards can then be categorized, and may actually be used by other students to aid them in deciding if they want to read a particular book. Every book which a child attempts, however, whether he finishes it or not, should be recorded. Both from the things that he has read and enjoyed, as well as those things which he has either started and not finished or which he has read and disliked, will come valuable information for the teacher in understanding this particular child.

If a child prepares reading cards, they should be kept either in a file which the child keeps at his desk or, if they are to be used by other children, in a file under each child's name at some place close to the table or shelf where the books are kept. They should not be allowed to be taken from the classroom. As the child prepares note cards and brings them to the teacher at the time of the individual conference, they are added to his file.

The teacher will most likely keep a manila folder on each child. At the time of the individual conference she will probably note the name of the book which the child is reading and the page on which he is reading so that she can keep up with his progress. Any notes concerning the child's attitude toward reading, particular strengths or weaknesses in reading ability, or needs for specialized skill instruction will be noted and placed in this file. The check list for skills by grade level found in Chapters 7 and 8 should be in the child's folder. This folder, together with a record of the books which he has read and the check of his skill should be passed on from grade to grade.

Planning Independent Activities, Group Activities, and Follow-Up Activities

The very principle of the personalized reading program will require that the teacher carefully plan independent activities from which the children will benefit. Basically, the first part of the planning will involve those activities in which the remainder of the class will participate while the teacher is working with some of the children individually. It is important to realize that these activities will not necessarily be individual activities, but that group activities will not be centered around the traditional three—good, average, and poor—reading groups.

Certainly, for at least part of each period when the teacher is engaged with other children, each child will read silently to himself from a book of his own choice. Upon completing a book, he will make a report of the title of the book, its author, and any other information which the class and teacher have previously decided will be helpful both to the child, the teacher and to other children who might want to read the book. The usual type of book report is not considered an activity which will encourage the child to read more and so should be avoided.

The child may join a group of other children who have read the same book to discuss his reactions to the book, sharing with others certain parts which are particularly interesting to him either by telling about them or reading them. He might join a particular group to tell them about the book he has just read so that they will know if they want to read it. Through class planning, certain procedures can be set up which include the things he should tell about the book, how much he might read from the book, and even what things he should not tell.

As the children had their individual conferences, the teacher may have noted the need for specific skill instruction on the part of several of the children. Either on the day she discovers this, or perhaps several days later when she has seen all of the children, she will ask these particular children to join together into a group which will then study the needed skill together. Once the skill has been presented, the group may work on their own either with or without the teacher's individual attention. They may actually work for a while on their own and then come back as a group to allow the teacher to check on how well the skill has been learned.

Essentially, during the individual conference, the teacher is checking comprehension on each child, his oral and silent reading ability, his word attack skills that are needed at that particular level and his reading habits and interests. This is accomplished mostly during the individual conference, with the assignments for individual work and the small group work designed to help him improve in any of these areas in which he may need help, or merely to improve his reading skills and develop his interest in reading.

Remembering what it is the teacher wants to accomplish with

the reading program helps in planning the activities which the students will engage in while she is busy with the individual conferences. Grouping is used in the traditional manner for skill presentation, but the group is formed only for a specific purpose and is disbanded as soon as that single, specific purpose is accomplished.

Interest groups are perhaps the most common type of grouping in the personalized program, and are usually conducted without need of the teacher's being in the group. The reason the student participates in an interest group is either to assist him in selecting material to read, or to allow him to share with others the material which he has read. The procedure to be followed in this type of activity can best be planned in advance by the group itself. The suggested procedure will probably be changed as the children become more skilled in techniques of arousing the interest of the others in the group. There is no particular need for the teacher to be in on such discussions for they are being done not for a grade, but either for the fun of sharing or for obtaining information.

Suggested activities for the remainder of the class during the time when the teacher is working with one student individually include (in addition to reading silently for pleasure and group work on skills and interest) such things as: keeping individual vocabulary lists of new or difficult words found in their reading; writing assignments either for a class newspaper or to provide information for other classes about their activities; preparation of research reports to be presented to the class at some time other than during the reading period; studying the derivations of words and their many meanings; and all of the enrichment activities normally used in an enriched classroom program.

Follow-up activities can be handled in several ways. Some teachers prefer to have a specific part of the period for this when she does not see children individually but when she can go to children at their seats, join in some of the group activities, plan with the children what they will do the following day when they are working individually, aid them in deciding what they might want to read next, check materials in and out, plan new group activities, and evaluate the activities of each child when he was working without direct teacher supervision.

The sharing of what one has read can be an activity that takes place during the time the teacher is working individually with a child, or it can be a planned part of the period at the end of each reading period. It is perhaps only a matter of preference and might well be used sometimes as an entire class activity at the end and other times as a part of the small group work. Maybe those books which would be of a reading level that anyone in the class would be able to read and of sufficient interest could be told about to the entire class, and those books either more difficult or of specialized interest could be shared in the small group discussion.

Other teachers do not have specific follow-up activity time. As the children complete certain activities, they select another book which they want to read or join with several other children much on their own without the direct supervision of the teacher. In this manner, the follow-up activity is generally going on at all times and can really not be distinguished from the regular independent activity. In this case, the teacher depends upon the individual conference alone to evaluate and suggest further activities for each child or group of children.

In some instances, certain reading areas have been designated and when a child is reading independently, he joins into that group. At least one good reader is assigned to each group and designated as reading helper. If the child needs help with a particular word while the teacher is having a conference, the reading helper will assist the child with the word. This practice is apparently not widespread, but is one way in which some teachers handle the problem of the child who needs help on a word before he can go on in his reading. Of course, if any of the children need too much help, it is an indication that he has selected material to read that is too difficult and at the next conference, the teacher should remind the child of the criteria which have been set up by the class to indicate material that is too hard, usually more than three or four new words per page, and then help him in selecting easier material.

The success of the teacher in planning with the children those activities in which they will engage themselves while she is busy with individual children will perhaps be a measure of the success or failure of the personalized program. Certainly, such planning should not be any more difficult than the planning of activities for any class in the more traditional three-group ability or achievement groupings. These activities must not be all teacher planned, for the teacher has neither the time nor the ability to adapt to the wide diversity of interests of the children. The activities should be planned with the children, perhaps in a period of time devoted only to planning such activities.

Specific types of follow-up activities which have actually been used in practice are described by Sharpe.[7]

I. *Fictional Stories*
  1. Recording
     a. Keep individual record of titles read; dates; pages.
     b. "Beginning book report": Title, author, publisher. List important characters: illustrate, name. For more capable learner: comment about the book—what liked or not liked; why someone else should read it.
     c. If book contains several stories, list titles of most interesting ones, as well as book title.
  2. Illustrating
     a. Illustrate main characters.
     b. Pictures of main events in sequence.
     c. Illustrate most exciting events, or best liked.
     d. Make book jacket for story.
     e. Make diorama of favorite part of story.
     f. Make miniature stage setting for exciting scene.
  3. Committee work
     a. Prepare a dramatization of part of the story.
     b. Prepare parts to identify characters in story.
     c. Make list of questions to ask others who have read the story.
     d. Prepare answers to such questions.

e. Report on books or stories relating to unit studies sections of basal readers.

f. Arrange book displays: "Our Favorite Books"; new and old books.

g. Classify book lists according to subjects; illustrate.

4. Oral reporting—audience situations

a. Show illustration and tell about it.

b. Prepare interesting part of story to read; tell why liked it.

c. Decide if story could be true; could not be. Choose selections from story to read orally to prove decision. Lower ability pupil could illustrate and tell to prove.

d. Interview adults concerning author; report orally.

e. Tell portion of story: predict how it might end, or make up different ending, or tell how reader would end it, and why, if he were the author.

5. Written activities

a. Write title or sentence for illustrations.

b. Write sentence which tells of author's illustrations.

c. Make list of unusual, how, or difficult words.

d. Write something about the author (upper grades).

e. Write answers to blackboard or mimeographed questions prepared by teacher; group; committee.

f. Creative writing: original poems, plays, stories, essays; illustrate.

g. Select important news and write a summary for class or school paper.

h. Make bibliography: organize for mutual interests.

II. *Factual Interests*

1. Recording

a. Make a record of what was done to follow directions of simple experiment.

b. Keep records of temperatures, weights, measures.

c. Title and pages where directions were found.

2. Research

a. To identify collections, such as shells, stamps.

    b. Make scrapbooks of pictures of collections—pets, animals, social studies interests, science.

    c. Find picture words to illustrate each letter of alphabet: find pictures to illustrate these words or draw own illustrations.

    d. Find stories which will answer questions of the group concerning social studies, science, other interests.

    e. Before taking a trip: plan what to see, how to go, places of interest to visit.

3. Committee work

    a. Groups work to find facts concerning interests.

    b. Organizing and recording information and realia.

    c. Organize bulletin board, book table, or collections.

    d. Classify book lists according to subjects.

    e. Illustrating: time lines, murals, experiments.

    f. Compile bibliography for background of current news events; arrange display.

4. Oral reporting—make preparation for the following:

    a. Tell about a simple experiment and results.

    b. Report findings concerning group interests which have been learned through trips or interviews.

    c. Tell about collections.

    d. Report interesting facts found when reading about interests.

5. Written activities

    a. Make lists of subject words: colors, food, phases of science, flowers, pets, etc.

    b. Make a "picture" dictionary illustrating picture or subject words.

    c. Find answers to questions of the group; list pages; make a bibliography file for reference.

    d. Record references to information found in library: pictures; junior encyclopedias, topical interests; include topic, pages, authorities, dates.

    e. Summarize information learned from charts, graphs, maps.

    f. Compile bibliography of mutual interests; make 3 x 5 card file for reference and expansion.

III. *Study Skills*
   1. Games
      a. Word drill, such as "I Know—I Do Not Know."
      b. "Bingo" type games.
      c. Following direction games for word drill.
      d. Matching words and pictures.
   2. Committee work, to study teams
      a. Word analysis exercise.
      b. Sight vocabulary practice.
      c. Phrasing and expression in oral reading.
      d. Help in speeding reading and skimming.
   3. Oral—with teacher
      a. Word analysis—structural, auditory, visual discrimination.
      b. Word meanings—reminding children of own experiences which will help get new meanings and mental pictures and ideas.
      c. Discuss special needs: prefixes, suffixes, unusual vowel sounds, rhyming words.
      d. Working out group discussion standards.
   4. Written activities
      a. Make own study word cards.
      b. Make list of unknown words; indicate location; check list with teacher.
      c. Find words that look alike.
      d. Find words that:
         —mean the same
         —mean the opposite
         —are written the same but have different meanings.
      e. Find and illustrate picture words.
      f. Choose a page in a story; make a list of all the words that begin with capitals; be able to tell why.
      g. Organize scrap books showing words of:
         —similar structure, beginnings, endings.
         —rhyming characteristics.

The Individual Interview or Conference

No phase of the personalized reading program is so important as the individual conference. It is at this time that the teacher either successfully reaches the child and succeeeds in teaching him to read, or fails to reach him and therefore fails to aid him in becoming a better reader.

The children come to the individual conference, either voluntarily or as directed by the teacher. Some people recommend allowing the students to come voluntarily at the time they have the need for either help from the teacher or have something which they particularly want to share with the teacher. In such a situation, if certain children do not voluntarily come to see the teacher once every three or four days, the teacher asks them to come for a conference. In some classes, the teacher puts the names of those children on the board each morning who will have the conference with her on that specific day.

Once the child is with the teacher in a one-to-one relationship, the teacher is in the position of justifying the program which hears the child read individually only once every three or four days, instead of the expected reading in a group to the teacher each day. There are certain things the teacher will want to know. She will ask the child what he is reading, if he likes it or not and why. She may ask him to tell her about it (as a comprehension check) and perhaps to read certain selections to see if the child is able to unlock new words.

It is particularly important that this individual period not become just another oral reading session, different only from the reading in a circle procedure in that no one is listening but the teacher and the material is not the usual textbook. This is not an oral reading period, although it is naturally expected that more oral reading will be expected from the lower grade level students than from the higher elementary grades.

As the teacher discusses the material with the child, gets to know him and his reading habits and interests better, she records pertinent information on the child's record. In addition to checking his comprehension and the level of difficulty of the material he is reading, she will probably also check his ability with particular words in the story that are difficult. (The students themselves may have prepared the list of difficult words from the story as they read it and brought this list to the conference.) All of this is recorded, as is the child's ability to use successfully the particular word attack skills felt to be necessary at the level at which he is reading. Such skills might include sounds of certain letters, seeing small words inside of large words, etc.

But the teacher is also responsible for watching for the child with emotional difficulties. It is not meant to imply that in the personalized reading program the teacher is expected to be able to cure severe emotional problems, for she certainly cannot. But the teacher is in a decidedly better position to come to know the student better individually, and to talk over with him any problems he may want to discuss with her. This added time with children individually should put the teacher in a better position to know when to refer particular children for any kind of special attention, whether it might be for special work in reading, speech correction work, mental testing to determine potentiality, or any other type of special referral.

The individual conference period may well be a remedial period for some children. The child who is far below the class level in reading may have to have very easy material in order to find success. In the personalized program, he is better able to find satisfaction in reading at his own level without the embarrassment of having to stumble along in material that is too difficult in front of his fellow classmates. But in order to help him, the teacher may have to work with him on basic skills at a very early level, or even at a readiness level. The advantage of the individual conference is that the teacher will at least have some time, admittedly too limited but nevertheless more than in the usual program, to work with the remedial reading case alone and in small groups with other children at his level.

The conference must not become a testing period for which the child feels he must prepare. It is instead a relaxed discussion period during which time the child and the teacher share together experiences. Too formalized a procedure will result in the conference being less successful. The teacher must remember, however, that oral reading should be preceded by silent reading, and should therefore ask the child to read those selections for her that he has already read silently, and not move the child ahead into material he has not read.

The individual conference is essentially a counseling session. The classroom teacher who has no formal training in counseling, as such, would do well to examine some of the literature on counseling techniques, as well as spend some time in in-service training developing this particular skill. So much depends upon the teacher's effective use of the short period of time which she has with each child that preplanning for the conference is absolutely essential.

SUMMARY

Organizing the classroom for any new procedure will, of course, take some time. It will, at first, perhaps be more rigid than later on when the teacher and children are adjusted to the program. Developing the organization pattern for the program with the children is essential. Arranging a spot in the room where the books can be placed so that the children will not interfere with the orderly conduct of the rest of the class when they go to select books is of major importance. The rules which are established might well be placed upon a chart and hung in the room in a somewhat permanent position.

Selecting reading materials is not nearly the problem which it might first appear to be. It is generally thought that about a hundred books should be in the classroom at all times, with three at about the reading level of each child. These books can come from either the school and public libraries, and the children's libraries themselves, or from second hand book stores.

Since the personalized reading program is a new one, the adequate keeping of records is vitally important. As the program has less rigidly defined procedures, only if the teacher keeps up with each child and records his progress will it be successful. She should be certain that the child is obtaining those skills and the type of training which he needs.

Planning the independent activities, group activities and follow-up activities will undoubtedly be a major concern to most classroom teachers considering this new program. Because of the flexibility which the program allows, as well as the fact that all children are expected to be reading at any time when they have finished their regularly assigned tasks, means that the program can aid the teacher with the over-crowded classroom. Careful planning of the independent activities should follow much the same pattern as has been necessary for the teacher to plan for the other two groups in the traditional basal reader approach.

The individual conference is the very core of the program. The skills with which the teacher handles this conference and imparts to the child those things which he needs in order to develop better skills and reading habits will determine the effectiveness of personalized reading instruction.

REFERENCES

1. VEATCH, JEANNETTE, "Individualized Reading For Success in the Classroom," *The Educational Trend,* No. 654, New London, Conn.: Arthur C. Croft publ., 1954, p. 6.
2. CROSSLEY, RUTH AND KNILEY, MILDRED, "An Individualized Reading Program," *Elementary English,* Vol. 41, January, 1959, pp. 16-20.
3. VEATCH, JEANNETTE, *Ibid.,* p. 7.
4. SPERBER, ROBERT, "An Individualized Reading Program in a Third Grade," *Individualizing Reading Practices,* MEIL, ALICE, editor, No. 14, *Practical Suggestions for Teaching,* New York: Bureau of Publications, Teachers College, Columbia University, p. 47.
5. CROSSLEY AND KNILEY, *op. cit.,* p. 17.
6. VITE, IRENE, "A Primary Teacher's Experience," *Individualizing Reading Practices, op. cit.,* pp. 37-38.
7. SHARPE, MAIDA WOOD, "Individualized Reading: Follow-up Activities," *Elementary English,* Vol. 36 (January, 1959), pp. 21-23.

Chapter Four

Beginning a Personalized Reading Program

The personalized reading program is new, and as such it presents some new problems. These can be overcome, and properly taken care of, should be no handicap to the program. Whether the program begins in a single class, or throughout the entire school, the entire faculty needs to know about it so that it can be interpreted to parents and children. The acceptance of the program by teachers not involved directly in it can be as much a factor in the success of the program as any other.

Concern needs to be given to the grade level at which the personalized program might begin. A discussion is included in this chapter of the ways in which parents might be introduced to this program and some of the information parents will want and are entitled to. Also included in the chapter is a list of the advantages and disadvantages of Personalized Reading Instruction and information available concerning the evaluation of those programs which have been in operation.

At What Grade Level Should Personalized Reading Begin?

The problem of when to begin is indeed a perplexing one. Is personalized reading better started after the child has attained some of the basic reading skills, or is it more difficult to operate an individualized program when the child must shift from one type of program to another? Although the entire idea of individualization in reading instruction is still too new to have been given the many trials that will be necessary before any final answer is found, it is possible that no answer will ever be forthcoming. This may well be one of those unanswerable questions, to be determined by each school system on the basis of attitudes and needs peculiar to that particular community.

The proponents of the personalized method of teaching reading insist that it should begin as soon as the child begins to learn to read. Perhaps this very beginning is an important part of the success of the program in establishing a stronger desire to read and accounts for the maintenance of the initial enthusiasm found among first grade children toward reading.

Rowe and Dornhoefer[1] discuss a program for first graders in St. Louis, Missouri, in an article in *Childhood Education*. Presenting both the principal's viewpoint and that of the teacher's, the general conclusion is that a personalized or individualized program may encounter many problems, but that they can be overcome and the results are well worth the effort.

Maxey,[2] writing in the *Instructor*, tells of another method of individualizing a first grade program. Each child is assigned a partner who reads about the same as he does. The two who read together take turns being listener. The teacher works with two at a time. She reports success with thirty-seven, but recognizes that a smaller group is to be preferred.

All of these discussions are reminders of the high degree of success attained by what was referred to as the "experience approach" to teaching reading so well explained in Lamoreaux and Lee's excellent book, *Learning to Read Through Experience*.[3] In the "experience approach" basal readers were not used in initial reading instruction and the programs were not unlike what is now being called the personalized approach. Perhaps the reason the "experience" approach did not develop into a method which differed from the basal reader approach was that there was no apparent way in which this could be continued on through the grades to include skill instruction at higher grade levels. Now, with a combining of the personalized methods and the experience approach it is possible that more and more use will be made of the many fine suggestions of Lamoreaux and Lee.

But if the personalized program does not begin in the initial states of reading, when then can it begin? At the demonstration school of Antioch College personalized reading has long been practiced in an ungraded situation. But the initial introduction to reading is done through primers and pre-primers. From then on the basal readers are used only as supplementary reading material.

An editorial note by Alice Meil[4] in Teacher's College *Practical Suggestions for Teaching* on individualized reading practices recognizes this problem of where to begin. She states that "many will readily grant the utter good sense of individualizing reading instruction in the upper elementary school where the range of reading ability is so great." This is the preface to a valuable discussion by Irene Vite[5] on "A Primary Teacher's Experience" with individualizing reading instruction.

Albert J. Harris, in *How To Increase Reading Ability,* states that he feels a personalized or individualized reading program "should be most difficult to operate in the first grade, because the children are less mature, less independent, less capable of self-direction, and less able to sustain attention than in succeeding grades."[6] Although Harris admits being "intrigued" by the success of some such programs, he nevertheless states that "in such a program, it is probably desirable to continue with a carefully arranged sequence of basal readers through the third-grade level."[7]

Perhaps the answer to the question, "When to begin?" cannot be answered other than to say there are examples of successful programs beginning with the child's first day in school. Other leading authorities apparently feel that waiting until after the child has acquired a basic sight vocabulary through the primer level is the time to shift away from the basal reading program to the individualized one. Still other reading authorities believe that the fourth grade is the time for the change-over. And indeed, there are those who believe that the personalized program is nothing more than an extension of the independent reading program which good teachers have always employed, and is most effective when used in conjunction with the basal reader approach.

How Can Parents Be Prepared for the Program?

Regardless of the grade level at which the personalized program begins, whether the child has been in a traditional basal reader program or whether this is his initial experience with reading, the personalized program is different from what he expects reading instruction to be. It is also different from what his parents expect reading instruction to be, and is almost certainly different from the way in which they were taught. For these reasons, a careful explanation to both children and parents must be given. The teacher who overlooks this preparation is very likely to be accused of not teaching reading by the over-zealous mother who wants the best possible instruction for her child. On the other hand, however, the parent who fully understands the program can do a great deal to assist the teacher in making the program a success.

The parent must understand that the primary goal of all reading instruction is to develop permanent interests in reading, as well as the necessary techniques and skills for reading. The value in being able to read is best measured in terms of how much the child reads, for the adult who knows how to read well, but is not interested in reading, has gained a skill which will be of little use to him. Parents must understand that the personalized program has as its main advantage the exposing of many different kinds of books to the child from the very beginning, because there are good children's books available which will be interesting and challenging to the children.

The parent must understand that this is not a method whereby the child will receive less of the teacher's attention, or will spend less time receiving reading instruction. By a careful breakdown of the time spent by the teacher with the children in the traditional three group, basal reader approach, it is possible to show that the child will actually receive more attention of an individualized nature in this new program than he did in the old.

A child in the basal reader program may read aloud each day, in a group of ten or more, for no longer than several minutes. In the personalized program, however, he receives individual attention for five or more minutes once every three days. This is more individual attention than he received in the basal program, even though he does not read for the teacher each day.

Care must be taken not to introduce the personalized plan as an attack on existing plans. To do this will merely bring forth critics of education to push for something different. It should be carefully explained as a new type of program which is being tried out, and not one which is meant to imply unfair criticism of present methods. If the teacher who is introducing the personalized reading program is not successful in explaining the program in terms of its ability to develop permanent interests in reading as well as adequate skill development, without having to attack existing methods, there is little likelihood that she will receive the cooperation of the rest of the school staff who are most likely waiting to see how this program works, and of those parents whose children learned in the basal readers to read well and to love reading.

Such administrative details as how grading is to be done and reported are of little importance other than the value placed upon grades by the community itself. In a new program, however, the teacher must carefully explain how this is to be handled. Since the teacher is to spend more time with each child individually in this new arrangement, it can easily be explained that grading will actually be fairer for it will represent more accurately what the child is doing and what he is capable of doing.

Even though the decision as to the type of reading program to be followed is a professional one to be determined by teachers and school administrators, and not parents, a change in the reading program is somewhat different. In the first place, parents have become particularly sensitive about the methods used to teach their children how to read and are likely to react quickly on an emotional level to any change which they do not understand. But of even more importance, in a personalized program there will necessarily be more reason for home-school cooperation as the child will not only take his book in which he is reading home with him, but will be encouraged to bring from home books which he will use in the classroom.

A letter explaining the new program to the parents, with an

opportunity for teacher-parent conferences to further explain the program, seems to be an effective manner in which the program can be initiated. Parent-teacher meetings serve as another way in which the purpose and goals of the program can be explained.

How Can Individualized Reading Programs Be Evaluated?

There is little actual research evidence to indicate that the personalized reading program is truly superior to the basal reader approach. But, on the other hand, neither is there evidence to support the belief that it is not superior. In philosophy it is certainly easy to determine that the personalized approach is sound, but the comparison of groups being taught by one method as opposed to another is always subject to some question. As has been discussed, most often research reports show the superiority of any new method. The very factor of change alone seems to make for improvement. Increased interest in a new program is always another contributing factor. Keeping these facts in mind, and remembering that the personalized program is not just one set of procedures but rather many adaptations of Olson's principles of seeking, self-selection and pacing, examination of the research literature has value.

Evaluation must concern itself with many factors. Such factors as improvement in both knowledge and application of skills is indeed important, and can in part be measured by determining grade level of reading at the beginning of the year and at the end of the year, but there are other factors which are of equal importance. These factors may easily be forgotten in an evaluation perhaps partially because they cannot be measured so easily. They include such intangibles as enjoyment of reading, interest in what Witty[8] has referred to as both the process and the results of reading, and the actual use of critical reading in everyday practice.

It is in these intangible areas that the personalized reading proponents claim the greatest gain. When the factors themselves cannot be carefully defined, for they relate to attitude which is one of the hardest possible areas of human behavior to describe, statistical evaluation is virtually impossible. Essentially, then, it appears that the personalized program cannot be truly evaluated in terms of its very strongest aspects, and must depend upon evaluation on those areas in which it is most like the basal reading program.

The very fact that the personalized reading program is an individual program adds to the difficulty in evaluating it. For the personalized program to be successful it must be flexible, and indeed different, and therefore the statistician is likely to be dissatisfied with the evaluation reports which are appearing in the literature.

The "action research" type of study is apparently the most common type of report available. This is the description of the program in operation in one particular grade or school system, and a report on how the teacher or author felt that the program helped the children make progress toward better reading. It is not mean to be indicative of a so-called "typical" situation, nor even of ideal conditions. It is more or less what happened in one situation. This type of reporting is of little real value for others when taken alone, but when combined with the reports of others in different situations and other parts of the country, the reports gain in value. It is mostly upon this type of research that the personalized program must now be evaluated.

Evaluation should probably be made in a variety of ways. Essentially, the types will probably be either according to (1) test results; (2) some measure of the number of books read and the variety of types of books read; and (3) some measure of attitudes of both parents and children toward the program and toward reading itself.

Test results may be used in a variety of ways. They are undoubtedly the easiest way to evaluate the program, although there is danger that test results will be misleading. It is most likely that in terms of the goals set up for the program, some tests would not be adequate measures of the kinds of things which the program considered important. Essentially, then, it is most important to consider the goals of the program in selecting the test to be used.

It would seem from an examination of the literature that the Gates Primary Reading Test is most commonly used as the measuring instrument for programs operating at the primary level. No one test is mentioned so frequently in the upper elementary grades. The results could be used to compare the progress of the group in the personalized program with another class of the same grade and age, and approximately the same mental ability, to determine the advancement made by each group. Another way would be merely to measure the progress of the class as compared with test norms to determine if one year's progress was made during the year. This could not be a valid measure of the brighter student for more than a year's progress would be expected normally, while less than a year's progress would be expected from the below average group. Such a comparison would provide the teacher with information as to the success of the program in teaching what the test assumed was important in the skills program. Such test results might also be compared with the progress the children had made in a previous year under the basal program. In this manner the either above average or below average learning rate of the class could partially be accounted for.

Vite[9] used the Gates Primary Reading Test and stated that under the new program all of the children were at their chronological age or above in reading ability. Olson[10] reported on a study by Dunklin at Columbia University in 1940 where experimental groups were set up which used personalized methods. At the end of seven months, the experimental group was almost half a grade ahead of the control group. In a study in 1948, Jones[11] reported that those children who were taught at their individual level were able to achieve greater amount of growth than comparable pupils taught as a group. This superiority was in arithmetic, spelling, and total achievement, as well as in reading.

The second method of evaluation, and one which is objective enough as one measure, but which must not be used alone as the criterion for determining the success of the program, is the number of books read by the children. Since the personalized program has as its very basic principle the presentation of, and stimulation to read, a large number of books, the teacher who feels that the program is a success merely because her pupils have read more books is operating under a false assumption. Quantity alone is not the measure of success, although it is hoped that mere numbers of books read will be some indication of ability to read and interest in reading.

Sperber[12] reports that in the third grade experimental group receiving personalized instruction each child had read an average of thirty-three books. In the ten other classes with the basal reading program, each child had read an average of slightly less than six books. This type of report is common to almost every report on personalized programs.

In addition to the number of books read, another evaluating factor might well be the diversity of the reading of the pupils. It is not at all unusual for elementary school children to become interested in one particular subject, such as dogs, horses, or science, and then want to read only in this area. The teacher in the individualized program should have the development of new reading interests as one of her goals.

An interesting evaluative technique is noted by Vite[13] in which she refers to the usual drop-off in reading ability over the summer months. She feels that children who have the personalized program do not lose ground over the summer months, probably because they have been more highly motivated to read for pleasure and have received guidance in knowing how to select material for themselves.

A third method of evaluation deals with attitudes. Such attitudes must be measured informally, but with care, questionnaires can be prepared which measure the attitudes of children toward the program, their parents' attitudes, and even the attitudes of teachers toward the program.

In addition to the attitudes of the children toward the program, their attitude toward reading itself is a measurable factor. Sperber[14] developed a reading attitude inventory consisting of twelve questions with three choices in each question of activities nine-year-old children engage in. One of the three choices dealt with some aspect of reading. Those in the personalized program chose more of the activities involving reading than did the children who had been in the basal reading program.

Frazier, Heacock and Thomas[15] report in *Educational Leadership* on a personalized first grade reading program which began with the pre-primer. The sight vocabulary was taught and the children took the book home each day. A child moved to a higher level book when he was ready to move ahead, and either re-read or read a new book on the same level if he was not ready to move ahead. At the end of the year there was no great difference in the test scores of the two groups, but more interest in reading was noted among the group in the personalized program.

Greenman and Kapilian[16] in an experimental program reported better than average test gains, wider range of reading interest, no labeling of students' abilities, increase in comprehension ability, enjoyment of reading by all children, and greater retention of skills and vocabulary. Such an enthusiastic report can hardly be overlooked.

The intangibles which indicate success of the program cannot adequately be measured. Perhaps they can only be noted, but they too have great value, perhaps far more than the more tangible results of standardized tests. Parkin[17] states this exceedingly well: "Then there are certain gains she (the teacher) cannot help observing: freedom of choice and the joy that accompanies it; release from the tethering gait of the group; release from the stigma of the group label; a relaxed attitude toward reading; the pleasure of making reading a live dynamic activity; more time for reading for the purposes that reading can serve; a change of emphasis from competition with the group to competition with one's self."

There has been little research, other than "action research," on the personalized reading program. As more people become aware of what such a program actually is, more research will be forthcoming. Veatch[18] says: "While teachers using an individualized approach are increasingly reporting highly significant gains in achievement along with startling changes in attitude toward the *instructional* reading program, it is undeniable that well-grounded research is needed. The next few years will undoubtedly see more and more attention to the evaluation of [personalized] individualized reading programs."

Advantages and Disadvantages of Personalized Reading Instruction

No program is without some disadvantages; the personalized reading program is certainly not an exception. In their support on this "new" approach, many of the proponents are making claims that are laudable but difficult to accept on any long time basis. Of course, there is virtually no evidence that the personalized program, separated from the basal reader program entirely, will produce the long term results which are desired. Perhaps some tempering of enthusiasm on the part of proponents of the personalized program will make it more acceptable to the many teachers who are desirous of doing the best possible job, but are determined not to be taken in by something merely because it is different.

The personalized program cannot and does not entirely eliminate reading difficulties. And yet, in article after article reporting the success of programs in operation, no mention is made of any child who did not either immediately or very quickly reach the proper level and develop a great love for reading. It would indeed be wonderful if we had now found the long sought after "cure-all." Perhaps at the expense of sounding pessimistic, it is obvious that this method is no "cure-all," either in eliminating reading problems or in developing permanent interests in reading. Some reporting on what is done with the child who does not make normal progress, and who does not respond to the individual approach, will strengthen the argument in favor of the personalized program.

But the personalized program is new, and while we like to think that the logical progression of ideas is from development of ideas to research on the value of such new ideas and then to putting these ideas into practice, such is not the manner of progression in education. All too often we neglect research findings, determined to make our own mistakes without benefitting from the experience of others. And then, when we believe in an idea, with or without research to support our belief, we put the program into practice. If anyone cares to question the wisdom of such a practice, we can usually support our faith in it by producing good results.

In the personalized program, much putting into practice has been effected, with virtually no research other than action research, with little or no experimental design or control. This can be questioned as the proper way to do such things, but when results then tend to support belief in the idea, there can be little criticism of the program. The very willingness to try new ideas deserves commendation, and reflects quite a change in education from the more rigid type of curriculum of days in the not too distant past.

This ability of the good teacher to make any program work is indicative of a very important principle. It is not nearly so important to have a good program as it is to have a good teacher. A poor teacher will be ineffective with any kind of program, while a good teacher can usually be effective with almost any type of program. The goal in education must be, of course, to have nothing but good teachers and to provide that teacher with materials and curricular programs which will be flexible enough so that she can do the best possible job. The combination of a good teacher and a good program is absolutely unbeatable.

In determining the advantages and disadvantages of the personalized program, the proponents of the personalized method score a very strong point when they answer many of the criticisms by saying, "Yes, but is that not also true and perhaps even more true under the basal reader plan, too?"

Interestingly enough, when a list of advantages and disadvantages of personalized reading programs are drawn up, there is great similarity between the list of advantages and the list of disadvantages. Such things as "good particularly for the gifted child" are listed as advantages by some and then by others as disadvantages. It is felt by some that under the personalized plan the teacher would have to strictly control the time of each conference, which would be difficult and perhaps unwise. If she did not, the pressures of time would cause her to slight the amount of time for the gifted child who was a good reader.

Generally speaking, the personalized program receives more favorable response from teachers than it does negative. In philosophy there is almost complete agreement with the principles inherent in the personalized program. However, there are many questions about the practicability of the program. Many teachers who oppose personalized reading feel that they have to justify their negativism by making alternate suggestions for some combination of the two methods.

DISADVANTAGES: One general area of disadvantages deals with the beginning of the program and describes what would indeed be problems, but which could be overcome as the program gained acceptance and becomes more wide-spread. The lack of reading materials to begin the program is of great concern to many teachers. The problems involved in having a child move into the program in one grade and out of it at the end of the year is troublesome to some teachers. The parent's concern because his child did not get to read for the teacher every day bothers some. But these must be classified as only temporary problems, and are ones which can certainly be overcome if by no other means than by operating a successful program.

The major objection or disadvantage of the program which the teachers express deals with the area of evaluation, both of the program itself and of the individual child's progress. In the personalized program teachers worry about how they will be able to measure the child's progress, how they could be sure that he is making progress, how they can be certain that he was not merely staying at the same level practicing how to do only what he already knew how to do.

The second major disadvantage seems to be concerned with the skills program. How would a teacher know what skills to teach if she does not have a manual, or if she was not provided with some listing of skills, how can she be sure of the material to use to help develop that particular skill? Basically, the questions here center around whether the teacher feels she is good enough to be depended upon to teach the skills without some formal guide. Many references are made to the need for a master teacher, and the feeling that the absence of a teacher's manual is indeed a disadvantage which may be too big to overcome.

The third general area of disadvantages seems to be concerned with the amount of non-teacher directed activity which will result as a necessary part of the personalized program. In very practical ways teachers tell of having forty or forty-five students crowded into a small classroom, where any amount of movement about by students is disturbing. Several first grade teachers have said that the children need to learn the group activity that comes as a part of the regular ability or achievement grouping in reading and are too immature to be able to keep themselves busily engaged while the teacher had individual or small group conferences. The discipline factor is mentioned, with several teachers readily admitting that while they know that student directed activities are the way in which "modern educators" feel learning best takes place, they are traditional in their methods and are actually afraid that they could not adjust to anything so "chaotic" as personalized reading.

Several other disadvantages are mentioned by teachers which are noteworthy. One is that the poor teacher can operate under such a plan without his weakness being as apparent, or as it was stated by a teacher, "It is too easy for a teacher to be lazy." This is in direct opposition to the comments by many teachers that such a program would involve much extra work and require much additional planning. Some teachers feel that it interferes with the correlation of the pupils' other work and others feel that help could not be given when it was needed as easily as in the regular program.

ADVANTAGES: The advantages which teachers state far outnumber the disadvantages, however, in both actual number and in length of responses. The areas do not separate themselves in discussing the advantages as clearly as the disadvantages do, but they can partially be grouped under four headings: developing interest in reading, progress at child's own rate, one-to-one relationship with each child, and skill instruction.

It is almost unanimously agreed by teachers that the personalized plan can develop greater interest in reading for pleasure. It must be recognized that even among teachers there is greater interest in not having to go over the same story year after year. It is believed that this greater interest in reading would be manifested by less anxiety in the reading situation and therefore more effective learning would take place. The relaxed condition of the child as he is doing something at a level at which he can succeed is often mentioned.

The one-to-one relationship with the teacher is recognized as a special advantage. More frustration is indicated by teachers by the lack of opportunity to help each child individually, the below average, average, and gifted, than on any other item. Teachers apparently see in the personalized program an opportunity to reach each child individually. It is felt that this one-to-one relationship takes care of such problems as the child who is absent on a particular day and missed certain skill presentation, and that better use was made of the teacher's time than just listening to children read.

"Being able to progress at his own rate" appeals to most teachers. Teachers refer to the gifted child who does not have to be held back, and to the slow learner who can find satisfaction in his own progress at his own level without having to be embarrassed because the material is at such a low level. The possibility of "more top and bottom" was the way in which one teacher expressed this flexibility of the program in order to meet the child at his level and be able to progress from there.

With respect to skill instruction teachers feel the personalized program offers many advantages. They felt that better silent reading habits are developed earlier in the personalized program. The most appealing part of skill instruction in this type of program expressed by a number of teachers is the fact that the child spent time working on his own weaknesses, and not on somebody else's. It is felt that the child learns to work independently, and to read independently, in the personalized program better than in any other program.

These advantages and disadvantages stated by teachers with only a limited amount of acquaintance with individualized reading cannot be taken too seriously. Some of the advantages and disadvantages reflect things which the teachers are not doing correctly in the regular basal program, while others reflect basic advantages and disadvantages of the program. Since the program is still in its infancy, the disadvantages will need to be weighed carefully by anyone thinking of starting a program. There will be other disadvantages which will arise in any situation, but the decision must be made on a local basis whether these disadvantages are over-shadowed by the advantages or whether the reverse is true.

SUMMARY

The personalized reading program is new on the educational scene. It is an important stage in the logical development of different types of educational provisions as more and more is learned about human behavior. The philosophical statement of the need for more individualization of instruction is best expressed in Olson's[19] statement of the way in which children learn: (1) seeking; (2) self-selection; and (3) pacing. An understanding of these concepts is basic to all good teaching.

Important to remember about the personalized program is that, while perhaps not a definite method defined by any set rules, it is nevertheless enough of a method that it can readily be distinguished from the independent reading activities found to be so effective as a means of increasing interest in reading. The personalized reading program is perhaps only a continuation of the independent reading activity, but it definitely is this plus something more. This something more is the inclusion of a systematic presentation of skill instruction.

The name "individualized" is unfortunate for it implies that group activities are not a part of the program. The name "personalized" better describes the program. The personalized reading program stresses individualization, as opposed to the basal program which is group oriented, but definitely includes much group instruction. The groups are, however, only established on a temporary basis and designed to meet immediate needs.

The danger of a new approach is that it will quickly become a "bandwagon," upon which every person unsuccessful in teaching from the basal reading program will want to climb. Personalized Reading Instruction is not a cure-all, and will be protected from those hunting for an easy way by the fact that beginning it is so difficult. In all probability, those who have had the most success with the basal program will also be those who will have the most success with the personalized program.

Good teaching, regardless of the program, is the key to successful reading instruction.

REFERENCES

1. ROWE, RUTH AND DORNHOEFER, ESTHER, "Individualized Reading," *Childhood Education*, Vol. 34 (November, 1957), pp. 118-22.
2. MAXEY, BESSIE, "Individualized Reading Program," *Instructor*, Vol. 62, (January, 1953), pp. 47, 78.
3. LAMOREAUX AND LEE, Learning to Read Through Experience.
4. MEIL, ALICE (editor), *Individualizing Reading Practices*, No. 14, Practical Suggestions for Teaching, New York: Bureau of Publications, Teachers College, Columbia University, p. 18.
5. VITE, IRENE, "A Primary Teacher's Experience," Chapter Two in *Individualizing Reading Practices*, Alice Meil, editor, No. 14, Practical Suggestions for Teaching, New York: Bureau of Publications, Teachers College, Columbia University.
6. HARRIS, ALBERT J., *How to Increase Reading Ability*. New York: Longmans Green, p. 116.
7. IBID, p. 119.
8. WITTY, PAUL, *Reading and Modern Education*. Boston; D. C. Heath and Co., 1949.
9. VITE, *op. cit.*, p. 42.
10. OLSON, WILLARD C., *Child Development*. Boston: D. C. Heath and Co., 1949, p. 139.
11. IBID., pp. 139-40.
12. SPERBER, ROBERT, "An Individualized Reading Program in a Third Grade," Chapter Three in *Individualizing Reading Practices*, Alice Meil, editor, No. 14, Practices Suggested for Teaching, New York: Bureau of Publications, Teachers College, Columbia University, pp. 45-51.
13. VITE, *op. cit.*, p. 41.
14. SPERBER, *op. cit.*, p. 51.
15. FRAZIER, ALEXANDER, HILSON, HELEN H. AND THOMAS, GLEN G., "Individual Reading in The First Grade," *Educational Leadership*, Vol. 16 (February, 1959), pp. 319-322.
16. GREENMAN, RUTH AND KATILIN, SHERAN, "Individual Reading in Third and Fourth Grades," *Elementary English*, Vol. 36 (April, 1959), pp. 234-7.
17. PARKIN, PHYLISS B., "An Individual Program of Reading," *Educational Leadership*, Vol. 14 (October, 1956), pp. 37-38.
18. VEATCH, JEANNETTE, "Children's Interest and Individual Reading," *The Reading Teacher*, Vol. 10, No. 3 (February, 1957), p. 165.
19. OLSON, WILLARD C., "Speaking, Self Type and Selection, and Pacing in Use of Books by Children," *The Packet* (Spring, 1952). Boston: D. C. Heath and Co., pp. 3-10.

Chapter Five

Determining Children's Reading Level

The importance of adequately determining every child's reading level cannot be minimized in either the basal or in the personalized reading program. Much depends upon the skill of the teacher in determining the reading level, and her sensitivity in interpreting the meaning of her findings. As with a medical problem, adequate diagnosis is vitally essential because it frequently indicates those steps which must be taken to bring about a cure.

It has often been found that children themselves are in a position to determine their own reading level about as effectively as anyone else. Demonstrations where children are asked, one at a time, to rate their own reading level—pretty good, not so good, just about average—clearly indicate their awareness of their supposed reading level. Almost without exception, the children can place themselves in the same group which the teacher then places them after extensive testing. This technique is not recommended as the final determination of grouping even in the basal program, but it nevertheless does have value for either the basal program or the personalized program.

There are distinct advantages in the personalized reading program in determining the child's reading level. In the basal program, in which the traditional three group pattern is established, each child must belong to some group. It is true that some children are frequently allowed to form a fourth or even a fifth group, but they must sensibly belong somewhere. The teacher who is uncertain as to which group a child belongs, for fear that the child will be hurt more by being moved back, places him in the lower group. If the child then demonstrates ability above this level the teacher is able to move him up. This "moving up" is certainly more sound psychologically than having to move him back. There is, nevertheless, a great danger that some children, and in particular primary age children will do the level of the work of the group in which they are placed, whether or not they are capable of doing more.

In the personalized reading program, however, this cannot happen. If the teacher encounters difficulty determining at what level the child is reading, because of the individual nature of the program, she is given ample opportunity to observe the child in many situations. If one book is too difficult, she may then soon move him into an easier book. Since the books are usually not marked in any way, the child suffers no loss of social status because he has gone into easier material, or in any way develops an attitude that he should work at this particular level. In the personalized program, since each child is both working at his level as well as "pacing" himself, there is not any danger of his working at the level of the group which is below his own particular level. He selects books which he wants to read, admittedly sometimes with directive guidance from the teacher, and reads at that level.

In the individualized or personalized reading program, it is not as necessary for the teacher to determine immediately the reading level of each child. Because he is selecting his own reading material, he plays a much larger part in determining the level at which he is going to read. The program does not have to be so rigid, nor do children have to be grouped on any such illogical premise as "one group is too large," or "but I am supposed to have three groups."

The teacher, of course, on occasion has to help the child select materials which will encourage the development of new reading skills and interests. Personalized reading is not a laissez-faire procedure, which assumes that each child will read at the highest possible level and always be seeking for a higher level

While this may actually be true of many children, there will be some children who, given a completely free choice, will always choose to read the easiest material they can find, and they may frequently follow a particular line of interest such as horses, science, or interplanetary travel.

Plateau reading is choosing to read books at one level, without progressing into more difficult or higher level books. This is not something new which can be associated only with personalized reading, for it has happened for many years. Librarians are frequently opposed to such books as the Tom Swift series, Nancy Drew mysteries, and the Hardy Boys series on the basis that children do not improve by reading so many books on the same level. This is certainly a legitimate complaint about such books, but does not mean that children should be denied the pleasure of reading them if they so choose. Children should be aware that they are reading at one level. They may need encouragement from the teacher in moving to higher levels. This does not mean that the teacher will tell the child that he cannot read any more of a certain type of book, or that he has to read any particular other book. There are far more subtle and effective procedures than this. Perhaps all of them come under the heading of good teaching techniques. It is not a difficult task to lead children to want to read certain types of material. The motivating force is often the desire to please the teacher. At the upper elementary levels the desire is partially to please the teacher, but also the beginning of the desire for "self-improvement."

Broadening the child's interest is not always so easy a task. Frequently it will be necessary for the teacher in the personalized reading program to utilize the interest type of grouping to encourage particular students to read more widely. Where the teacher's encouragement may not in itself be effective, the desire for group approval and the desire to participate in the group discussion of a particular book, will often expand the child's interest.

Particularly with upper elementary children, but sometimes with primary children, establishing an interest in a particular author will guide children away from a strong interest in a particular topic. Often by making available books on related subjects, the child can be guided away from any single interest. This does not mean that interest in a particular type of reading is unwise, for exactly the opposite is true. Reading along one line of interest, to exclusion of all other areas, is what should be discouraged.

Factors Which Influence Reading Level

There is no such thing as an exact reading level for any child. Each child actually has many reading levels, depending upon a variety of factors. Even these various reading levels fluctuate from time to time.

Teachers have for too long felt that reading level can be measured exactly. They have perhaps been motivated to react in this way by the demands of parents and school administrators who insist that the reading level of the child be recorded on some kind of permanent record. Unfortunately reading is not a single skill, but is a combination of many factors. Arriving at some medium grade level of each of these various skills is an approximation of a reading level. Any belief that more than a mere approximation of reading level exists is false.

The interest which the child has in the material read will influence his ability to read it. The usual type of story found in basal readers, which is certainly not representative of the type of child found in lower economic groups, and may not even be representative of the type of child from higher economic groups, has little appeal. Fast moving, adventure-type stories appeal to most elementary school boys and, on material of this type, they can read at a higher level than they can on material of the basal reader. Girls seem to like much of the material in the basal reader which may account for their supposedly better reading ability at the elementary school level.

Familiarity with the material is another factor which influences reading level. Because of lack of experience, unfamiliar happenings in the stories will result in lower reading level scores. Over-familiarity results in inflated scores. Examples of the type of new material which may produce inflated scores are stories about the history of certain athletic contests such as baseball, basketball, and football. Boys who are greatly interested in these areas have often read widely at what might be labeled as being above their grade level and consequently cannot actually read other material at this level.

A girl who was very fond of pets was tested on a paragraph on the Durrell Analysis of Reading Difficulty. This particular paragraph was about "The Uses of Kites," but the girl read the story as "The Uses of Kitties." Thinking that she would discover from context that she was missing this word, she was allowed to read on. Instead of discovering her mistake, she became more and more interested in the story, reading it without error—other than the obvious mistake on the key word. Her comprehension on the story, which was actually above her reading level of other paragraphs designated as the same level of difficulty, was one hundred per cent, allowing for this slight mistake on the word "kites." Because of her special interest in cats, she was able to read at a level which would ordinarily be considered too difficult for her. This essentially means that when children want a particular type of information, they are able to rise to heights in reading which would otherwise be impossible.

Another factor which influences reading level is the situation in which the child must read. It is not unusual to find children who can read better at home than they can in the classroom situation. In these cases there is often difficulty in explaining the reason for concern over the child's reading level. In other instances, reading in the home is actually poorer than it is in the classroom. In a situation such as this, the schools sometimes are criticized by parents who have actually caused the problem themselves.

It has long been known that in the tutoring or clinic situation, some children, particularly those with emotional difficulties, are able to read better in the individual situation than they can either in the home or in the classroom. Tutors have sometimes been criticized for reporting too high a reading level for a child, when actually the factor which has influenced the level is the presence of other children or tensions under which the child is placed when he is asked to read. So that this will not happen, remedial clinicians today often lead children from individual instruction into small group instruction before returning them to their regular classroom. It is clearly demonstrated that gains made in the clinic situations are more readily carried back into the classroom if a short period of instruction in small groups is added at the end of the individual instruction.

Tutoring often influences reading level greatly. Summer tutoring, which sometimes claims as much as three years gain in relatively short periods of time, actually brings together for the child the skills which he has already learned. The great progress which he makes then is not due entirely to the tutoring itself, but is due to a type of unlocking or putting together of skills which the child already knows. The value of such type of work must not be underestimated, although neither should tutors believe that they have actually taught the child all these things he now knows but did not appear to know before.

The child's physical condition also influences his reading level. Glandular inbalance, poor nutrition, lack of sleep, and poor stamina are all factors which tend to make the reading level of the child appear lower than it actually is. Only if the child is in the best possible physical condition can the teacher adequately determine his reading level. Because it is often impossible to know the condition of the child, a program which determines his reading level on the basis of any single or even a number of tests is often inaccurate. The personalized reading program allows for long term type of determination. The basal program is more rigid in its demand that children be placed in some group early.

The physical factor which most often influences reading level adversely is poor vision. Just exactly how teachers can be adequate vision screening specialists is indeed a perplexing problem. The large number of children who are reading problems because of vision difficulties of long duration is astounding. To place the blame upon the teacher, however, is asking more from the regular classroom teacher than she can be expected to do.

At the time of admission to the school every child should have a thorough physical examination, including both visual and auditory checks. This should be more than a perfunctory height and weight type of examination. It should be as thorough as possible, including the tentative noting of possible areas of difficulty which might later be followed-up with a thorough examination if the child encounters difficulty in learning. These areas might be such factors as thyroid inbalance as indicated by over- or under-weight, possible visual or auditory defects, or neurological examinations indicated by hyperactivity or short attention span. The classroom teacher's role would then be merely to supply observational data on those areas which are in doubt. The use of such devices as the orthorater and tele-binocular have limited value in the primary grades, except as screening devices. When administered by untrained lay people, who do not understand the learning limitations of young children, the tests are worthless. The Snellen Chart, which has frequently hung in the room many months, may be little more than a test of memory rather than vision.

Frequently the child's desire to remain in books with larger print are an indication of his particular visual needs. If his vision has not matured to the point where he is able to easily discriminate between words, then he should never be placed in books with smaller print. This does not necessarily mean that the child needs glasses, although visual examination would be wise, but may merely indicate a lack of physical maturation which only time will overcome.

Another factor which, while it does not directly concern itself with determining the child's reading level, is nevertheless important in understanding reading level of the child. If the child is not capable of reading better than he is, then remediation or efforts to push him to a higher level will at best meet only with limited success. Children may be artificially boosted to higher reading levels above their innate ability level, but these boosts will be only temporary and, as the pressure is removed, the child will drop back to a lower level.

One teacher reported that after completing the basal book for each group, she then shifted into a personalized program. The main value of the personalized program to her was the aid in determining the reading level of the children. To her surprise, in several instances, she found that children were achieving at too high a level in the basal reader because of pressure either from parents or from the environmental situation. In the personalized program the children actually dropped back to a lower level where they could read with understanding and enjoyment. Being concerned with these students dropping back to a lower level, she checked their comprehension at the higher level and found that it was not satisfactory. Because of superior mental ability, the students were able to devise answers which were often correct, but the higher level was too difficult for them.

The innate mental ability of the child will determine the limit to which his reading level can be developed. In most instances, the child's reading level will not approximate his mental level. In those cases where the reading level does come close to the innate mental ability level, the teacher must be careful not to apply pressure. Over-achievement is at best a difficult thing to accomplish and may actually be emotionally harmful to the child.

Teachers must remember that the reading level is not rigidly set and that it may be influenced by many different factors. Understanding this flexibility of the reading level makes the need for a flexible type reading instructional program even more apparent. It is true that there may be freedom of movement between ability groups in the basal reader approach, although there is great question as to how a child in one level can ever actually get to the next level, if by the time he has learned to read as well as the other children in the next group, they have moved on to a still higher level. In the personalized reading program, such grouping problems do not arise, since the only grouping is of a temporary nature for a specific purpose and is disbanded as soon as the purpose is accomplished.

The need is not so much for a definite reading level for each child, which can be recorded on test or record blank, but instead there is a need for an approximation of reading level in each of a variety of situations and in each of a variety of reading skills. An oral reading score might be obtained for a child reading in a group of his peers, another oral reading score for a child when he is reading to the teacher alone, and still another reading score when he is reading outside of the classroom. But the important thing to remember is that a reading level score is only an indication of what the child is actually achieving. The teacher's responsibility is to aid the child in learning to read material beyond this point. To the extent that she does this, along with developing the desire to read these materials, she will be successful as a teacher of reading.

Achievement Level

There are two distinct types of tests which measure reading ability. One, which is most frequently used, determines reading level. The other, of much greater value to the classroom teacher, is a diagnostic type test which attempts to measure a wide variety of reading skills. Considering the time devoted to the administration and scoring of standardized tests, far more should be obtained which will be of help to the teacher in aiding the child than merely a score which is of questionable validity. Considering first standardized reading tests, certain factors about them need to be reviewed:

1. Standardized reading achievement tests, because of their objective nature, often result in inflated scores. The total reading level which the child obtained on the usual standardized tests runs six months to one year above the child's actual independent reading level. The brighter child can guess more intelligently than the slower child, and consequently will receive an even higher score.

2. Test results should be used to indicate progress by using alternate forms before and after instruction. The real value of group achievement tests then is their value to measure progress, not to determine the instructional reading level.

3. The usual achievement type reading test measures reading vocabulary and comprehension, and not the specific types of reading skill. The teacher, in selecting a test, should do so on the basis of that test's ability to measure those things best which she is teaching.

4. Most standardized tests result in measuring childrens'

ability to work under pressure. Reading is not necessarily a speed type of activity, particularly at the elementary school level, and a test which makes this factor too important results in a less reliable measure.

5. The use of national norms as a potential goal is very misleading. Depending upon the abilities of the children, such goals are unrealistically low. Where children's innate abilities are below those of the children using the national reading norms, then the goals are too high. Schools are operating under a false assumption when their goal is to get every child above the national norm, for when this happens the national norm will only be raised. More sensible norms are class norms, and an evaluation of each child's relative position in the class in terms of his innate ability.

6. Many tests which are administered in public school are essentially diagnostic tests, although the scores are usually recorded only as a total reading score. In this case, these tests count only as achievement level tests with no actual diagnostic value. The reading section of the Wide Range Achievement Test, referred to as the "Rat" by most psychologists, is a good example of a test containing no diagnostic value. The Wide Range Achievement Test is merely a carefully graded list of words of increasing difficulty. The number which the child can read successfully indicates a grade level of reading ability. The test is easy to administer, of short duration and easy to score. Its validity as a reading test is somewhat questionable, for it actually measures word calling ability. It is not alone in this, however, and has value when it is recognized as a grade level of word calling ability test. Too frequently, however, both teachers and psychologists use such results to indicate reading level. Great danger can result when classroom teachers use this to indicate instructional level.

Being used widely in many elementary school classrooms are such informal reading paragraphs as those found in *My Weekly Reader*. The vocabulary in these tests, although somewhat controlled, has a tendency to be too easy. The scores are usually higher than the child is able to read independently. This can be misleading to the teacher, the child, and his parents. Another method of determining the child's reading level, of a more informal nature than the easy standardized test or the *Weekly Reader* type test, is to have the child read from graded material. The basal reader type material, somewhere within the book rather than the beginning which is often only the preceding level material, with a careful check for comprehension, is often very meaningful in determining a reading level. Obviously, the best way to check the child's reading level is to have him read at that level. If he is unsuccessful, then his reading level is at a lower grade level. If he can read the material easily, he can then go into the next higher graded reader. Selecting particular paragraphs for him to read at this level will indicate if this is his reading level. For the child to be able to read without help from the teacher, he should encounter no more than two or three new words per page. If he encounters more words than this, the material is too difficult. Reading independently, he will either miss comprehension or give up.

Informal reading in the inventory developed by Betts demonstrates this method of determining reading level. When used properly, it is a most valuable means of determining reading level and will yield the instructional level which is of the greatest benefit to the teacher.

The Betts Reading Clinic
257 West Montgomery Avenue
Haverford, Pennsylvania

INFORMAL READING INVENTORY: FORM B-4
(The ABC Betts Basic Readers, Second Edition, 1958-61)

Name _____ Examiner _____

Age _____ Grade _____ Date _____

INSTRUCTIONS

Independent Reading Level. This is the level at which the pupil reads on his own with no signs of difficulty: lip movement, finger pointing, etc.

Teaching, or Instructional, Reading Level. This is the highest level at which the pupil reads under teacher supervision, without signs of difficulty.

Frustration Level. This is the level at which the pupil is blocked by inadequate phonic skills, lack of information, or the inability to think about what he is trying to read.

Hearing Comprehension Level. This is the highest level at which the pupil can understand material read to him.

Procedure. Pupils are observed as they read at successive levels of graded materials—starting at a level where they show no signs of difficulty.

To estimate the starting level for this Informal Reading Inventory, use the results of the Informal Word Recognition Inventory. Begin this I.R.I. at least one reader level below the point at which the pupil hesitates or makes an incorrect response on the I.W.R.I.

For each selection, use (1) the preparation to introduce the pupil to the selection, (2) the comprehension questions to guide the silent reading, (3) the oral rereading suggestion to observe rhythm, interpretation, etc.

Record all breaks in rhythm, incorrect responses, symptoms of difficulty, and other observations in this booklet.

Battery of Inventories. This battery includes (1) Informal Inventory of Interests, (2) Informal Word Recognition Inventory, (3) Informal Inventory of Phonic Skills, (4) Informal Inventory of Concepts and Thinking Abilities, (5) Informal Reading Inventory.

Specific help is given on construction, administration, and interpretation of both individual and group inventories in "Informal Inventories: Manual." See also Betts, Chapter 21 in *Foundations of Reading Instruction,* Revised 1957 (American Book Co.)

SUMMARY

Estimated Levels
Independent _____

Teaching (instructional) _____

Frustration _____

Hearing comprehension _____

Estimated Needs

Interests

Phonics

Thinking

Other Observations

Reprinted with permission of the authors, Carolyn M. Welch, Supervisor, In-Service Teacher Education, and Emmett A. Betts, Director, The Betts Reading Clinic.

Third Pre-Primer: *All in a Day,* page 58

A. Preparation

Direct attention to the illustration. Ask, "What does the man in the picture have? (A little house) Continue by having the pupil read the title. Ask, "Which person in the picture is mentioned in the title of this story? (Father) Use the comprehension questions to guide the silent reading.

B. Silent Reading (29 words)

Fun with Father
"Sue," said Father.
"Here is a little toy house.
It is for you."
"Oh, Father," said Sue.
"A little toy house for me!
I like it."

Comprehension

1. Who is the first speaker? (Father)
2. What is the little girl's name (Sue)
3. What did Father tell Sue? (He has a little toy house for her.)
4. What does the word *it* stand for in the last sentence Father said? (The toy house)
5. What does the word *you* stand for? (Sue)
6. How did Sue feel about receiving the toy house? (Surprised) (She liked it.)

C. Oral Rereading

Read aloud what Sue said that showed she was surprised. (Second paragraph)

Primer: *The ABC Up the Street and Down,* pages 122-123

A. Preparation

Call attention to the illustration and the title on page 122. Ask, "Where do you think this story takes place?" (At a school) "Find Sue in the picture. What is she holding?" (A duck) "To whom is Sue speaking?" (A little boy) Use the comprehension questions to guide the silent reading.

B. Silent Reading (66 words)

"Oh, hello, Freddie," said Sue.
"Will you please look after my duck?"
Then Sue ran into the school.
Soon the boys and girls came out.
The boys had airplanes and trains.
The girls had big dolls
and little dolls.

They all had something
for the mothers and fathers to see.
Freddie looked at all the toys.
But he did not look after
the little yellow duck.

Comprehension

1. What is the little boy's name? (Freddie)
2. Why is Sue talking to Freddie? (She wants him to do something.)
3. What did Sue ask Freddie to do? (Care for her duck)
4. Then what did Sue do? (Ran into the school)
5. What happened next? (The children came out of the school.)
6. What did the boys have? (Airplanes and trains)
7. What did the girls have? (Big dolls and little dolls)
8. Why did the children bring out their toys? (To show to their parents)
9. Did Freddie do what Sue asked him to do? (No. He looked at the toys instead of watching the duck.)
10. What do you think will happen to the duck? (It may get lost.)

C. Oral Rereading

Read aloud each sentence that names a toy carried by the children. (p. 123, lines 2, 3, 4)

First Reader: *The ABC Around Green Hills,* page 162

A. Preparation

Check the pupil's knowledge of clues to seasons—clothing, sled, snow, etc. Ask, "During what time of year does this story take place?" (Winter) Notice whether or not the pupil relates the illustration clue (on the sled) to the title. "What do you think the title of this story means?" (The name of the sled) Use the comprehension questions to further guide the silent reading.

B. Silent Reading (62 words)

Fly Fast

One cold morning little Freddie
saw Mr. Day coming out of the store.
Mr. Day was holding a very big bag.
"Hello!" called Freddie.
"Would you like me to take

that big bag home for you?
I can take it on my new sled."
   Mr. Day looked at Freddie's sled.
On it was the name FLY FAST
in gold letters.

Comprehension

1. Who is the little boy? (Freddie)
2. What time of day is it? (Morning)
3. Whom did Freddie meet this cold morning? (Mr. Day)
4. What had Mr. Day been doing before he met Freddie? (Buying things in a store)
5. What did Freddie offer to do for Mr. Day? (Take home his big bag)
6. How was Freddie going to help Mr. Day? (By taking the bag on his sled)
7. Did Mr. Day accept Freddie's offer right away? (No)
8. What did Mr. Day do instead of answering Freddie? (He looked at the sled.)
9. What did Mr. Day see on the sled? (The name *Fly Fast*)
10. How did this story get its name? (From the sled)
11. Was the sled old or new? (New)
12. Find two words that show the sled belonged to Freddie. ("my" in "my new sled", and "Freddie's" in "Freddie's sled")

C. Oral Rereading

Read aloud the question Freddie asked Mr. Day.
(Lines 5 and 6 of first paragraph)

Second Reader: *The ABC Over a City Bridge,* page 204

A. Preparation

"Look at the picture and decide what time of year you think it is."
(Summer) "Where is this family?" (In the garden) Use the comprehension questions to guide the silent reading.

B. Silent Reading (87 words)

A Trip to Harbor City

Summer had come to Red Oaks.
The days were hot. It was time for
children to wear sun suits.
   Peter and Betty Woods had been growing
fast. They could no longer wear

their last summer's play suits.

Mrs. Woods said, "Maybe Father will
drive us to Harbor City. Then we could
buy some summer clothes at the City Fair."

"I must reach my office early,"
said Mr. Woods. "I'll gladly drive you,
if we can get to the city by nine o'clock."

Comprehension

1. What time of year is it? (Summer)
2. Where does this family live? (Red Oaks)
3. What are the names of the children? (Peter and Betty Woods)
4. What problem did Peter and Betty have? (They needed new play clothes.)
5. Who had a suggestion for solving the problem? (Mrs. Woods)
6. What was her suggestion? (To ride with Mr. Woods to Harbor City and buy some clothes at the City Fair.)
7. On what condition did Mr. Woods say he would take the family to Harbor City? (If he could arrive at his office by nine o'clock)
8. If the distance from Red Oaks to Harbor City requires one hour's drive, what time would the Woods family have to leave their house? (Eight o'clock)

C. Oral Rereading

Read aloud the paragraph that tells why Peter and Betty needed to buy new summer clothes. (Second)

Third Reader: *The ABC Along Friendly Roads,* page 252

A. Preparation

Have the pupil look at the illustration on page 251. Ask, "Do you know the kind of American Indians that lived in homes like these?" (Cliff dwellers) "In what part of our country did the cliff dwellers live?" (Southwest) If the pupil needs help on the last question, he may skim the fourth and fifth paragraphs on page 251 to locate the answer. Use the comprehension questions to guide the silent reading of page 252.

B. Silent Reading (118 words)

In each village on the cliffs there was a large meeting room. To enter this room, too, the Indians had to climb onto the roof and descend through an opening.

Inside the round meeting room, a fire of juniper logs

burned in the middle of the floor. Beside the fire sat the wise men of the tribe. They sang songs and told stories.

Around the walls sat children of all ages. They listened eagerly to the wise men.

The men told stories to explain why the world is the way it is. They explained the thunder and the moon and the stars. They explained the animals, too, and told why each one was different—some wild, some gentle.

Comprehension

1. What did each cliff-dweller village have? (A large meeting room)
2. What was unusual about the entrance to this meeting room? (It was in the roof of the room.)
3. In what way was this meeting room used? (The wise men of the tribe sat around a fire, singing songs and telling stories.)
4. Who else could be found in the meeting room? (Children)
5. Why were the children there? (To listen to the stories and to learn things)
6. What were some of the things the children learned about nature? (They learned about thunder, the moon, and the stars.)
7. What did the Indian children learn about animals? (Why each one was different)
8. What two words were used to describe the different kinds of animals? (Wild, gentle) Name a wild animal you think these Indians knew. (Mountain lion)

C. Oral Rereading

Read aloud the one sentence that summarizes, or gives the main idea of, what the wise men told in their stories. (Fourth paragraph, first sentence)

Fourth Reader: *The ABC American Adventures,* pages 296-297

A. Preparation

Have the pupil look at the illustration on page 296. Ask, "What river is this selection about?" (Amazon) "Where is the Amazon located?" (In South America) "Find the mouth of the Amazon on the map. What is it?" (The place where it empties into the ocean.) "Find the headwaters on the map. What are headwaters of a river?" (Smaller rivers and streams that feed into the river.) Use comprehension questions to guide the silent reading.

B. Silent Reading (157 words)

Mighty River of Brazil

The greatest river in the world lies in South America, running thousands of miles across Brazil to the sea. From the time of its discovery to the present day, strange tales have been told of the mighty Amazon.

These tales began with the naming of the river many years ago.

One of the early Spanish explorers thought that the long-haired native men he saw there were women, and he was surprised to find them fierce fighters, as well. He had heard in his own country many tales of strange, warlike women who were called Amazons. And so he named the South American river the Amazon.

No other river in the world carries so much water as the Amazon. It gathers the waters from half of South America and sends them in a great yellow flood out to sea. It is so deep that heavy ocean liners can travel it for two thousand miles.

Comprehension

1. Through which country does the Amazon flow? (Brazil)
2. What is one of the strange tales about this river? (How it got its name)
3. Who named the river? (A Spanish explorer)
4. Why did he use the name Amazon? (The Spanish explorer thought the long-haired native men were women. He had heard about warlike women called Amazons—so he named the river Amazon.)
5. Why is this river considered by the author "the greatest river"? (It carries the most waters of any river in the world.)
6. How far can ocean liners travel up the Amazon? (2000 miles)
7. If you went 2000 miles west (or east, north, or south) from where we are now, where would you be? (Use a globe to verify the answer.)

C. Oral Rereading

Read aloud the sentence that tells where the Amazon River gets its water. (Page 297, 2nd paragraph, 2nd sentence)

Fifth Reader: *The ABC Adventures Here and There,* page 355

A. Preparation

Have the pupils look at the title on page 354 and tell what it meant by "Outer Space." Ask, "At the present time, what is in outer space that has been put there by man?" (Satellites) "How has man been able to send a satellite into outer space?" (By rockets) Use the comprehension questions to guide the silent reading on page 355.

B. Silent Reading (131 words)

Take a tube, sealed at one end. Put into it a charge of something that will explode. As the blast blows out the open end at the back, the tube jumps forward. The gases made by the exploding charge push against the walls of the tube in all directions. Since they cannot get out forward, the tube runs away and leaves them behind. That's a rocket.

The Chinese found this out about the year 1200, when they invented gunpowder. That first gunpowder was very poor, as far as exploding power went. It burned slowly instead of going off all at once with a bang. So when it was placed in tubes, the tubes moved forward, carrying some of the unburned powder instead of blowing up.

And the Chinese had invented rockets!

Comprehension

1. What shape is a rocket? (Tube-shaped, cylindrical)
2. What is placed inside? (A charge that will explode; an explosive)
3. Describe both ends of the rocket. (The one end is pointed and closed. The other end is left open.)
4. What happens when the charge explodes? (The gases push against all sides of the rocket, escaping through the opening and forcing the rocket forward by the pointed end.)
5. When was the first rocket made? (1200) How many years ago was that?
6. By whom was the rocket "invented"? (The Chinese)
7. What was an important discovery that made the Chinese rockets work? (The discovery of gunpowder.)

C. Oral Rereading

Read aloud the sentences that explain why the Chinese rocket did not explode when the gunpowder was ignited. (2nd paragraph, 2nd and 3rd sentences)

Sixth Reader: *The ABC Adventures Now and Then,* pages 278-279

A. Preparation

Have the pupil read the title and tell what a scientist is. Use the comprehension questions to guide the silent reading.

B. Silent Reading (212 words)

An Early Scientist

The huge cathedral was silent except for the sound of scattered footsteps on the stone floor. Here and there men and women were kneeling. The young student, Galileo, rose to leave. As he did so, his glance fell upon the great lamp hanging above him.

Someone had just come to light the lamp. In order to do so more easily, he drew it toward him. When he let it go, it swung back and forth, back and forth. The young man watched with growing interest.

Galileo noted that although the swinging became less and less as it died down, the time of each swing neither increased nor lessened. But how could he be sure? There were no watches in those days, more than three hundred years ago. How could he measure exactly the length of time it took the swinging object to make each swing?

His heart beat excitedly. The beat in his body! It was so regular he could use it as a timepiece. He did, and found he was absolutely right. The lamp, swinging like the pendulum of a big clock, took the same time to make its first large movement as the last small one. The swing was as regular as the beat of his pulse.

Comprehension

1. Who is the scientist in the story? (Galileo)
2. Where was Galileo when the story opened? (In a cathedral)
3. What is a cathedral? (A very large church, often in Europe)
4. What attracted Galileo's interest? (A swinging lamp)

5. What did Galileo notice about the swinging lamp? (That each swing took about the same time)

6. How did he time the swings? (By using his own heart beat—his pulse)

7. What decreased as Galileo watched the lamp—the times of the swings or the distances of the swings? (The distances of the swings)

8. Approximately what year did this story take place? (Any year between 1560 and 1660. The date given in *Compton's Pictured Encyclopedia* is 1583.)

9. Would the speed at which the lamp moved decrease or increase as the lamp stopped swinging? (Decrease)

C. Oral Rereading

Read aloud the sentences that give two conclusions Galileo drew from his experience timing the swinging lamp. (Page 279, last paragraph, last 2 sentences.)

Junior High School: Adapted from Center and Persons *Experiences in Reading and Thinking* (Macmillan), page 179

A. Preparation

Have the pupil read the title. Ask, "What will this selection explain?" (Why shells produce pearls) "What is a pearl?" (A lovely beadlike gem used in jewelry.) Use the comprehension questions to guide the silent reading.

B. Silent Reading (121 words)

Why Shells Produce Pearls

Centuries ago, people were puzzled to know how pearls were formed, and the ancients had many fanciful stories and myths regarding them, but today we know just how and why shells produce pearls, although all are not formed in exactly the same way. But in every case pearls are formed when some foreign matter becomes lodged in the shell and the animal covers it with the same material as the lining of the shell, or the "nacre" as it is called. For this reason, the pearls are always of the same color and luster as the interior of the shell, so that the more beautiful and lustrous the shell, the more beautiful and lustrous is the pearl.

Comprehension

1. What do we know today that people centuries ago did not know about pearls? (How and why they are formed)
2. What is necessary to form a pearl? (A bit of foreign matter inside a shell)
3. What is meant by "foreign matter"? (Something that does not belong inside the shell)
4. What is the animal that "covers it"? (The oyster or whatever creature lives in the shell)
5. What does the animal use to cover the foreign matter? (Material which the animal uses to line its shell)
6. What is this material called? (Nacre)
7. What two characteristics does the pearl have in common with the interior of the shell in which it is formed? (The color and the luster) What does luster mean? (The brightness or shining quality of something)

C. Oral Rereading

Read aloud the part of the sentence that tells how the people centuries ago explained the formation of pearls. (First sentence, 2nd clause)

High School: Adapted from Center and Persons *Practice in Reading and Thinking,* page 363

A. Preparation

Have the pupil read the title and the subtitle. Ask, "What is this selection about?" (The human eye) "How does the author describe the eye in the subtitle?" (Nature's happiest invention) "Does the author want you to interpret the term *invention* literally or figuratively?" (Figuratively) Use the comprehension questions to guide the silent reading.

B. Silent Reading (111 words)

The Human Eye: Nature's Happiest Invention

Mother Nature polished off her happiest invention the day she took a sphere about the size of a ping-pong ball, implanted therein a few optical gadgets like those in a dollar box camera, and labeled her product the human eye.

Nature practiced a good deal on the animal kingdom before she perfected her apparatus. She gave the eagle a set of eyes which are virtual telescopes, able to distinguish tiny objects from incredible distances. The zebra has eyes with horizontal pupils, the better to see while grazing with its head to the ground. The bee distinguishes ultraviolet light to which the human eye is blind.

Comprehension

1. Whom does the author credit with the invention of the eye? (Mother Nature)
2. What shape is the human eye? (Round) Which word tells you the shape of the human eye? (Sphere)
3. What is the size of the human eye? (That of a ping-pong ball) Use your hand to show the size of the eye.
4. What parts of the eye are similar to those of a box camera? (The pupil, the shutter opening; the iris and the lens for focusing; the retina, the film; etc.)
5. According to this author, how did Mother Nature perfect her invention? (By experimenting on animals)
6. What is an unusual characteristic of the eagle's eye? (The ability to see objects at great distances) What does "incredible distances" mean? (Unbelievable distances)
7. How does the zebra's eye differ from the human eye? (It has a horizontal pupil. The pupil of the human eye is round.)
8. What can the bee see that man cannot? (Ultraviolet light rays) What does the prefix ultra mean? (Beyond a given limit) What does *ultraviolet* mean? (Beyond the violet rays in the spectrum)
9. What is the author's attitude toward his topic—the human eye? (Slightly humorous in crediting Mother Nature—but greatly respectful of the structure of the human eye.)

C. Oral Rereading

Read aloud the sentence that best gives the author's opinion of the marvelous structure of the human eye. (First paragraph)

Betts discusses various reading levels as "independent, instructional, and frustration." The independent level is that point at which the child can read on his own without having to depend upon the classroom teacher or his parents to help him over the words. It is the level at which the child is able to select materials on his own and read them with understanding and appreciation. The personalized reading program will operate to a large extent at the independent level. The child's instructional level in the basal reader is somewhat higher than the independent level. At the instructional level, the child is not expected to know all of the words. He is expected to use those skills which he has been learning to unlock the new words. In the personalized program, since the child is reading so widely, it is likely that the child will meet a sufficient number of these words at the independent level, so it is expected that his reading in the personalized program may be at a slightly easier level than it would be in the basal text.

The frustration level of reading is that level at which the child must have constant help in order to be successful. Most standardized reading tests indicate a score which is actually at the frustration level. It means that the child, with the greatest possible effort, can comprehend, even at a lower level, some of the material. It is not a satisfactory instructional level and should be avoided for it develops discouragement within the child rather than any appreciation for reading.

DIAGNOSTIC READING TESTS

There are three rather distinct types of diagnostic reading tests. To the extent that these somehow arrive at a total reading score, they are not diagnostic tests. To the extent that they attempt to give a variety of levels in different types of reading skills, they are diagnostic. The standardized type of diagnostic test is, of course, the most familiar. Of less familiarity to classroom teachers, and more widely used in clinic situations are those tests which might be called semi-standardized. The more valuable type to the classroom teacher than any other, however, is the informal type of test which depends upon the teacher's skill both in knowing what to look for and sensitivity to the child's reading behavior.

Standardized type diagnostic reading tests, depending mainly upon word meaning and paragraph comprehension, attempt to analyze each of a variety of types of reading skills for both primary and elementary levels. For the test to be of diagnostic value, the form should be administered to the child which most closely approximates his reading level rather than his actual grade level.

The best example of the semi-standardized type of tests is the Durrell Analysis of Reading Difficulty. This is an individual test, administered by the teacher to one student at a time. Its main purpose is to diagnose the child's difficulty and not merely to determine a reading grade level. Graded levels are provided in oral reading and comprehension, silent reading and comprehension, word analysis ability, word recognition ability, spelling, handwriting, phonics instruction and listening comprehension. It is not necessary to always administer every part of the test, but the administration of a complete test provides a thorough diagnostic measure of the child's reading ability, and frequently outlines clearly the pattern to be followed in correcting the child's reading difficulty.

The diagnosis of a child's reading ability is divided into a number of areas. Most of these are oral reading and comprehension and silent reading and comprehension. But other essential abilities such as sight word recognition and ability to unlock new words must also be considered.

In measuring oral reading level, the child reads aloud to the teacher and she then asks comprehension type questions. If he is able to call words at a higher level than he is able to comprehend, this should be noted on his record. His reading orally, however, is determined by the level at which he can successfully read, attacking new words, and comprehending with a satisfactory degree of proficiency.

It is not unusual for the basal reader three-group approach to develop better oral than silent readers. This comes about because the teacher must have the child reading aloud in order to know how he is doing. Because the teacher is dividing her time equally between groups, only when the child reads aloud can she determine if he is making the expected progress. To further this encouragement in oral reading, parents have come to expect that unless the child reads each day for the teacher, he is not being taught reading. When the child goes home, his parents frequently check on his reading ability by having him read aloud.

At the beginning stage of reading instruction, much dependency is placed upon oral proficiency. This should not continue for too long or it will become a permanent habit. Reading aloud does, of course, provide the child with an audience situation, often deadly both to the teacher and to the other children. As for actually developing reading ability, however, oral reading does little of this.

Oral reading essentially is used only as a method of checking to determine if the child is reading. Without a comprehension check, however, it is actually of little value. It does not determine if the child is understanding what he is reading.

Certainly most of a child's reading throughout life will be silent and the development of good silent reading skills begins in the latter part of the first grade. In many instances oral reading is being used too long, and the child actually develops a dislike for reading silently. It is not unusual for reading clinics to find large numbers of children who are reading at a level two or three years higher in oral reading than they are in silent reading. This is an absurd situation which should not be allowed to develop.

There is less danger in the personalized program that oral reading will be overemphasized. Because the children spend so much of their time reading material which is selected by themselves, more opportunity for developing silent reading skills is offered. The program itself stresses silent reading. A teacher must, of course, frequently check comprehension to be assured that the child is not skipping material.

The teacher should check to determine the level of oral reading and comprehension and the level of silent reading comprehension. Both oral and silent reading levels are determined by comprehension, and not by the ability to call words. It should certainly be noted if there is any wide discrepancy between the child's word calling ability and his comprehension level in oral reading, but in silent reading, comprehension checks must depend upon comprehension entirely. Rate of reading silently is given little particular concern until the fourth grade. Then, so long as it does not take a child an unreasonable amount of time to read silently, it is probably not considered as an essential skill taught until the sixth grade level. At this point the child is taught to adjust his rate for the material he is reading and purpose for which he is reading.

The child's ability to read sight words should be regularly checked. There are a large number of words which a child knows, not because of their initial sounds or any specific word attack skills, but merely by rote memory. These are called basic sight words. By the middle of the third grade level, the child should be expected to know by sight the 220 words listed by Dolch.

In addition to the child's oral and silent reading and comprehension, and ability on basic sight words, the teacher must be concerned with the child's ability to unlock new words. Essentially, word attack skills can be divided into:

1. Little words inside of big words, both in compound words and in larger words containing smaller words.

2. Phonic ability in initial positions, final positions and medial positions.

3. Ability to spot and pronounce prefixes, suffixes and root words.

It is not meant to imply that all children at grade level can do all these things. Careful following of the skills chart, developed in Chapters 7 and 8, will indicate to the teacher the levels at which these skills should be taught. Even though the child has been presented certain of these skills, however, it is not unlikely that an occasional review of them will help both in his word attack procedure in reading and in his spelling.

Types of Reading Difficulties Which Can Be Observed

In oral reading there are a great number of things for which the teacher must watch. She must be alert to the child's hesitation, skipping of words, changing of words, and inserting words. She needs to pay attention to what the child does when he comes to a word which is difficult, noting particularly whether the child is having difficulty at the beginning of the word or at the end of the word. It is not infrequent to discover that children in oral reading will leave off endings of words, but in an effort to put on a good show can glide on over the material so quickly that it is hardly noticeable.

Checking eye span is sometimes an aid in helping the child read with more expression. This is accomplished by having the child read aloud. When he is in the middle of a sentence, the teacher covers the remainder of the material. The child then tells the words which are covered. The child's eyes should actually be two words, perhaps even more, ahead of where his voice is. If he is looking exactly where his voice is, he is reading word by word usually without any expression. Merely pointing out to the primary age child that his eyes should be ahead of where his voice is will sometimes eliminate the problem of lack of expression in reading. The use of tape records sometimes accomplishes much the same purpose.

In silent reading, there is less for the teacher to watch for. Certainly, however, lip movement and whispering should be detected. It is not unusual for first grade children to have lip movements until they learn that this is not silent reading. So long as the child is moving his lips, or is whispering, he is actually only reading orally. Putting his finger to his lips and teaching him how not to move his lips will avoid the development of a habit which will later severely retard his reading rate.

The number of fixations per line in silent reading can be checked by the classroom teacher by the use of a small pocket mirror which is held just above the page which the child is reading. With the teacher sitting next to the child she can observe his eye movements and count the number of fixations per line. If the child is fixating on each word, he is actually reading word by word which will result in poor comprehension. He needs to be taught to read groups of words both for better skill and comprehension.

Unless he is extremely slow, silent reading will only be noted. Little attention will be drawn to rate of reading until the child is perhaps in the fifth or sixth grade. The most important thing in silent reading is, of course, good comprehension.

Hesitation on sight words, or ability to sound out words, should be corrected. Basic words need to be learned almost entirely by rote. Devices by which this can be done are described in detail in Russell and Karp's excellent book, *Reading Aids*

Through The Grades.

The absence of any word attack needs to be noted, or any errors in methods of word attack. In the initial consonant sound, recognition of confusion between "b" and "d" and "p" and "q" can easily be detected. Confusion of the sound of certain letters needs to be noted.

Reversal of either letters or words needs to be carefully watched, particularly at the second grade level. The first grade child may often make such errors which usually can be easily corrected. Beyond this level, it will often take direct teaching to straighten out the child having difficulty with left-right progression on reversal of individual letters.

The informal inventory developed by Betts demonstrates a type of check list which the teacher may best develop for each child. Its value is far greater than any standardized test. Careful following of the informal inventory will not only find the difficulties, but will actually provide a rather definite type of program for the child in order to overcome the difficulty.

Determining Potential Reading Level

Of importance to teachers of reading in the personalized program or the basal program is to determine the actual capability that the child possesses. To expect the child to achieve at a level beyond where he has the innate ability to do so, is expecting the impossible. The pressure needed to try to get this child up to grade level will result in unpleasant attitudes toward reading, as well as lack of success on the part of the child. It is necessary for the teacher to know what each child is capable of doing, both for helping him in setting his own goal as well as setting the goals of her instruction.

The personalized program has a great advantage for the child in allowing more freedom in pacing himself. It is nevertheless important, however, that the classroom teacher know if his goal is realistic. For just as the teacher must not expect too much from the below-average child, so must the teacher of the bright child not lead him into thinking that less is expected from him than he is capable of.

The traditional group I. Q. test is of little value in helping the teacher in the reading situation. Because the group intelligence test is essentially only another type of reading test, the poor reader is immediately penalized. This is particularly true of the upper elementary level but is also true to a lesser degree of the primary level test. Although there is less evidence that it is true, it is certainly likely that the above average child both benefits from his reading ability and is benefited in his reading by superior ability. To rely on group I. Q. results, particularly with poor readers, would do great injustice.

The Stanford Binet Form LM (1960 edition) is a valuable tool for the trained examiner. An individual test should be administered to every child having reading difficulty in order to determine as nearly as possible his actual potential level. This test cannot be administered by the classroom teacher, however, which lessens its value. The poor reader will certainly be penalized even on the Stanford Binet, but the qualified examiner can actually diagnose the reading difficulties with use of the Binet and the report will indicate to what extent his reading disability has interfered with the results of the test.

In 1959, the Peabody Picture Vocabulary test was published. The author has administered it to more than 500 children with reading difficulty in Chattanooga, Birmingham, and Montgomery, and has found it to be especially effective with upper elementary children who are having reading difficulty. The results correlate highly with the Stanford Binet, but neither the Binet nor the Peabody correlate with group I. Q. tests of upper elementary poor readers.

The Peabody Picture Vocabulary Test is administered individually, with no reading ability required on the part of the student. It can be administered by a classroom teacher with only a minimum of training. For children with reading difficulties in elementary school, it is highly recommended as a means of measuring the potential reading level of the child.

The most valuable tool which a classroom teacher has at her disposal to determine potential reading level is a measure of the child's listening comprehension. If the child is able to understand material read to him of a particular grade level, then he is potentially capable of reading at this level. Understanding is essentially what mental ability is, and the simple device of reading to a child from graded material and having him answer questions about it indicate the level at which he could be expected to read if instruction were provided in the proper way.

This use of listening comprehension may seem like an oversimplification of the mental ability concept, but it nevertheless provides a reliable measure of what the child is innately capable of achieving. A comprehension check on material read to the child must measure understanding and must rely upon rote memory.

The reason for determining potential reading level is so that the teacher will know how much below his potential level the child is actually reading. It is not likely that many children will achieve up to their potential level but a somewhat commensurate score should be expected. A part of the individual conference with the child would be to determine the potential level and make the child aware of what he is capable of doing.

Determining Children's Interests

The best means of determining a child's interest is, of course, from observation. The personalized reading program allows the teacher time with each child individually in the reading program so that she knows each child better. It would not be out of order for the teacher to ask the child about those things which he likes to do. Observing the child during the rest of the school day and after school serves as clues to the child's specific interests. No interest inventory will measure interest better than the teacher's observation.

So that the teacher will have some guide as to the child's interests, it is not unusual to follow some type of formal inventory. One of the best is that prepared by Witty.

WITTY INTEREST INVENTORY

Teachers' and Clinicians'
CHILD STUDY RECORD
Paul Witty and David Kopel
Northwestern University Psycho-Educational Clinic
Evanston, Illinois
Revised by Paul Witty and Anne Coomer, 1948
Form VI. Pupil Report of Interests and Activities

Part 1. *The Interest Inventory*

Name .... Date of birth .... Age ....

Grade .... School .... Teacher .... Date ....

These questions are to find out some of the things boys and girls do and how they feel about certain things. Answer each question as accurately as you can. If you do not understand a question, you may ask your teacher about it.

1. When you have an hour or two that you can spend just as you please, what do you like best to do? ....
....

2. What do you usually do:
    After school? ....
    In the evening? ....
    On Saturdays? ....
    On Sundays? ....

3. At what time do you usually go to bed? ....
    When do you get up? ....
    Are you ever tired in the morning? ....Sometimes?........Often?........
    Are you ever late for school? ....Sometimes?........Often?........
    Do you ever have headaches? ....Sometimes?........Often?........
    Are you ever absent from school because of illness? ....
    Sometimes?........Often?........
    Do you ever cry? ....Sometimes?..................Often?..................
    Why do you cry? ....

4. In the space below write the full names and ages of your close friends.
    ....
    ....

    Underline the name of your best friend. Do you have many friends or few? ....
    Do you have a nickname? .... What? .... Do you like it? ....
    What do you like to play best? ....
    Would you rather play by yourself, with other boys, girls, boys and girls. Underline.
    Do you fight with your friends? Never, sometimes, often. Underline.
    Do you have as much time to play as you would like? ....
    Do you have any brothers or sisters? Write their names and ages here:
    ....
    ....
    With which of them do you play? ....
    Does your father or mother ever play with you? .... What? ....
    Do you like to be with your mother much of the time? ....
    With your father? ....

5. To what clubs or organizations do you belong? ....
    ....
    What do you do in your club? ....
    ....

How long have you been a member? .... Are you an officer? ....
Where do you meet? .... When? ....
Do you go to Sunday School? ....
Do you take any kind of special lessons outside of school? ....
What kind? .... Do you like them? ....
How long have you been taking lessons? ....
Is there another type of lesson you would prefer to take? ....

6. What tools, toys, playthings do you have at home? ....
....
Which do you like best? ....
Do you let other children use your toys? .... If not, why? ....
Is there any tool, toy, or equipment that you especially want? ....
What? ....
Do you have a workshop? ....
Are you carrying on any experiments? .... What? ....
Do you ever give shows? ....

7. Do you receive spending money? .... How much? ....
Regularly or occasionally? ....
Do you have a job after school or on Saturdays? ....
What do you do? ....
How many hours each week do you work? ....
Have you ever earned any money? .... How? ....
How do you spend the money you receive or earn? ....
Do you save money? .... How? ....
Do you have chores or other regular duties to do at home? ....
What? ....
Do you enjoy these duties? .... Do you like your home? ....

8. How often do you go to the movies? .... With whom, usually? ....
What are the names of the two best movies you have ever seen?
a. .... b. ....
Underline the kinds of pictures you like best:
comedy western "sad" news love serial mystery gangster
educational society cartoons
Who is your favorite actor? .... Actress? ....
If you were going into the movies, what kind of parts would you like
to play? ....
What stage plays have you seen? ....
Do you prefer movies or plays? Underline.

9. Have you been to a farm? .... A circus? .... A zoo? ....
A museum of art? ....
Other museums? ....
Have you been to an amusement park? ....
Have you ever been on a picnic? ....
Do you ever go to concerts? .... How often? ....
Have you ever taken a trip by boat? .... By train? ....
By airplane? .... By bus? .... By automobile? ....

By bicycle? .... Where did you go? ....

....

....

Where did you go during your last summer vacation? ....

....

    Underline *once* the places you *liked* and would like to see again:
    underline *twice* the places you *did not like.*
    To what other places would you like to go? ....

....

Who takes you to different places, or do you go alone? ....

10. What would you like to be when you are grown? ....
     What would your father and mother like you to be? ....

11. What is your favorite radio program? ....
     Second? .... Third? ....
     How much time a day do you spend listening to the radio? ....

12. What is your favorite television program? ....
     Second? .... Third? ....
     How much time do you spend each day watching television? ....

13. Do you have a pet? .... What? ....
     Are you making any collections? .... Of what? ....
     Do you have a hobby? .... What? ....

14. Do you like school? ....
     What school subjects do you like best? ....
     Second? .... Third? ....
     Do you take any electives? .... What? ....
     What school subjects do you dislike? ....
     What do you do best in school? ....

15. About how much time each day (outside of school) do you spend do-
     ing school work? ....
     Do your parents help you with this? Never, sometimes, often. (Under-
     line.)

16. Suppose you could have three wishes which might come true, what
     would be your first wish? ....
     Second wish? ....
     Third wish? ....
     Have you told these wishes to any one? .... to whom? ....
     Have any of your wishes ever come true? ....
     Have you ever pretended to be someone else? .... Who? ....

17. Do you dream at night? Never, sometimes, often. (Underline.)
     What do you dream about? ....
     Are your dreams pleasant? ....
     Are you ever frightened by dreams? ....

18. What things do you *wonder* about? ....

....

19. Are you afraid of many things? ....
    Name some of the things you fear ....

20. Do you enjoy reading? ....
    Do you like to have someone read to you? .... Who? ....
    Apart from lessons, about how much time each day do you spend
      reading? ....
    Do your parents encourage you to read at home? ....
    What are the names of some books you have been reading during the
      last two months? ....
    ....
    ....
    Draw a line through the names of those books which you did not finish.
    Do you have a card for the public or school library? ....
      How often do you get books from the library? ....
    How many books do you have of your own? ....
      Name some: ....
    ....
    What other books would you like to own? ....
    About how many books are there in your home? ....
    Underline the kinds of reading you enjoy most: history, travel, plays,
      essays, adventure, stories, science, poetry, novels, detective stories,
      fairy tales, mystery stories, biography, music, art.

21. What newspapers do you read? ....
    What parts do you like best? ....
    Name the comic strips you read and underline your favorites ....
    ....

22. What magazines are received regularly at your home? ....
    ....
    Underline those which you read.
    Name your favorite magazines: ....
    Name the comic books you read and underline your favorites ....
    ....
    Where do you get your magazines and comic books? ....
    ....

The purpose in determining the child's interest, of course, is to aid the teacher in selecting reading materials in which the child might be interested. It does not mean that the child will develop new interests from the use of the inventory but is a beginning point from which the teacher can work. If the teacher is unable to determine specific interests, part of her program must be to help the child develop such interests.

SUMMARY

It is an extremely important part of the teaching of reading to determine the child's reading level and his reading needs. To believe that there is any one reading level for the child, however, is a false assumption. Betts' discussions of independent, instructional, and frustration levels of reading are extremely helpful in understanding the child's reading level.

The achievement type of test which provides a reading level needs to be understood as something different from the diagnostic type of test. More important than standardized tests is the teacher's ability to observe the child in a variety of reading situations. She must know the types of ability to look for, as well as types of difficulty that she needs to be aware of. The wide use of informal inventories is strongly recommended, particularly for teachers who are working in a personalized program where they will have the time to work with children either individually or in groups on the basis of specific needs.

In order that the teacher will know what to expect from the child, an adequate determination of his potential reading level is essential. This can best be done by the use of a variety of different scores rather than relying upon any one score or observation. The determining of interests of the children themselves should be a part of all good reading programs. While it is not absolutely necessary for basal programs, it is so much an inherent part of the personalized program that the teacher must do it.

To the extent that the classroom teacher determines the child's reading level properly and his reading needs, she will be able to help him. With use of the personalized method, she is given an opportunity to use those things which she knows about children. Only to the extent that she adequately understands the child, will she be able to help him enjoy both "the process and the results of reading."

Chapter Six

Selecting Children's Books

It is of utmost importance that classroom teachers in the personalized reading program, or in the basal reading program, become as familiar as possible with children's literature. Because of the great dependency upon material which will be of interest to the students in the personalized reading program, the teacher has as one of her major responsibilities the making available of a wide variety of reading material. If a teacher does not know how to select children's material, or from where such materials can be obtained, then there is little likelihood that she will be successful in the personalized program. This very same problem, however, has undoubtedly existed in the basal reading program.

The classroom teacher must select books in many different areas of interest. Part of an elementary school teacher's duty is to encourage reading in a wide variety of areas. Only to the extent that the teacher has made available in the classroom materials covering different areas of interest can she hope to be successful in developing for each pupil a diversity of reading interests. Availability of interesting books in a variety of areas is one of the easiest ways to broaden one's reading horizon.

The teacher must not only be aware of materials in different areas of interest, she must also be aware of different interest levels of books. As children progress through the elementary grades they have both increased experiences as well as improved reading skills. Animal stories, for example, are of great interest to beginning readers. This interest shifts, at least for the brighter students, to an interest in biographies at the upper elementary level. The teacher must be aware of the interest level of books, as well as whether they are particularly valuable for use with boys or girls.

In addition to being concerned with the areas of interest, and interest levels of the material itself, the teacher must also be aware of the different reading levels of the various books. In the personalized reading program, it is necessary that the teacher have a number of books which will be of interest and challenging to children at each of a large number of different reading levels.

This does not mean the teacher will never buy more than a single copy of any one book. The initial order would most likely never contain more than an order for one copy of a book, but after the teacher has come to know a particular book and found it to be of high interest to a large number of students, a number of copies might be ordered. In the personalized program it is not unlikely that the teacher will order five or six copies of some of the books of more general interest.

The purpose of this chapter is to present classroom teachers with information about obtaining children's books. This information is ordinarily of concern only to librarians. If classroom teachers are to develop libraries within their rooms, and to aid in developing school libraries, they must be aware of the sources of books. More so in the personalized program than in the basal reading program, the classroom teacher must know about children's books. Included in this chapter is a list of the publishers of children's books who will readily send catalogs upon request. This list is followed by a discussion of the types of material which are available from each of the publishers. The chapter includes those approved book lists as well as a discussion of several books which would be of help to teachers in selecting children's books. Because of the importance of having books which have bindings that are durable, and ordering books in the most economical manner, there is a discussion of book wholesalers and prebound books. Mention is made of the various reference books available, as well as the publishers of the leading basal readers.

PUBLISHERS OF CHILDREN'S BOOKS

Listed below are those publishers of children's books who will readily mail catalogs and listings of available books for children.

Abelard-Schuman, Inc., 404 4th Avenue, New York 16, N. Y.

Abingdon Press, 810 Broadway, Nashville 2, Tenn.

Associated Publishers, Inc., 1538 9th St., NW, Washington 1, D. C.

A. S. Barnes & Company, 232 Madison Ave., New York 16, N. Y.

Binfords & Mort, Publishers, Binfords & Mort Bldg., 124 NW 9th Ave., Portland 9, Ore.

Bobbs-Merrill Company, Inc., 724-730 N. Meridian St., Indianapolis 7, Ind.

Bruce Publishing Company, 400 N. Broadway, Milwaukee 1, Wis.

Camp Fire Girls Inc., 16 E. 48th St., New York, N. Y.

Children's Press Inc., Jackson Boulevard & Racine Ave., Chicago 7, Ill.

Criterion Books, Inc., 257 4th Avenue, New York 10, N. Y.

T. S. Denison and Co., Inc., 321 Fifth Ave. South, Minneapolis 15, Minn.

Dial Press, Inc., 461 4th Ave., New York 16, N. Y.

Dodd, Mead & Company, Inc., 432 4th Avenue, New York 16, N. Y.

M. A. Donohue & Company, 711 S. Dearborn St., Chicago 5, Illinois

Doubleday & Company, Inc., 575 Madison Ave., New York 22, N. Y.

Duell, Sloan & Pearce, Inc., 124 E. 30th Street, New York 16, N. Y.

E. P. Dutton & Company, Inc., 300 4th Avenue, New York 10, N. Y.

Fideler Company, 31 Ottawa Ave., NW, Grand Rapids 2, Mich.

Follett Publishing Company, 1255 S. Wabash Ave., Chicago 5, Ill.

Friendship Press, 257 4th Ave., New York 10, N. Y.

Girl Scouts of the U.S.A., National Headquarters, 830 3d Ave., New York 22, N. Y.

Harcourt, Brace & Co., Inc., 383 Madison Ave., New York 17, N.Y.

Harper & Brothers, 49 E. 33rd Street, New York 16, N. Y.

Hastings House, Publishers, Inc., 151 E. 50th St., New York 22, N. Y.

Heritage Press, 595 Madison Ave., New York 22, N. Y.

Holt, Rinehart & Winston, Inc., 383 Madison Ave., New York 17, N. Y.

Houghton Mifflin Company (Riverside Press, Cambridge) 2 Park St., Boston 7, Mass.

Alfred A. Knopf, Inc., 501 Madison Avenue, New York 22, N. Y.

J. B. Lippincott Company, 227-231 S. 62nd Street, Philadelphia, Pa.

Little, Brown & Company, 34 Beacon St., Boston 6, Mass.

Longmans, Green & Company, Inc., 55 5th Ave., New York 3, N. Y.

Lothrop, Lee and Shepard Co., Inc., 419 Park Ave. South, New York 16, N. Y.

David McKay Company, Inc., 55 5th Ave., New York 3, N. Y.

The Macmillan Company, 60 5th Ave., New York 11, N. Y.

Macrae Smith Company, Lewis Tower Bldg., 225 S. 15th St., Philadelphia 2, Pa.

Julian Messner, Inc., Publishers, 8 W. 40th St., New York 18, N. Y.

Thomas Nelson & Sons, Copewood & Davis Sts., Camden, N. Y.

Noble & Noble, Publishers, Inc., 67 Irving Place, New York 3, N. Y.

National Safety Council, Inc., 425 N. Michigan Ave., Chicago 11, Ill.

Orion Press, Inc., 30 5th Ave., New York 11, N. Y.

Parnassus Press, 33 Parnassus Rd., Berkeley 8, Calif.

The Platt & Munk Company, Inc., 200 5th Ave., New York 10, N. Y.

Popular Mechanics Company, 200 E. Ontario St., Chicago 11, Ill.

Prentice-Hall, Inc., Route 9W, Englewood Cliffs, N. J.

Rand McNally & Company, Box 7600, Chicago 80, Ill.

Random House, Inc., 457 Madison Ave., New York 22, N. Y.

The Reilly & Lee Company, 14 E. Jackson Blvd., Chicago 4, Ill.

William R. Scott, Inc., 8 W. 13th St., New York 11, N. Y.

Charles Scribner's Sons, 597-599 5th Ave., New York 17, N. Y. (refer orders to 525 Main St., Belleville, N. J.)

Sheed & Ward, Inc., 840 Broadway, New York, N. Y.

Simon & Schuster, Inc., 630 5th Ave., New York 20, N. Y.

Vanguard Press, Inc., 425 Madison Ave., New York 17, N. Y.

The Viking Press, Inc., 18 E. 48th St., New York 17, N. Y.

Frederick Warne & Company, Inc., 210 5th Ave., New York 10, N. Y.

Ives Washburn, Inc., 119 West 40th St., New York 18, N. Y.

Franklin Watts, Inc., 699 Madison Ave., New York 21, N. Y.

Westminster Press, Witherspoon Bldg., Philadelphia 7, Pa.

Albert Whitman & Co., 560 W. Lake St., Chicago 6, Ill.

John C. Winston Company, 1006-1020 Arch St., Philadelphia 7, Pa.

The World Publishing Company, 2231 W. 110th St., Cleveland 2, Ohio

Whittlesey House, 330 West 42d St., New York 36, N. Y.

Henry Z. Walck, Inc., Publishers, 101 Fifth Ave., New York 3, N. Y.

Webster Publishing Company, 1154 Reco Ave., St. Louis 26, Missouri

Abelard-Schuman, Inc. (6 West 57th St., New York 19, N. Y.) lists in their catalog all of their books which are in print, alphabetically by author, regardless of classification. After each description is a notation concerning the category, either juvenile, fiction or non-fiction, or teen-age. The two special series are the Ram's Horn books of Jewish interest, and Life of Science Library.

The Abingdon Press provides an enjoyable catalog, with a careful description of all of their new books, and with an annotated listing of earlier publications. The description of the new books includes even the exact size of the text as well as the age and grade level of the material, its publication date, binding, number of pages and price. In addition to their listing of new books, they also have an excellent listing of picture books, several titles in the read-aloud books, easy to read books, recreation books, books beyond seven, non-fiction in the Makers of America series for ages eight and up, and religious books for boys and girls.

Associated Publishers, Incorporated, publishes books on the Negro. The books are not listed by grade level, most of them being at the adult level, although there are several under a juvenile books listing.

The A. S. Barnes & Co., Incorporated, includes publications of the Thomas Yoseloff Company and the Sagamore Press. The Golden Cockerel Press is also included in this catalog. Of concern to teachers are the Barnes Wonderful World Books. A few other books are for children at the six-year level, but most of their books are for age nine and up.

Publications of Binfords and Mort are concerned specifically with books on the Northwest. The catalog does provide a graded list for schools and libraries of books for juveniles. There are several listings at the primary grades, others at grades 3 and 4, at grades 5 and 6 and at grades 7, 8 and 9.

The Bobbs-Merrill Company provides a catalog of a large

number of books. The "Childhood of Famous Americans" series contains at the present time 124 titles, ranging in reading levels from grades 3 to 6. They are in new format with color illustrations. In addition to the "Childhood of Famous Americans" series, Bobbs-Merrill also publishes a wide selection of juvenile books for the preschool level up through high school. A recent addition to the Bobbs-Merrill Company books are the Raggedy Ann stories. The books are from the preschool level on up through the primary grades. There are 14 titles in this series. Another publication of the Bobbs-Merrill Company is the "Best of Children's Literature," compiled and edited by Nila B. Smith, Hazel C. Hart and Clarabelle Baker. There are six books in this series, ranging in age from 5 up through 13.

The Bruce Publishing Company publishes the Catholic Treasury Books. This is a selection of 21 titles for readers from the ages 10 to 14. The stories are taken from Catholic history and include "True to life biographies and dramatic stories of historical events which will make the reader proud of his Catholic heritage." For very young readers, Bruce Publishing Company has the "Christian Child's Stories." These books are for boys and girls in the preschool age through primary grades and offers religious reading for Catholic children.

Camp Fire Girls, Inc. offers a wide variety of materials of interest to girls of ages seven and up. The material is relatively inexpensive, and will provide the classroom library with hard-to-find material designed especially for girls.

Children's Press, Inc., states as its purpose "to aid the educator in his search for supplementary and individualized reading material to support his curriculum." The catalog of Children's Press lists books in a variety of ways. The author-titled descriptive lists group books by grade level. Another listing is by subject and unit study guides. The listing includes both reading level and interest level of the various materials. Children's Press publishes the "True Books" and the "I Want To Be" books. An affiliated company of Children's Press is Melmont Publishers. All Melmont books are prebound in washable book cloth and are sold at a single price.

Criterion Books begin at about age eight. The materials are

of high interest, but the vocabulary range is perhaps higher than the lower level which is stated.

The T. S. Dennison Co. publishes a new series of children's books written and designed for children from ages five to nine. The type is especially prepared for primary age children, and the books contain numerous illustrations.

The Dial Press has just presented its first list of Dial Junior Books. The department intends to publish books for boys and girls from the preschool age through the teen-ages. These will be books of an informational type, story books and picture books on all subjects of interest to children.

Dodd-Mead publishes a catalog of Science Books. These are graded and are mostly for grades 7 through 12, although there are some excellent ones available for grades 4 through 6. The "Science in Your Life" section contains most of the ones for 4 through 6 grades. The "World Around You" and "Astronomy" sections also contain books for children in fourth grade and up.

The M. A. Donahue Company publishes a number of books which would be useful in the classroom. They are not graded as to particular level, but cover a number of topics which would be of interest to elementary school children.

The prebound juvenile publications of Doubleday & Co., include a large number of books which the classroom teacher would find of value.

The catalog of Duell, Sloan & Pearce, Inc., lists books by headings: Animals & Animal Stories, Regions of America; Fiction, Regions of America; Non-Fiction; American Folkways; Sea and Sailing; Homer Croy's Books of the West; Indians and Indian stories; and others for high school students. The books are grouped by these categories, but include the age level to which they would be of interest. Most of the books would be no lower than the fifth or sixth grade level, so the catalog would be of particular interest to upper elementary teachers.

Dutton Books for Children and Young Adults lists all of the publications in the graded list for ages three to 14 and over, from kindergarten through grade 12. The picture story books and easy reading are listed in the first section, for the beginner reader in the next section, the middle grades in the next section, the upper grades in the next section, and for older readers in the higher section. One section of Dutton's catalog which would be of special interest to the teacher in the personalized program is entitled, "Meet The Authors of Dutton's Books for Children and Young People." By using this material to introduce authors to the children, more interest could be established in the books themselves.

The Fideler Company publishes supplementary geography material. With these supplementary textbooks are also film strips and pictures. The material is at the upper elementary school level.

Follett Publishing Company has a catalog of a wide variety of material from kindergarten through grade 9. The Follett "Beginning-To-Read" Books contain 17 titles. A new series of "Read-To-Know" books is now being developed. The catalog includes "Good Read Aloud Books," Animal Stories, and Social Studies. At the fourth grade level, Follett books include the "Farm Life" series, the "What Is It?" series, the "Big City" books, "Children of the World," stories in which girls are the central figure, and others in which boys are the central figure. This is a catalog which all teachers will want to see before placing their book orders.

Friendship Press is the publishing imprint of the Commission on Missionary Education of the National Council of the Churches of Christ in the U. S. A. To determine the exact reading level of the publications of Friendship Press is somewhat difficult, although there are certain books which are obviously at the kindergarten level, such as the Little Playmate books and others at the primary and upper elementary level.

The Girl Scouts of the U. S. A. publishes a large number of paper-back, inexpensive materials of high interest to girls. For upper elementary girls interested in girl scouting, including some of these books which they might choose to read in the classroom library would be very effective.

In addition to listing in some detail the publications of their new books, Harcourt, Brace & Company publishes a catalog of books for boys and girls which includes a complete list of all of their publications, arranged in alphabetical order of their authors. The books include a large number for all ages of elementary children beginning at ages six up through 12.

Harper & Bros. publishes a catalog of books for boys and girls. Those with the Harpercraft library binding meet textbook specifications and "are guaranteed for the life of the sheets." Their publications include the "I Can Read" books and the "Early I Can Read Books." There are 18 titles in the "I Can Read" series and two in the "Early I Can Read" series. The "Boys' Life" series includes four titles. Two of the books in the "I Can Read" series are science books by Sellfam, "Plenty of Fish" and "Seeds and More Seeds."

Hastings House includes books mostly of concern to teachers in the fourth, fifth and sixth grades and higher.

Holiday House books for young people are cataloged by author and classified by grades and subject. There are a wide variety of books at all elementary grade levels, particularly at the early primary grades.

Holt, Rinehart & Winston, Inc., a combination of three well-known publishers now producing juvenile books under the combined name, include a "Book to Begin On" series for ages six to eight, the Pogo series for children age six to nine, and a number of other titles.

Houghton Mifflin Co. publishes a large number of books for children at all reading levels, beginning at about the second grade. The "North Star" series contains 23 titles and deals with themes of the nation's heritage. The series by George Corey Franklin totaling now 13 titles in all ranges in interest from third grade on up. Piper Books contain 12 books and range in interest level and ability level at about the upper elementary grades (grades 4, 5 and 6).

The Alfred A. Knopf Company publishes Borzoi Books for Young People. Since 1957, the flat picture books for very young children have been made available in reinforced editions only. In addition to a thorough description of their new publications, the catalog also includes a listing by categories for younger readers, intermediate readers, and older readers. It also includes a list of those books which are eligible for purchase under the

National Defense Education Act in the fields of science, mathematics, and modern foreign languages.

Little, Brown & Co., which includes the Atlantic Monthly Press Books, includes in their catalog publications for children from grades 1 through grade 9. There are a number of books listed for the first three grades entitled "Easy-to-Read Books," including some picture books.

The catalog of J. B. Lippincott Company is divided into three major grade classifications: books for preschool and grades 1, 2, 3; books for grades 4, 5, and 6; and books for grades 7, 8, and 9. Their series of "Easy-to-Read Books" for the beginner reader include some 12 titles. These stories are "told in easy words and short sentences, are set in good size type, and have attractive illustrations. There are about 19 books in their More Picture Story Book series. Lippincott also makes available on request Librarians' Guides for Elementary and Junior High School, library cards on books which they have published, biographical sketches of authors, and supplementary books relevant to the National Defense Education Act. Lippincott publishes the delightful books of Munro, Leaf and Lois Lensky, among many others. In addition to their author-title index, the catalog also includes a special subject index, books for slow readers by grade level, and sight-saving books.

Longmans, Green & Company publishes Young America's Heritage Books. Their catalog contains a graded list of Longmans' junior books. These books are for readers from age 8 through 16. There are no books for primary children listed in the catalog. The catalog includes, in addition to the regular publication, the Andrew Lang Color Theory books for upper elementary age children. Their publication, "The Pageants of History," would be of use to the upper sixth grade students. In their catalog there is a chronological index entitled "Making America," beginning with America Gets Started; The Colonial Period and Before; America Fights for Freedom; The Revolution; America Fights Again: The War of 1812; America Pushes Back the Frontiers; American Settlers Make Themselves At Home; America Fights for Unity: The Civil War; One Nation Indivisible: After the Civil War; Some Men

Who Helped to Build; Life in America Today; Young Americans at Work; and American Problems. Another chronological index entitled Ancestors Yesterday, Neighbors Today includes books on the Rise of Civilization of the Ancient World; The Roman World; Living in Medieval Times; The Age of Discovery and Transition; Age of Rebellion; Beginnings of Modern Democracy; Living in the World Community of Nations: Europe; Living in the World Community of Nations: Asia; Great Leaders Belonging to the World; Folk and Fairy Tales: Reflection of the People's Culture. In addition to the author-title index, there is also a Geographical Index of Other Lands and a Geographical Index of U. S. This catalog should be of particular interest to upper elementary teachers in selecting materials which would correlate with their social studies units.

Lothrop Books are published by Lothrop, Lee and Shepard Co., Inc. In addition to the description of their new books, the catalog includes a complete check list by author and a complete check list by title. This includes the age level of the book, its classification and price.

The Macmillan Books for Boys and Girls includes a list of picture books, books for beginning readers, illustrated story books, and many others. The M. Sasek books are actually travel books for children from ages eight and up. Macmillan has a "New Children's Classics" which includes 21 titles of children's classics in "new format, with fresh bindings and illustrations." These are particularly for ages ten through 16. The "Lands and Peoples Series" tells in reading level of children from ages ten and up an account of a country and its people. In addition to listing the books by age level, they are also listed under the headings of history, geography, and biography. Books which are of interest to all ages include such headings as: Story Collections, Special Interest Books, Poetry, Religious Books, and Nature Books.

Macrae Smith Company publishes a complete catalog including their adult books as well as those for children. Their catalog includes a number of books for children of sixth grade and above, but only a few for earlier ages.

The David McKay Company publishes a catalog of books

for children and young adults. Teachers would be interested in several of the titles.

The Julian Messner Company publishes a catalog on books for children and young people. The listing of titles is arranged according to subject, interest, age levels, and grades. Each book is marked in the catalog with a short description and the grade levels which it would be of interest to by categories such as adventures, animals, artists, writers and poets, aviation, biography, etc. Some of the materials are at the primary grades but the catalog will be of particular interest to upper elementary teachers.

The catalog of the National Safety Council lists a wide number of publications on Safety which will be of interest to school age students. Some of the pamphlets would be of the reading level of upper primary children, but most of the materials would be for upper elementary age level students.

Noble & Noble Publishers, Inc., publishes Rainbow Classics. These are books for upper elementary level. They also have a picture dictionary for primary grades and the Rainbow Dictionary for Grades 1, 2, and 3.

Nelson Juvenile Books include the Nelson Picture Biographies for ages eight to 11 and other junior books.

The Orion Press publishes only two books for children— *Italian Fables* and *Fairy Tales*.

Parnassus Press has only a limited offering of books for children. "Quality, not Quantity" is the emphasis according to the publisher. There are a number of books at the early elementary level in which teachers will be interested.

Platt & Monk Company publishes books categorized preschool through grade 3, grades 4 to 6, and grades 7 to 12. They also include a number of materials, under the heading Educational Activities, which will be of interest to teachers. The puzzles, riddles, and quizzes which they publish should be of special interest.

Popular Mechanics publishes a number of books which will be of special interest to upper elementary boys. The Science Career Books, "There's Adventure," includes nine titles. Such titles as *There's Adventure in Atomic Energy* and *There's Adventure in Jet Aircraft,* make this a very appealing type of material. Other materials about shop work, hobbies, and sports make this material of interest to upper elementary students.

Prentice-Hall Junior Books include books for all ages. Although the actual number of books published by Prentice-Hall is not great, there are a number which will be of interest to elementary school teachers.

The G. P. Putnam's Sons publications include those of Coward-McCann and the John Day Company. Extensive listings of Putnam's books for the elementary level make this a valuable catalog. Coward-McCann's books for girls and boys includes a large number of books as well as a graded list and a subject index. John Day has just announced a new series by favorite authors entitled "The Reason Why" series.

Rand-McNally publishes a large number of books for children at each grade level. The catalog includes a description of each of these books and also a subject index.

Random House publishes a catalog on books for boys and girls. Their catalog is divided into three sections: complete annotated list of books grouped by grade level, title index, and new books. The different series which Random House publishes are: "Beginner Books; Picture Books; Easy-to-Read Books; Legacy Books; All-About Books; Landmark Books; World Landmark Books; Shirley Temple Editions; Looking Glass Library; and Teen-age Fiction." The "Beginner Books" are for those children who are at the very beginning levels of independent reading. It includes the delightful books of Dr. Seuss, *The Cat in the Hat* and *The Cat in the Hat Comes Back.* The beginner books will be popular from first grade on up. The "Easy-to-Read" Book series will probably be of interest to teachers from second grade on up. "Legacy" Books are "exciting diversions of the great and enduring myths, legends and folktales of long ago, retold by famous storytellers of today." This series will be of particular interest to upper elementary teachers. The All-About Books are science books for boys and girls from grades 5 to 10. There are 32 titles in the series, ranging through all areas of science. The Landmark books are primarily for social studies materials in the fifth to tenth grades. At the present time, there are 90 titles in this series. With the Landmark series are Enrichment Records and film strips. The World Landmark books are for readers age 12 and up and are about "the great events and personalities who have been turning points in history." There are 43 titles in this series. The Looking Glass Library contains "great works of children's literature which have been out of print or difficult to obtain in book stores." There are ten titles in this series at the present time. They are for children of ages eight and up. The title index includes the division of material into fiction and nonfiction, and by age levels. Random House is a source of a great many books which are of particular interest to children at all of the elementary levels. Each teacher should have a Random House catalog from which she can read a description of all of the books.

The Reilly and Lee catalog lists a limited number of books for juveniles. The age range of their materials includes some that will be of interest to elementary school teachers.

Sheed & Ward are publishers of religious materials for children of all ages. There are a large number of publications, many of which are of the Catholic faith.

The Charles Scribner's Sons catalog, "Books for Young Readers," includes materials from preschool age through high school. The extensive listing by author and title and by subject matter makes it easy for classroom teachers to locate desired materials. The grouping by age level, includes an annotated description of the book. All of the new Scribner picture books and books for younger readers are in the Scribner Durable Binding. The Scribner Illustrated Classics includes 33 titles. Most of these would be of interest to upper elementary grade teachers. The Willow Leaf Library includes "distinctive new editions of our famous books that have been among those that are best loved by children." There are seven titles in this series at the present time. These are books for upper elementary grade children.

Simon & Schuster, Incorporated are publishers of the Golden Book Encyclopedia as well as the American Heritage Junior Library, the Big and Giant Golden Books, the Golden Beginning Readers, the Golden Adventure Books, Guild Press Books for Catholic readers, Golden Nature Guides, L. W. Singer Books and the Golden Library of Knowledge. Most of the books mentioned are for upper elementary readers. The Golden Beginning Readers, however, containing eight titles, are for children in grades 1 and 2. These materials are published under the Golden Press, Inc., rather than Simon & Schuster, although they are one company and the same mailing address is used.

Vanguard Press publishes a catalog including both adult and juvenile books. There are a number of titles which will be of particular interest to elementary school teachers.

Viking Press publishes a catalog of junior books. In addition to a large number of publications which are carefully described, the catalog also includes a graded list of a large number of materials and a subject index. Teachers in the elementary school at all grade levels should have this catalog to use in ordering books.

The Henry Z. Walck Company was established as a new publishing house for children's books for preschool age through teen-age in 1958. All of the titles which were formerly published by Oxford University Press are now published by the Henry Z. Walck Company. The catalog includes an annotated list of their publications by the author's name including a description of what is in the book, the number of pages, date of publication, its price and the age level to which it would be of particular interest.

The Frederick Warne Company has a selected list of picture books for children which should be of particular value to first grade teachers.

The Ives Washburn Junior Books Catalog includes a number of books which would be of interest to elementary school children. Most of the publications would be for upper elementary children.

The Franklin Watts Company publishes several series of interest to elementary students. The Watts International Series is the imprint on American editions of "outstanding and contemporary books for boys and girls from overseas." These are books for children from kindergarten level on up. In addition to their other books, the Franklin Watts Company is best known to elementary school teachers for their "first book series." At the present time, there are more than one hundred first books. Areas covered by first books include arts and literature, science, social studies, language arts, transportation, communications, and recreation.

In addition to their textbook material, Webster Publishing Company has some reading material which would be of interest to the classroom teacher. The Webster Classroom Science Library is an example of this. It includes 18 science books covering more than 500 different topics. These inexpensive short books at an easy reading level would make excellent material for the classroom teacher to make available to the children.

The Westminster Press publishes a check list of books for children and youth and for young adults. This includes all of their publications, the materials beginning for children in grades 3 of age eight and goes up through age 15 in grade 10, and includes a few young adult publications.

The Albert Whitman Company, pioneers of easy reading books, publishes a catalog, "Better Books for Boys & Girls," which states the exact grade level at which the book should be used. Most of the publishers group the books by varying ages, frequently meaning that the books can be used at the lowest grade level but more likely will be read by the average student at the higher grade level. In the catalog of the Whitman Company, there are more than 20 listings at first grade level, an additional 20 at the second grade level, third grade level, fourth grade level, and on up through the eighth grade.

The Whittlesey House Books for Young People are published by McGraw-Hill Book Company. The Whittlesey House publications include a large number of books in science for children at kindergarten to grade 3, grades 4 to 6, and up. There are a large number of books published by Whittlesey House of all types.

The John C. Winston Company publishes a catalog which includes their books for boys and girls as well as their adult books and religious books. It also includes the Tell-Well Books of Bill and Bernard Martin.

The World Publishing Company has a catalog of "Children's Books." This includes the Rainbow Classics for upper elementary and above age level as well as many other books for children of all age levels.

The Young-Scott Books, published by William R. Scott, Inc., Publisher, has a complete list of Young-Scott books arranged by subjects. There are a great many books of interest to primary grade teachers in this catalog. There are some books for upper elementary level, although the major emphasis is on the primary grade publications.

APPROVED BOOK LISTS

Authoritative sources of children's books are frequently recognized by publishers. Either by the use of abbreviations or symbols which are explained from the catalog of the publisher, individual books are identified as having been included in certain of these lists. It would be wise for each teacher to have these lists herself, so that she would not have to depend upon the publishers for classifying material, but could go about selecting books from those approved lists.

Not every book which a teacher selects must be from an approved list. For a book to be on an approved list, it must have rather general appeal, be of a literary quality, have a somewhat controlled vocabulary, and meet other rigid requirements. In some instances, teachers will want books which have only regional appeal or provide a very specialized type of information which she particularly wants to use with her class. In both instances, the books will probably not be on any of the book lists. This does not mean that the books are of a low quality and should not be ordered.

The most widely accepted book list is that of the American Library Association, (50 East Huron Street, Chicago 11, Illinois). The American Library Association has prepared the following four lists of approved books:

1. American Library Association Book List.
2. American Library Association Basic Book Collection for Elementary Grades, 1960 Edition.

3. American Library Association Basic Book Collection for Junior High Schools, 1960 Edition.
4. Basic Book Collection for High Schools, 1957 Edition.

The Children's Catalogue is published by the H. W. Wilson Company (950 University Avenue, New York 52, N. Y.). The Ninth Edition of the Children's Catalogue was published in 1956, and at the present time there is a 1957-1959 supplement. The H. W. Wilson Company also publishes a standard catalogue for high school libraries, of which there is a seventh edition published in 1957.

The Independent Schools Education Board publishes a junior book list. Also, the Library Journal, Junior Libraries, approves certain books.

The Horne Book Magazine is published bi-monthly (585 Boylston St., Boston 16, Mass.). The Horne Book Magazine is a magazine containing reviews of outstanding children's books and articles of an almost literary quality themselves dealing with books and reading for children.

The Association for Childhood Education has prepared a "Bibliography of Books For Children" listing "more than 2,000 titles including old favorites in the best books for children published through December 1957." The price of this book list is $1.50 and can be ordered from the Association for Childhood Education International, 3615 Wisconsin Avenue, N.W., Washington 16, D.C. Books are classified according to content under the following headings:

Animals of All Kinds   Life in the United States
Biographies for Boys & Girls   Music
Collections of Modern Stories   Picture Story Books
Fanciful Stories and Folklore   Plays
Games, Hobbies & Sports   Poetry for All Tastes
Holidays to Celebrate   and Moods
Informational Books for the   Reference Books
  Social Studies   Religion
Life in Other Countries   Science

The titles are listed under each of those subjects stated above.

They also include an age classification, the author of the books, publisher, and price. The bibliography is 125 pages long.

Another publication of the Association for Childhood Education International is "Children's Books—For $1.25 or Less." This is a complete revision of the classified list of approved books which cost $1.25 or less. It is 36 pages long and may be ordered from the Association for Childhood Education (address listed above) for 75 cents.

The National Council of Teachers of English has prepared a number of reading lists. *Adventuring With Books* for grades from kindergarten through sixth grade was published in 1956, with a 1958 supplement. *Your Reading*, prepared by the National Council of Teachers of English, is for grades 7 through 9. It was first published in 1954 and a 1956 supplement is available.

The Horne Book, Inc. (585 Boylston St., Boston 16, Mass.) has several publications which are of particular interest to teachers.

Books Are Vacations, compiled by Lois R. Markey, is "An Annotated Reading List for Ages 8 to 12." Sections on nature, science, poetry, fantasy, fiction, biography, and music books, among others. The price of this publication is 75 cents.

Children's Classics, compiled by Alice M. Jordan, is a narrated list of sixty of the "Best Books Ever Written for Children" and is recommended for parents who want to build a good home library. It is also 75 cents.

The Horne Book Crier of November-December 1959 (a bimonthly news sheet issued by The Horne Book, Inc.) contains The Horne Book's Honor List. It is based on children's books of 1954 through 1958 and contains a wide variety of different types of books. The divisions into which the books are divided are: Picture-Story Books, Poetry and Rhymes, Legends and Folk Tales, Tales of Fantasy and Imagination, Stories for the Younger Children, Stories for the Middle Years, Stories for the Older Boys and Girls, Biography and History, and Nature and Science.

For teachers who want to select books which are related to the content areas which they are studying there is no better source than Eloise Rue's *Subject Index to Books for Primary Grades,* 1943, First Supplement, 1946, and *Subject Index to Books For Intermediate Grades,* 1950.

CHILDREN'S BOOK AWARDS

There are a number of awards each year for children's books. The winners of these awards can usually be depended upon to have high interest appeal to children. Since they are selected by authorities in children's literature, who have available all of the recent publications, prize winning books should be made available to elementary children. In addition to the Newbery Medal and Caldecott Medal, there are the New York Herald Tribune Awards and the Regina Medal.

The Caldecott Medal Award was established in 1937 for the best illustrated books for children published each year. Listed below are the Caldecott Medal Awards since 1938.

Title	*Author*
1938 Animals of the Bible	Dorothy Lathrop
1939 Mei Li	Thomas Handforth
1940 Abraham Lincoln	Ingri and Edgar D'Aulaire
1941 They Were Strong and Good	Robert Lawson
1942 Make Way for Ducklings	Robert McCloskey
1943 Little House	Virginia Burton
1944 Many Moons	James Thurber and Louis Slobodkin
1945 Prayer for a Child	Rachel Field and Elizabeth Orton Jones
1946 Rooster Crows	Maud and Miska Petersham
1947 The Little Island	Golden MacDonald and Leonard Weisgard
1948 White Snow, Bright Snow	Alvin Tresselt and Roger Duvoisin
1949 The Big Snow	Berta and Elmer Hadar
1950 Song of the Swallows	Leo Politi
1951 The Egg Tree	Katherine Milhous
1952 Finders Keepers	Will and Nicolas
1953 Biggest Bear	Lynd Ward
1954 Madeline's Rescue	Ludwig Bemelmans
1955 Cinderella	Marcia Brown
1956 Frog Went A-Courtin'	John Langstaff

1957 A Tree Is Nice   Janice Udry
1958 Chanticleer and the Fox   Barbara Cooney
1959 Nine Days to Christmas   Marie Ets

The Newbery Medal was established in 1921 for the most distinguished contribution to American children's literature each year. Listed below are the Newbery Medal Award winners:

Title	*Author*
1922 Story of Mankind	Hendrik Van Loon
1923 Voyages of Dr. Dolittle	Hugh Lofting
1924 Dark Frigate	Charles B. Hawes
1925 Tales from Silver Lands	Charles J. Finger
1926 Shen of the Sea	Arthur B. Chrisman
1927 Smoky, The Cowhorse	Will James
1928 Gay-Neck	Dhan Gopal Mukerji
1929 Trumpeter of Krakow	Eric P. Kelly
1930 Hitty	Rachel Field
1931 The Cat Who Went to Heaven	Elizabeth J. Coatsworth
1932 Waterless Mountain	Laura Armer
1933 Young Fu of the Upper Yangtze	Elizabeth F. Lewis
1934 Invincible Louisa	Cornelia Meigs
1935 Dobry	Monica Shannon
1936 Caddie Woodlawn	Carol R. Brink
1937 Roller Skates	Ruth Sawyer
1938 White Stag	Kate Seredy
1939 Thimble Summer	Elizabeth Enright
1940 Daniel Boone	James Daugherty
1941 Call It Courage	Armstrong Sperry
1942 Matchlock Gun	Walter D. Edmonds
1943 Adam of the Road	Elizabeth Janet Gray
1944 Johnny Tremain	Esther Forbes
1945 Rabbit Hill	Robert Lawson
1946 Strawberry Girl	Lois Lenski
1947 Miss Hickory	Carolyn Sherwin Bailey
1948 Twenty-one Balloons	William Pene DuBois
1949 King of the Wind	Marguerite Henry
1950 Door in the Wall	Marguerite deAngeli
1951 Amos Fortune, Free Man	Elizabeth Yates
1952 Ginger Pye	Eleanor Estes
1953 Secret of the Andes	Ann Nolan Clark
1954 . . . And Now Miguel	Joseph Krumgold
1955 Wheel on the School	Meindert DeJong

1956	Carry on, Mr. Bowditch	Jean Latham
1957	Miracles on Maple Hill	Virginia Sorenson
1958	The Witch of Blackbird Pond	Elizabeth George Speare
1959	Onion John	Joseph Krumgold

Books of Particular Interest to Teachers

A book which must not be overlooked by teachers is by Nancy Larrick, *A Teacher's Guide to Children's Books.* Charles E. Merrill Books Inc., Columbus, Ohio, 1960. In addition to providing valuable information for teachers in selecting books for children, *A Teacher's Guide to Children's Books* also includes many aids for the teacher in her "teaching of reading" program. Particularly in the personalized program can this book be of value. The first chapter deals with "Children and Books in the First Grade." This describes those activities relating to reading to children which develop readiness for reading. "As Children Begin to Read" describes those activities and reading materials which will be of interest to children in grades 2 and 3. "Extensive Reading in the Middle Grades" deals with reading on many levels and lists the many types of books available at each level. The section entitled "Bringing Children and Books Together" provides a much broader concept of reading than merely reading more books. The activities will be of particular help to all teachers. Part Three, "Taking Stock of Your Reading Program," tells about how a book is made and selecting books for children. Part Four deals with favorite books of boys and girls and books teachers themselves will find valuable.

Another excellent source of books for children is that by Nancy Larrick entitled, *A Parent's Guide to Children's Reading.* This book published by Doubleday in 1958 can be obtained in either the hard binding or in pocketbook edition. It was a project of the National Book Committee in cooperation with eighteen other national organizations. It presents a complete guide for parents to the selection of children's books, as well as a discussion of the learning-to-read process.

A 1960 publication of the American Library Association, *Let's Read Together,* is the first publication of the Library Association containing a selection guide for parents. More than

500 titles are included for children from the various early ages to those 15 years old. They are arranged in 24 subject areas and contain, in addition to a description of the book, complete buying information. Although designed primarily for parents, *Let's Read Together* is also valuable for classroom teachers in ordering books for use in the personalized program or in the supplementary phase of the basal program.

One of the major problems of ordering children's books for use in the classroom is the durability of their binding. Frequently, children's books in the trade editions have attractive covers which will not withstand the great use to which they will be subjected in the regular classroom. Rebinding of such books, which is practiced widely with adult books in most libraries, provides a durable type cover, but takes away the appeal of the publisher's cover. An older book which has been rebound, without the advantage of the appealing picture cover, can still be used with children, but will not be so widely accepted as if it had its original cover.

Books to be used in the classroom, which will be read by many children and receive more wear than it would in any home library, should have either a special reinforced library binding or the special publisher's binding for classroom use. The cover should be of cloth, resistant to water and dirt smudges.

Prebound books cost slightly more than the regular edition of the book. The binding of the prebound book is much more durable than regular binding, and is to be highly recommended for all purchases by teachers for classroom use. Some of the books are published in sturdy bindings, or school editions, by the original publisher. When this is not true, it is worth the additional cost to buy the books from a company which prebinds the books. Carl J. Liebel and New Method are the leading prebinding companies. Each of these companies, as well as other companies which prebind books, publish a "replacement" catalog as well as a current catalog. The current catalog lists all of the new books which are available in the prebound edition from these publishers. The replacement catalog, however, lists only those books which have been found to be good sellers. In a sense, the replacement catalog would be of particular interest to teachers because it indicates that these books have already been widely accepted by teachers and children. It would certainly be hoped that a teacher would not rely entirely upon a replacement catalog but when ordering from this type of catalog she can feel some assurance that the book has been widely accepted by children and teachers.

The Carl J. Leibel Company is a specialist in prebinding juvenile books from all publishers. They provide books for schools and libraries with a "quality binding." All books of other publishers, whether in their catalog or not, can be ordered through this company with their special "prebound" cover. Most preprimers, primers, and supplementary readers of the leading textbook publishers, which appeared originally with paper covers, can be ordered by the Leibel Company with a library binding. These are listed in their catalog "Prebound Books for Boys and Girls, 1960 Replacement Catalog" (1236 South Hatcher Avenue, LaPuente, California). The Prebound Books for Boys and Girls, Fall, 1960 Catalog lists those books to appear in the fall of 1960 by leading publishers. The title of each book is listed with its author and a brief description of the story. The age range of children who will be interested in this book is given, the month of its publication and its original publisher. The price of the prebound edition is slightly higher than the publisher's list price.

Carl J. Liebel, Inc., of LaPuente, California publishes a "comprehensive bibliography of elementary books on science and mathematics selected to conform with the provisions of title 3, National Defense Education Act of 1958 (Public Law 864)." The bibliography is divided into two main sections called: Science and Arithmetic and Mathematics. The science section is divided into the following classifications: Non-fiction (for students), fiction (for students), professional reference (for the teacher). The arithmetic and mathematics section is alphabetized by last name of the author. The reading level by grade is given for each book except those for the teacher. There is a special section entitled "Conservation." Conservation on the biography-individual section is arranged alphabetically by the name of the person whom the book is about. The subject headings roughly correspond with the subject covered in any elementary science textbook series.

New Method Book Bindery, Inc., Jacksonville, Illinois publishes an annual replacement catalog. New Method is a distributor of prebound books, and not a publisher. Books of all publishers are included in their catalog. The New Method catalog lists books by the last name of the author, and includes the publisher and the age levels for which the book is recommended.

Distributors of prebound books publish an annual replacement catalog, and a current catalog in the fall and spring of each year. Classroom teachers should request these catalogs if they are in a position where they are able to order books from such companies. If they cannot order books through these companies because of state regulations, or their orders are very small, they should borrow the catalogs from their librarians in their systems in order to have a guide to the children's books which are available.

STATE TEXTBOOK DEPOSITORIES

In some states it is necessary for classroom teachers to place orders through State Textbook Depositories. In many instances, library funds which teachers are allowed to spend must be spent on materials available through these depositories. To the extent that the depository makes books available at a lower cost, they provide a great service. When some unknown employee of the depositories makes substitutions without consulting teachers, they are doing the teacher a disservice. If books are not available through the depository which the teacher wants to order, they should be allowed the freedom to order through the publisher.

Listed below are the state textbook depositories and their addresses:

ALABAMA—State Textbook Depository, Southside Station, Tuscaloosa

ARKANSAS—Arkansas Book Co., 2101 Bond Street, Little Rock

CALIFORNIA—Vroman's California School Book Depository, 367 S. Pasadena Ave., Pasadena 2, Branch at 560 Mission St., San Francisco 5

FLORIDA—Florida School Book Depository, P.O. Box 36, Station G., Jacksonville

GEORGIA—Georgia School Book Depository, 441 W. Peachtree St., N.E., Atlanta

IDAHO—The Caxton Printers, Ltd., Caldwell

KANSAS—The Kansas Book Co., Inc., 911 Adams St., Box 641, Topeka

LOUISIANA—A. K. Kilpatrick, 1400 Arkansas St., Monroe

MISSISSIPPI—School Book Supply Co., 116 E. South St., Jackson

NEW MEXICO—New Mexico School Book Depository, Inc., P.O. Box 4128, Santa Fe

NORTH CAROLINA—North Carolina School Book Depository, Inc., Raleigh

OKLAHOMA—Jasper Sipes School Book Depository, Inc., 17 Main St., Oklahoma City 2

OREGON—J. K. Gill Co., 408 S.W. Fifth Ave., Portland 4

SOUTH CAROLINA—The R. L. Bryan Co., 1440 Main St., Columbia 1

TENNESSEE—Tennessee Book Company, 126 Third Ave., Nashville 3

TEXAS—Lone Star School Book Depository, 707 Browder St., Dallas 1

UTAH—Utah–Idaho School Supply Co., 155-157 S. State St., Salt Lake City 1

WASHINGTON—John W. Graham & Co., 435 North 34th St., Seattle

The E. M. Hale & Company of Eau Claire, Wisconsin, provides a wide variety of books at a 40 per cent discount off list price. All of the E. M. Hale & Company books have either cloth or special reinforced library binding. The catalog from E. M. Hale & Company is one with which all teachers should be familiar. The books are listed by title, by author, and by series. They are also listed by groups. The following are books of the Cadmus Series and are books for children from kindergarten through Grades 8. The Cadmus Series, available through E. M. Hale & Co., contains 420 titles.

Group K includes books for kindergarten and Grades 1 and 2. Group 1 refers to Grades 1, 2, and 3.

Group 2 refers to Grades 2, 3, and 4.
Group 3 refers to Grades 3, 4, and 5.
Group 4 to Grades 4, 5, and 6.
Group 5 to Grades 5, 6, and 7.
Group 6 to Grades 6, 7, and 8.

Also available from E. M. Hale & Co., are Landmark Books. There are 57 Landmark titles available. Landmark Books are of either the American Landmark series or the World Landmark series. The American Landmark Books are for Grades 5 through 8, and the World Landmark Books are for Grades 6 through 9. The E. M. Hale edition of the Allabout books are for intermediate grades. There are 33 titles in this series at the present time.

The E. M. Hale & Company also has available the Hale Magic Window books. There are 17 in this series at the present time. These books are for teenagers. Through Golden Windows Anthology is a series available through E. M. Hale & Company. This includes ten titles ranging from kindergarten through Grade 8.

The Baker and Taylor Co. (Hillside, New Jersey) is the oldest and largest exclusive book wholesale center in the United States. They stock more than 60 thousand different titles. The Baker and Taylor cumulative library catalog of "Desk Books for Boys and Girls" contains 2700 titles of books for children. The list of 2700 books is compiled in the offices of Library Journal and Junior Libraries. The catalog is divided into five parts: (1) Preschool to third grade, (2) Grades 4 to 6, (3) Grades 7 to 9, (4) Special subjects, (5) Indexes.

Other Materials

In addition to the publishers of children's materials already mentioned, the classroom teacher should also know of the leading children's encyclopedia, dictionaries, maps and atlas. By being readily available within the classroom, the children will learn how the material can be helpful. With so much additional opportunity in the personalized program to do independent research, the need will be greater than ever for reference materials.

Basal readers will still be available in the classroom, even though the teacher has changed over entirely to the personalized program. When certain skills need to be worked upon, the teacher might bring together those children into the particular story in the basal reader in which the skill is emphasized.

SUMMARY

One of the most frightening features of the personalized reading program is, "Where do I get the materials?" The list of children's publishers given in this chapter should provide the teacher with enough catalogs from which to choose good children's books. Already existing libraries within schools and individual classrooms will be a good beginning, but it will be necessary to add a great many books, both of different reading levels and of different areas of interest.

Purchasing books has too often been a task placed upon the teacher without sufficient instruction as to what types of bindings should be ordered, how books can be ordered economically without sacrificing durability, and from what source the best discount may be obtained. If a teacher is to follow the personalized program, she must become versed in children's literature, as well as the mechanics of ordering books.

The cost of materials for the personalized program might initially seem prohibitive, but the resourceful teachers should have little difficulty obtaining books from libraries, second-hand book stores, and the children themselves. Beginning will, of course, be the hardest time. Once an adequate room library is established, keeping up with new books will be an easy and enjoyable task. Materials for the personalized program should actually cost no more than the cost of basal texts, and will eventually perhaps cost even less.

The teacher must not content herself with merely using someone else's book list. With the great abundance of fine material appearing, the teacher should carefully select materials to fit the needs and interests of her particular children.

Chapter Seven

Primary Grades Reading Skills

The success of the child in learning to read depends primarily upon how effectively he learns the essential reading skills presented in the first three grades. For this reason, particular attention must be given to reading instruction during these years. If the child learns to read well during these years, he will encounter little if any difficulty in the succeeding grades. If he fails to learn to read in the primary grades, however, it is most likely that he will have academic difficulties throughout his school career.

The basic foundation upon which a child's reading ability is built depends to a large extent upon his readiness to learn. If the child is not ready for formal instruction, it would be wise for him either to remain out of school another year or to repeat kindergarten. It is better that the child enter the first grade, when formal reading instruction begins, ready to learn, rather than meeting failure in the formal reading situation of the first grade and having to repeat. In those instances where the child does enter the first grade before he is ready, the teacher should keep him in a readiness program, and then in the next year carry him on into the first grade reading program. Depending upon a great many other circumstances, of course, it is often wise to have him repeat at this time. Retention at grades above primary level is both ineffective and may actually result in even lower achievement levels than before retention.

Because reading skills in the primary grades are so vitally important to the child's ability to read effectively at higher levels, the teacher must move slowly. She must be certain that each child is mastering those skills which are essential to more advanced reading. There must be a logical, sequential development of skills. Only if these skills are presented when the child is ready for them, in a manner which does not skip over certain skills, can he be expected to build an effective foundation for reading skills.

It must be recognized that learning reading skills is not the final goal, however. The teaching of skills is intended to help children read better. If skill instruction is isolated from reading itself, it is likely that all the children will not be able to make the needed connection between the two. It is not unusual to find children who are able to do some of these reading skills well but who do not know how to read. When skill instruction is not an integral part of the reading process, it is little more than another subject added to the curriculum which has little carryover either to reading or spelling. The goal of reading instruction is, of course, to help children know how to read well and to enjoy reading. To the extent that they read on their own, either to obtain information or for pleasure, the instruction is successful. How well the child has mastered reading skills is only an indication of his reading ability, and is definitely not the sole criterion by which reading ability should be measured.

It is not enough even to insist that skill instruction should be a part of reading instruction. Reading instruction itself must be a part of a still bigger picture. The language arts area, which includes reading, writing, spelling, and listening must be considered as a total unit. Reading is only one part of this language arts area and must be kept in proper prospective.

The fragmentation of the language arts program into a large number of isolated subjects will result in less effective teaching and an actual waste of badly needed time. With pressure upon schools becoming greater and greater to teach more and more subjects, the classroom teacher cannot afford the time to break each subject down into many unrelated parts. It is necessary that she teach children to relate those things which they learn in one subject into useful learning experiences for mastering other subjects.

As isolated subjects, spelling, writing, and reading are each so much an entity unto themselves that the child cannot hope to remember all of the things that are to be learned. Phonic instruction, for example, should obviously be helpful both to reading and spelling. As spelling is practiced, there is no reason why writing should not also be practiced. The total language arts approach is not only sensible, it is absolutely necessary if the classroom teacher is to be successful either in a personalized reading program or in the basal reading program.

There is some disagreement among educational authorities as to whether or not reading skills should be presented to all children. Certain children in each grade already know how to read material at that grade level. Whether or not these children should be taught the skills at that level is a controversy among reading specialists which will perhaps never be resolved. One solution would be to present all of the reading skills to all of the children, regardless of their actual reading level so long as it is at least at grade level, with the idea that even though the student may not need these skills at this particular point, he will need them later. This author believes that the reason why so many bright children are such poor spellers is that they have missed the skill instructions in phonics at the primary grade level because they did not need it at that level to read or spell. But when they reached a higher level, they needed the phonic skill but did not know it. It is certainly true that brighter children will not spend so much time as average and slower learning children on the reading skills. It is important, however, that the skills be presented to the pupils if their achievement level is at least at grade level. If it is found that the student already knows the particular skill, then no time need be spent drilling on it. If the child does not know the particular skill, however, some time should be spent actually practicing the skill to be sure that it is mastered. The slower children will undoubtedly need more of this rote drill, but the initial presentation should be made to all the children.

Perhaps the major criticism of the personalized reading program has been that it does not pay careful attention to the teaching of reading skills. Whether or not the teacher actually follows the manual, in the basal reader program, the teacher is guided through a pattern of skill presentation. The fact that many teachers do not use the teachers' manual, or change from one basal series in one grade to another is a problem of application and should not be considered a weakness of the basal reading program itself. The personalized reading program does allow for more flexibility of program so that it is possible for skill instruction to be neglected. The experienced teacher, however, should know those skills which she would need to teach. The beginning teacher is not in a position to know these skills quite so well, however. But both the experienced teacher and the beginning teacher need some kind of guide to follow in a more condensed form than the teachers' manual, whether they are teaching in the personalized program or in the basal reader. The material presented in the next two chapters is intended to provide this type of guide.

Chapter 7 deals with those reading skills presented in the primary grades. Regardless of what grade level a teacher may actually be assigned to, she needs to know the skills of the grades above and below her. Whether the teacher is a first grade or a third grade teacher, she is likely to have children at the readiness level. Material presented in this chapter is intended mainly for primary teachers, but should be of concern to upper elementary teachers who have children reading at the primary level.

The author feels strongly that the most important part of this chapter is the section on readiness. If the child is adequately prepared for formal skill instruction, he will encounter success in it. Initial success in the learning to read process must be recognized as a major factor in good reading. Initial failure in the learning to read process is probably the major cause of subsequent failure in all academic areas.

Following the section on readiness is a section on first-grade reading skills. This is followed by second-grade reading skills, and then third-grade reading skills. By arranging these skills at grade level, the author does not mean that he expects all children in each of the grades to be reading at this level. The teacher should be concerned with the skills mastered by each particular child, and should work accordingly with him. His actual grade placement may be little more than an indication of his chronological age. It is a foolish teacher indeed who insists that because she has a third-grade class she is going to insist upon every child reading at third-grade level. Such a situation would indeed be ideal, but in practice it does not exist.

Skill instruction should not go beyond the child's actual grade placement, however. The goal is to move each child through the skill instruction at his own pace, neither speeding him up to get him through it more rapidly nor dragging it out while the rest of the class catches up. In the personalized program, skill instruction is geared to the child's own ability to learn. Once the child has mastered the skills at his grade level, no new skill instruction is presented. Skills from previous levels are checked upon and if they have not been fully mastered, they are relearned. It is true, of course, that the brighter child will acquire some of the skills of a higher grade level in an incidental manner. This is not to be discouraged, but neither should the teacher in any way formally present the skills of the higher grade levels.

While the author does not believe that grade skipping is a desirable practice for bright children, if it is to take place because of special conditions in isolated cases, presentation of the skills described in this chapter at the level to be skipped should take place before the child is moved into the next higher grade. Material found in this chapter should aid a teacher in preparing a child for a higher grade level.

At the end of each section is a copy of a check list which is recommended for each child at each reading level. The skills listed at each level are those which are to be learned at that level. Once they have been mastered, the child is ready to move to the next level. Copies of this check list, which may be obtained by writing to the author, should be kept in each child's folder. Looking at the child's previous records, it is possible for the teacher to determine exactly those skills which have been presented to him as indicated by the teacher's check. In some cases it will be necessary to review or actually reteach certain of the skills, but by noting whether or not the skill has been checked, it is possible for the teacher to determine if this skill is a new one for the child or one merely to be relearned.

At the beginning of each year after the child has completed his first year in school, the teacher would be wise to review briefly those skills which were presented and learned at the preceding level. This might be the first type of group which is established. As the skills are reviewed, the teacher will quickly come to know those children who have thoroughly retained those skills which they have learned, as well as those who will need more review work on the skills of the earlier level. Remembering that the purpose of establishing groups in the personalized program is to accomplish a particular goal, these groups will be disbanded as soon as the review skills have been covered.

READINESS LEVEL SKILLS

Vocabulary: Word Recognition

During the readiness period, it is important that the child become interested in words. The bright child usually does this at the preschool level when he begins asking his parents what words on signs mean. The first interest is in, of course, familiar words which are seen around the school room. The teacher can aid in the development of this interest in words by placing labels upon familiar objects.

Frequently teachers prepare a chart for each child which includes pictures of the child, art work which he has done, or objects which belong to him. In large manuscript print is the child's name. He learns, of course, to identify his chart from the familiar pictures and objects and then to read his own name. He may then learn to read the names of his friends.

The child learns in the readiness period to say the names of the individual letters. Although there has been in the past some disagreement as to whether it is important for the child to know the names of the letters and numbers, this opposition has died out in the past few years. Particular attention needs to be given to such letters as "b" and "d," "p" and "q." Whether or not the child knows the names of the letters in sequence is not nearly so important as being able to identify them.

At the readiness level it is important for the child to learn how to match letters and match words. By listing in two columns different letters, the child should be able to draw a line from the word in the column on the left to the word in the column on the right which is the same. This can be done in a variety of ways but should begin with matching either single letters or words that begin the same. The teacher can then lead into matching words and can then even mix words and letters. She can also include capitals and small letters when the child has learned to match these.

Vocabulary: Word Meaning

The teacher should pay particular attention at the readiness level to aiding the child in developing a speaking vocabulary which is adequate to convey his own ideas. This can best be done in as informal a situation as possible. The sharing period, at which time each child shares with the other children in the group, some experience or possession newly acquired, provides for a free flow of ideas. The child should be helped at this time to add those words which he needs to express his ideas.

At the sharing period time, as well as during the rest of the school day, the teacher should help all of the children become interested in correct pronunciation. Certain sounds such as "gr" and "wh" are more difficult to make and may not be possible for many children at this level. It is important, however, that the child develop a desire to imitate the correct speech pattern of other children. The emotional factors which may be involved here complicate the picture if the teacher attempts to eradicate certain speech problems, but it is important that she make all children aware of the need for correct pronunciation even if she cannot actually correct some of the difficulties.

Children in the readiness program need to learn to associate pictures to words. They do this by the use of labels, both on objects and on the children themselves. The technique of identifying new words by picture clues should be encouraged. This does not mean that the child is actually reading the words but rather that he is reading the picture. The purpose here is not to develop reading vocabulary, but is instead intended to help him grasp the concept that printed words represent objects and actions.

Perceptive Skills: Auditory

Children at the readiness level must learn to reproduce pronounced two and three syllable words. The teacher says the word and the child reproduces it. This is the beginning of instructions in syllables and must not wait until the child is in the fourth or fifth grade. At this point, he is mainly listening for the number of syllables in the word.

Although the child has already learned that the printed word represents an object, at the readiness level he needs to learn that a printed word may also represent a spoken word. This can most easily be taught by using the child's own name. As the readiness period progresses, and the child becomes familiar with the other children in the room, other children's names can be used.

It is important for children to learn to hear the differences in familiar words. (Such as "chimney" and "chair," "pen" and "pin," "weather" and "whether," etc.) He must also be able to hear the word that is long or short, and he able to distinguish between them. (Such pairs of words given aloud as "elephant and boy," "dog and giraffe," etc.) The child should be able to tell which of the two words is longer and which is shorter.

At the readiness level, the child should be taught to hear certain sounds. Even though he may not be able to reproduce the sounds at this level, he should nevertheless be able to pick out the word that begins with that sound. Later on he should be able to find words that end with that sound. The most difficult task in this sequence is learning to hear the sound in the middle of the word. This is, of course, readiness for formal phonic instruction. Until the child can hear the sound, it is foolish to begin phonic instruction which has the child making the sound.

The ability to hear rhyming words is an essential part of the readiness program. Although it is not necessary that the teacher do anything more than refer to the word "rhyme" in an incidental manner, finding words and making words that sound alike helps develop phonic readiness. The use of such children's books as Dr. Seuss's *Horton Hatches the Egg* can aid in this process. When read to a class, rhyming couplets such as those found in *Horton Hatches the Egg* provide many learning experiences. After the teacher has read the couplet which is repeated over and over where Horton says, "I meant what I said, and I said what I meant, an elephant faithful one hundred per cent," the children quickly begin to repeat this rhyme. Indicating that the two words end in the same sound provides the first introduction to the concept of rhyme.

Dr. Seuss is also a favorite source for the introduction of unusual words. His delightful book, *If I Ran the Zoo,* provides many strange sounds as does such of his books as *Bartholomew and the Obleck.*

Perceptive Skills: Visual

The child at the readiness level learns to use picture clues. There are many objections to "reading the picture" at the higher grade levels which are certainly justified. At the readiness level, however, this is a technique for teaching the child to be observant and use reasoning power in aiding his word attack techniques.

The child should learn to recognize the names of the different colors. He should also learn sizes of objects, being able to distinguish big from little, tall from short, etc. He should know whether or not an object is square or round.

At the readiness level, he is introduced to the concept of configuration. He is taught to observe likeness and differences in letters and words. By drawing boxes around certain letters, and around words, he learns which letters are above the lines and which ones are below the line.

At the readiness level the teacher needs to stress left-right eye movement. Practice in moving from left to right and back to the left again can be taught in a variety of ways. Some teachers have effectively used even comic strips to teach left-right progression.

Comprehension: Interest

In order to develop good comprehension in reading, the child must be interested in reading. This is not an attitude which is learned but is actually "caught" by the child from his parents, teachers and peer group. Only if the child wants to learn to read is it likely that he is going to have a successful initial reading experience. Practically every first grade child enters school with a desire to learn to read. This initial enthusiasm is sometimes lost if the teacher does not actively work to maintain it.

Particularly important to primary age children is the attitude of their parents and their teacher. If the child has observed no reading in the home, and the teacher herself expresses no particular interest in reading other than as a subject to be taught, it is not likely that the child himself will have any particular enthusiasm for reading. One of the most effective means by which teachers are able to transmit to the children a love of reading is to read to them.

The selection of materials to read to children is of the utmost importance. But of even more importance, however, is that the teacher read something. If at all possible, the teacher should select material which will in some way be suited to the interest level of the children whom she is teaching. If such materials cannot be found, read something. The great wealth of children's literature appearing today should make it quite easy to find some material which would be of interest. A particularly good story to read to children at this level is *Petunia,* about a silly goose who thinks that owning a book is the way to be wise. After many misadventures, she discovers that merely carrying a book under one's arm does not make one wise, but that one must know how to read.

It is important for comprehension that children develop an attention span which is sufficiently long for them to be able to understand what is being read to them. The teacher may need to point out to the children the need for quietness, and for them to pay attention. These are things which are learned.

Some children learn them only in a direct teaching situation, and not incidentally from the other children.

Comprehension

In developing comprehension, the children must learn to pay attention. The teacher can develop techniques for helping the children pay attention by asking simple questions before she starts reading, and encouraging them to listen for the answers. The children should know the names of the main characters in the stories which have been read to them. They should be able to relate the main idea of the stories, and come to reasonable conclusions about the value of the story, its being either a fairy story or a true story, or to provide a reasonable conclusion.

They should be able to keep a series of events in proper sequence. Retelling the story is one technique for having the child do this. Another technique is to ask the children which of two points retold to them came first.

The child at the readiness level should learn to use complete sentences. It is not necessary that he know the component parts of the sentence, but his sentences should be more than merely declarative statements.

He learns in the readiness period to work independently for short periods. The group process is certainly valuable, but also valuable is the ability to follow directions at his desk for himself. He also learns at this level to begin at the front of the book. He must also learn that he reads from the left-hand page first, and, of course, proceeds from left to right within the sentence.

Oral Expression

A child must be able to express himself spontaneously. He should be able to remember five-word sentences which he repeats after hearing. He should be able to make up simple endings for stories and should be able to use new words which are presented and explained to him.

As simple as these readiness activities may sound, their importance cannot be overly emphasized. This readiness period may extend no longer than the first week for some of the chil-

BARBE READING SKILLS CHECK LIST

READINESS LEVEL

_____   _____
(Last Name)   (First Name)

_____   (Name of School)
(Grade Placement)

_____   _____
(Age)   (Name of Teacher)

I. Vocabulary:

A. Word Recognition

1. Interested in words _____

2. Recognizes own name in print _____

3. Knows names of letters _____

4. Knows names of numbers _____

5. Can match letters _____

6. Can match numbers _____

7. Can match capital and small letters _____

B. Word Meaning

1. Speaking vocabulary adequate to convey ideas _____

2. Associates pictures to words _____

3. Identifies new words by picture clues

3. Observes likenesses and differences

   in words _____

   in letters _____

4. Left-right eye movements _____

III. Comprehension:

A. Interest

1. Wants to learn to read _____

2. Likes to be read to _____

3. Attention span sufficiently long

A. Auditory

1. Can reproduce pronounced two and three syllable words _____
2. Knows number of sounds in spoken words _____
3. Can hear differences in words _____
4. Able to hear length of word (Which is shorter? boy - elephant) _____
5. Able to hear sound:
   At beginning of word _____
   At end of word _____
   In middle of word _____
6. Hears rhyming words _____
7. Aware of unusual words _____

B. Visual

1. Uses picture clues _____
2. Recognizes:
   Colors _____
   Sizes (big, little; tall, short) _____
   Shapes (square, round, triangle) _____

1. Remembers from stories read aloud:
   Names of characters _____
   Main ideas _____
   Conclusion _____
2. Can keep events in proper sequence _____
3. Uses complete sentences _____
4. Can work independently for short periods _____
5. Begins at front of book _____
6. Begins on left hand page _____
7. Knows sentence begins at left _____

IV. Oral Expression:

A. Expresses self spontaneously _____
B. Able to remember five word sentence _____
C. Able to make up simple endings for stories _____
D. Able to use new words _____

Teacher's Notes:

dren, and it may actually extend throughout the first year for other children. Its length depends to a great extent upon how effectively the readiness program has been presented. Teachers should be firm in their decision to develop the readiness program before formal reading instruction begins.

The personalized reading program provides the greatest opportunity for determining the length of the readiness program. It allows these children who are ready to cover quickly the readiness program to go on into formal reading, while it provides the teacher with the freedom of movement to develop reading by means of the experience chart method for the remaining children. The very excellent book, *Learning To Read Through Experience,* by Lamoreaux and Lee, is an absolutely essential guide for teachers who are following the personalized program at the first grade level without the benefit of the basal reader.

FIRST GRADE LEVEL READING SKILLS

The sequence from pre-primer to primer to first grade reader found in most basal series presents numerous problems. Perhaps the greatest problem is that it presents "reading" to the child in an almost nonsense fashion. By constant repetition of awkward phrases such as "Come, Come" and "Look, Look" the child soon realizes that even though he may be reading, the story certainly has little appeal to him. In the personalized reading program, the teacher may by-pass the pre-primers and primers by use of experience charts, developed for the children at their level of interest, and incorporate many of the same words which are considered essential at this level.

The vocabulary control in the pre-primers and first readers probably reflects the greatest contribution of the basal reader series. Listed below are those words which Olive Reeve found to be common to most of the basal pre-primers. It would be wise for the teacher in the personalized reading program, or even one using the basal reading approach, to keep these words before her. The words should be used in blackboard assignments and in speaking conversation whenever possible. They should not be used in meaningless sentences, but repetition should come from a wide variety of tasks assigned throughout the day in the classroom procedure. It would be wise for the teacher to recheck and see that the children have mastered most of these words before they move on to the next higher list.

a	cowboy	have	morning	something
airplane		he	my	splash
an	daddy	help		stop
and	did	her	near	surprise
apple	dinner	here	no	
are	dish	hide	not	table
at	do	home		thank
away	dog	house	oh	that
	down		on	the
baby		I	one	three
ball	father	in		to
be	fast	is	party	toy
bed	find	it	pie	two
big	fine		play	
birthday	fish	jump	pretty	up
blue	for		puppy	
boat	funny	kitten		want
bow-wow			ran	we
	get	like	red	what
cake	girl	little	ride	where
call	give	look	run	will
can	go			with
cap	good	make	said	work
car	good-by	may	see	
Christmas	green	me	she	yellow
come		mitten	show	you
cookies	has	mother	sleep	your

The words listed below are those which Reeve found to be common to most of the first grade readers in the most widely used reading series. With the child reading widely, it should not be necessary to, in any artificial way, present many of these words. An occasional check to see that the child is acquiring in his reading vocabulary most of the following words would be helpful, however. At the end of the first grade, before he enters into second grade level reading material, it would be wise to use these words as a check list.

a	eat	jump	party	to
about		just	play	too
again	farm		put	toy
all	fast	kitten		two
am	find	know	rabbit	
and	for		ran	up
are	from	laugh	red	us
as	fun	let	ride	
at	funny	like	run	walk
away		little		want
	get	long	said	was
baby	girl	look	sat	water
back	give		saw	way
ball	go	make	see	we
be	good	man	she	went
big	good-by	many	so	were
birthday		may	some	what
black	had	me	something	when
blue	happy	mother	soon	where
boat	has	Mr.	stop	white
boy	have	must		wish
but	help	my	take	who
	her		thank	will
call	here	new	that	with
came	him	night	the	
can	his	no	them	yellow
come	home	not	then	yes
could	house	now	there	you
cow	how		they	your
		of	this	
day	I	on	three	
did	in	one	took	
do	is	open	time	
dog	it	out	tree	
down		over		
duck				

Vocabulary: Recognition

By the end of the first grade, the child should be able to identify practically all of the words in the lists above, both on word lists and in various reading material. These are essentially words which a child should know by sight, and not ones on which he has to use word attack skill. The teacher should check to be certain that the child will recognize these words both in small letters, as well as when the first letter of the word is capitalized or all of the letters of the word are capitalized.

Vocabulary: Word Meaning

The teacher should frequently check to determine if the child is understanding the meaning of words which he is reading. In the personalized reading program, where the child is selecting his own reading material, there is a greater chance that he will encounter words which may have new meanings for him. The teacher should rely upon the child's own list of words which he has kept while reading, and should occasionally take words from the child's reading and ask him for meaning of them.

It is not enough only to understand what these new words mean. The teacher must also work with the child in using these new words in his speaking vocabulary. It is quite possible that this is a type of group activity which could be carried on while the teacher is having individual conferences. There are a number of different play situations which could be developed using the new words which each child would contribute. Perhaps seeing which child could make a sentence using three of the new words, or even a larger number, would be a way of interesting the students not only in the words which they had encountered, but also in the words which the other children had come across.

Word Analysis: Phonics

During first grade instruction, the children should learn to recognize and make the sound of the nineteen initial consonants which make only one sound (b, d, f, h, j, k, l, m, n, p, q, r, s, t, v, w, x, y, z). It is best to teach these nineteen initial sounds one at a time, providing two examples (such as "b" as in ball and boy, "d" as in day and dog, "f" as in fan and full, etc.). The vowel following the initial consonant should not be the same in the two words used as samples. Brighter children will quickly begin providing other examples, but for average and slower students, it is most likely that they will like having two words on which they can always rely. Phonics should not be taught in isolation, even with single words, but should be taught along with words which are then used in sentences. As these initial sounds are taught, it is well to teach the child to blend the initial sound with the already learned sight words.

Once single initial consonants are learned, the teacher should make the child aware of the sound when it is in the final position. (Such as a*t*, ta*p*, etc.) He then needs to be made aware of the single consonant sound in the medial position.

Once single initial consonants have been learned in initial, medial, and final positions, it is wise to introduce the names of the vowel. This introduction is actually only done in an incidental way, for formal presentation of vowels will come at early second grade level. The brighter students will be able to use vowels in the introduction of consonant blends.

The following consonant initial blends are then introduced: st, tr, fr, sm, sn, sw, tw, dl, gl, fl, pl, cl, sh, ch, wh, th.

They are, of course, not all introduced at one time, but are introduced over a period of many months. This will probably occur toward the end of the first grade.

It is probably wise to point out to the students that they can decide if the initial sound is to be a single consonant sound or a blend by going up to the first vowel. If there is only one letter before the first vowel, then it is an initial single consonant, but if there are two or even three letters, it will be a blend.

Without a doubt, by this time, some of the students will have asked why the letters c and g have been left out. For those students who are ready, the two sounds of "c" and "g" are presented in an incidental fashion. Formal instruction in the two sounds of "c" and "g" will come at second grade level.

Word Analysis: Structure Analysis

At first grade level the child is taught to notice the endings of words. The "s," "ing," "ed" endings are taught. The three sounds of "ed" in the final position are learned. The sound of the final "ed" can either be "ed" as in want*ed*, "d" as in mov*ed*, "t" as in lik*ed*.

Children learn in the first grade to recognize compound words. Such words as "into," "good-by," and "upon" are presented to the child. He is then asked to pick out two words in the combination. This can best be done in the child's reading material rather than in a formal lesson. If he has difficulty doing it, however, he should be grouped with other children in the room having the same difficulty and taught in the group.

Since families have already been introduced, the child should have no difficulty in seeing little words in big words. Such words as *fall, sold, rat, fill,* and *for* are samples of words which a child will come across in his reading which a teacher might use to check the child's ability to spot these little words.

Word Analysis: Word Form Clues

Attention at this level needs to be given to upper case and lower case letters. The length of words should be brought to the child's attention as well as double letters in words (such as bigger, fatter, etc.).

Word Analysis: Context Clues

The child at the first grade level needs to learn that frequently new words can be figured out by using context clues. This, as using picture clues, can be a helpful word attack technique but should be used only as a last resort. The initial sound should always be used before resorting to context or picture clues. In this manner the child will not call "lion" "tiger" merely because there is a picture or context which indicates a ferocious animal.

Comprehension

The child at the first grade level extends his understanding that printed symbols represent objects or actions. This may be accomplished by labeling objects, as well as labeling pictures which show action. This understanding is absolutely essential before any further comprehension in reading can be developed.

The child should learn to follow printed directions. This can be developed with the entire class by putting on the blackboard each morning printed directions which students must follow. Exercises or group activities using mimeograph sheets or experience charts are helpful, telling the children in printed directions to find the boy's house, draw a picture of the boy's boat, or any number or variety of such activities. The ability to follow printed directions must be developed. In the personalized reading program, the teacher is provided with a natural situation which will make the directions to be followed much more meaningful to the children.

Before students read particular stories of their own selection, the teacher should provide them with simple questions which they are to answer from their reading of the material. This will necessitate the teacher's being familiar with much of the material available in the room. She will not necessarily need to have read everything, but as the year progresses, she will become familiar with more and more of the material. The questions which were used in the story for one child can then be used again as another child reads the story. Giving the questions to the children first will teach them to concentrate on the material better, organize their thinking, and give them a very obvious purpose for reading carefully.

Children in the first grade need to learn to draw conclusions from given facts in the reading material. This can be done by telling how they think the story will end or what will happen next. Writing their own endings to stories, using the facts which have been presented, will aid in developing this ability.

The child must of course be able to recall what he has read. If he cannot, this indicates either too rapid reading or too difficult material. If upon re-reading, the child still cannot recall what he has read, the material is too difficult for him. While reading material at a sensible rate is important, no attention should be given to speeding up a child's reading at this level. It is important for a child to be able to recall what he has read orally, but he must also be able to recall what he has read silently. In the personalized reading program there is more attention to silent reading at an earlier level than in the basal reading program. In the basal program, the child must read aloud before the group to demonstrate his reading proficiency, while in the personalized program he demonstrates reading proficiency by reading aloud to the teacher in the individual conference.

In order that the child have an understanding of what he has read, he must not only recall the facts but must be able to place them in the proper sequence. When more than one child has read a particular story, they can list the main facts on separate cards, then mix the cards and place them in proper sequence. This is one technique of developing the idea of what happened in the correct order.

Along with giving children questions for which they are to find the answers as they read, they may sometimes be given questions after they have read the material and told to find where the answers are. This will involve not only recalling that something did happen, but knowing about where it is in the story. Asking what happened and then telling the child to look for the place where this happened is a rather meaningless activity. It would be better to ask the child to find where a certain character is described or where certain things were said. In this way, the exact wording of the author can be brought out. The questions therefore should be of the type that will require answering in the exact words of the author rather than something the child can answer from his own memory.

Oral and Silent Skills: Oral Reading

In oral reading the teacher should watch to see that the child uses correct pronunciation, correct phrasing, and proper enunciation to give the author's meaning. As a child reads, he should have good posture, and handle the book appropriately. It should be a proper distance from his eyes, and at an angle of ninety degrees for a line drawn from his eyes to the page. He should understand simple punctuation marks such as periods, comma, question mark, and exclamation point.

Oral and Silent Skills: Silent Reading

In silent reading, of which the child will do a great deal in the personalized reading program, he must read without vocalization. This means using neither whispering nor lip movements. Careful observation must be made of the child's silent reading to detect these things. If the child can be corrected at the first grade level, the habit will not become established. Too often

BARBE READING SKILLS CHECK LIST
FIRST GRADE LEVEL

_____ (Last Name) _____ (First Name) _____ (Name of School)

_____ (Age) _____ (Grade Placement) _____ (Name of Teacher)

I. Vocabulary:

A. Word Recognition

1. Recognizes words with both capital and small letters at beginning

2. Is able to identify in various settings the following words usually found in preprimers:

a	do	jump	show
airplane	dog	kitten	sleep
an	down	like	something
and	father	little	splash
apple	fast	look	stop
are	find	make	surprise
at	fine	may	table
away	fish	me	thank
baby	for	mitten	that
ball	funny	mother	the
be	get	morning	tree
bed	girl	my	to
big	give	near	toy
birthday	go	no	two
blue	good	not	up
boat	good-by	oh	want
bow-wow	green	on	we
cake	has	one	what
call	have	party	where
can	he	pie	will
cap	help	play	with

2. Knows single consonant sounds in final position (hat)

3. Knows single consonant sounds in middle position (seven)

4. Names of vowels are introduced

5. Knows sounds of initial consonant blends (listed in order of difficulty)

sh___	fr___	cl___	sw___
st___	wh___	gl___	tw___
bl___	th___	sp___	
pl___	ch___	sm___	
tr___	fl___	sn___	

B. Structural Analysis

1. Knows endings
ed sound as "ed" in wanted
ed sound as "d" in laughed
ed sound as "t" in liked
ing
s

2. Recognizes compound words (into, upon)

3. Knows common word families:

all___	et___	an___	ay___
at___	en___	ill___	ake___
it___	in___	ell___	or___

C. Word Form Clues

1. Notices capital and small letters

2. Notices length of words

III. Comprehension:

A. Understands that printed symbols represent objects or actions

B. Can follow printed directions (Find the boy's house.)

C. Can verify a statement (See if Sandy ran away.)

D. Can draw conclusions from given facts (What do you think happened then?)

E. Can recall what has been read aloud

F. Can recall what has been read silently

G. Can place events in sequence

H. Can remember where to find answers to questions

IV. Oral and Silent Reading Skills:

A. Oral Reading

1. Uses correct pronunciation
2. Uses correct phrasing (not word-by-word)
3. Uses proper voice intonation to give meaning
4. Has good posture and handles book appropriately
5. Understands simple punctuation:
   period (.) —
   comma (,) —
   question mark (?) —
   exclamation mark (!) —

B. Silent Reading

1. Reads without vocalization:
   Lip movements —
   Whispering —
2. Reads without head movements

— cookies   — home   — red   — your
— cowboy   — house   — ride
— daddy   — I   — run
— did   — in   — said
— dinner   — is   — see
— dish   — it   — she

Only additional words found in six of seven leading primers were:

— about   — fun   — night   — they
— again   — had   — new   — this
— all   — happy   — now   — too
— am   — him   — of   — us
— as   — his   — put   — walk
— back   — how   — rabbit — was
— black   — just   — sat   — water
— boy   — know   — saw   — way
— but   — laugh   — so   — went
— came   — let   — some   — were
— could   — long   — soon   — when
— cow   — man   — take   — white
— eat   — many   — them   — wish
— farm.   — Mr.   — then   — who
— from   — must   — there   — yes

(List prepared by Olive Reeve, Whitewater (Wisc.) State College.)

II. Word Analysis:

A. Phonics

1. Recognizes single initial consonants and can make their sound:

b —   k —   q —   w —
d —   l —   r —   x —
f —   m —   s —   y —
h —   n —   t —   z —
j —   p —   v —

children reach upper elementary grades either whispering or moving their lips, which greatly interferes with both their reading rate and comprehension; however, by this time the habit has become so much a part of them, it is very difficult to break. The child should read silently without moving his head, but instead by moving only his eyes.

When a child has learned the skills which are necessary for the completion of first grade level reading, he is ready to practice these skills by reading more materials of his own selection and reviewing these skills. He should not be moved to the second grade level skills until he is ready to be placed in the second grade. Teaching skills before a child reaches that grade level only interferes with the teacher's program at the next higher level. In the basal reading program, it may be sometimes necessary to move on to the higher level reader since so much importance is attached to books with numbers on the outside cover. In the personalized reading program, however, there is no justification for teaching skills at a higher level, for the child is allowed to select those books which interest him and which he can read. If they are of a higher level, there is no reason why he should not be encouraged to read them. His skill instruction, however, will be geared to his grade placement level.

SECOND GRADE LEVEL READING SKILLS

Much of the child's reading through most of the first grade has been from experience charts, the blackboard, experience stories, preprimers and primers which he has selected himself, and a few very easy books. By the time the child has reached the end of the first grade level, he is able to read enough words so that he can enjoy an ever increasing number of good books. (See listings of books for this level in Chapter Six). Up until this point the child's learning to read process has been governed mostly by those activities described by Lamoreaux and Lee in

Vocabulary: Word Recognition

During second grade level reading instruction, the child's reading vocabulary increases rapidly. The most valuable list of words which the second grade teacher has to rely upon are the 220 basic sight words prepared by Dolch. These words make up 75 per cent of all the reading that the child will do in the elementary grades, and 50 per cent of all the reading which he will do in his entire life. These words are ones which the child should know by sight and which he should not have to use his word attack skills upon. Before the child goes into third grade reading level skills, he should know practically all of the words in this list. These words are arranged in columns of increasing difficulty. Attention should be given to the words in Column I first, continuing on to the next column as the preceding one is mastered. Many of these words will be learned by the child incidentally in his reading, but those which are not learned in this way should be taught formally to him during second grade reading level instruction.

Column I	*Column II*	*Column III*	*Column IV*	*Column V*
and	at	all	an	find
are	away	am	after	gave
can	big	around	as	got
come	blue	black	be	has
funny	down	but	brown	know
go	for	by	cold	let
he	good	call	did	live
is	green	came	fly	made
jump	have	do	from	many
like	here	eat	give	may
little	in	fast	going	new
look	it	get	had	now
my	me	going	help	over
of	not	into	him	put
play	on	make	her	that
red	one	no	his	them
run	ran	old	if	then
said	saw	out	its	they
see	three	was	round	walk
the	too	who	so	when
this	we	she	soon	went
to	will	some	ten	were
up	yellow	stop	under	what

During second grade reading level instruction, the child learns to use word form clues as a means of helping him attack new words. One of the biggest problems with children at this level is that when they come to a new word they either put the book down as being too difficult or skip over the word and read on. By stressing word attack skills, children learn to read independently. Learning to recognize the shape of the word is one of the best means of word attack. This is called "configuration," and can best be demonstrated by drawing boxes around the words and pointing out similarities and differences between words which are confused. Care must be taken to point out that such words frequently confused as "was" and "saw" and "on" and "no" have the same configuration. If the child persists in confusing words of this type, it is an indication that left-right progression has not been established firmly. Usually this can be corrected by use of the kinesthetic method as described by Grace Fernald in *Remedial Techniques in Basic School Subjects.* Having the child touch the left side of the page each time before he begins to read often helps him remember to begin on the left.

The child should regularly use initial consonants and consonant blends as a means of unlocking new words. Sounds of these letters and blends have been taught at first grade level, but will have to be reviewed at second grade reading level with emphasis being placed upon their use. Visual similarity of rhyming words such as call, fall, and ball need to be pointed out. A review of final consonant blends, with careful attention to the child's ability to use this skill, is essential.

During the second grade reading level, the teacher should be conscious of the child's need to use structural analysis. The teacher must watch for and use, as a method of word attack, the child's ability to read little words in big words such as *many, ball,* etc.

Compound words such as barnyard should be recognized as two words put together. The child needs to know possessives and word endings such as: 's, ed, ing, t, er, est, y and ly. Apostrophes need to be taught and learned thoroughly as in I'm, I'll, and can't.

Vocabulary: Word Meaning

During second grade reading level instruction, the child needs to become aware of the multiple meanings of words. These do not have to be difficult words, but can be simple words already in the child's reading vocabulary such as top, being used as the toy, or the top of a man's hat, or fast as a fast runner, not eating, a fast color, etc.

The child is introduced to the meaning of the word "synonym," and is instructed in learning a number of simple synonyms. Examples of these would be jolly and happy, sad and unhappy, etc. He is also instructed in learning opposites, such as up and down, fast and slow, etc. While synonyms or opposites are learned readily, words pronounced identically but with different spellings and meanings present more difficulty. The teacher might present this to the entire class, for they will all need many repetitions in order to distinguish between such homonyms as rode and road.

Word Analysis: Phonics

At this grade level the child should know all consonants and blends taught in the first grade, in the initial position, medial position, and final position. He should know the following word families:

ou as in out	ur as in fur	ew as in new	ack as in back
ow as in show	ir as in bird	ight as in night	uck as in duck
oi as in oil	oo as in balloon	ind as in find	
oy as in boy	oo as in book	eck as in neck	
er as in her	aw as in straw	ick as in sick	

In second grade level reading instruction, the sound of the short vowel should be taught. The short vowel should be learned before the sound of the long vowel. Because the long vowels essentially only say their own name, it is much easier if the short vowels are learned first. The long vowels can then be learned without any difficulty. If the reverse procedure is followed, great difficulty will be encountered in teaching the short vowel sounds. The short vowels can be remembered better if the child is taught at least one word which begins with each of the short vowel sounds.

It is helpful for the child to learn the use of the letter "y."

When it is at the beginning of a word it is a consonant and makes the sound which the child has already learned as the initial consonant sound of the letter "y." When the letter "y" is in any position in the word other than the initial position, it usually acts as a vowel. (For example, "y" as in yard is a consonant, but in bicycle the "y" is a vowel.)

The child learns in the second grade reading level that "c" and "g" in the initial position each make two sounds. It is very likely that this has been introduced to some of the children in the first grade level, but probably will not be mastered by the average child until the second grade reading level. When "c" is followed by "a," "o," or "u," it makes the sound of the letter "k." (As in candy, cold, and cut.) When "c" is followed by "i," "e," or "y," it makes the sound of the letter "s" as in cents, city, or bicycle. In the same manner, the letter "g" makes two sounds. When followed by "a," "o," or "u," it makes the hard sound (guh) as in game, got, and gun. When "g" is followed by "i," "e," or "y," it makes a sound of the letter "j" as in gentle, ginger and gypsy.

There are many rules of phonics which can be learned. The most essential of these are perhaps the following four.

1. A single vowel in a word or syllable is usually short.
2. An "e" at the end of a word usually makes the preceding vowel long.
3. A single vowel at the end of a word or syllable is long.
4. When there are two vowels together, the first is long and the second is silent.

Structural Analysis

The child learns at the second grade reading level to identify roots or base words such as *mine*s, *mind*, and *minor*. He must recognize word endings such as "en" as in waken, "ful" as in careful, and know how these endings influence the word.

In addition to learning these things in order to be a better reader, he often needs to know them to help him in spelling. Such rules as changing "y" to "i" and adding "es" are most helpful. He must know to double the final consonant before adding "ing."

It is important for the child at this level to know in spelling that the final "e" is dropped when adding "ing." He must also know contractions such as "isn't," "I've," "I'm," "you're," and "let's." He needs to become familiar with possessives such as: Bob's, Janes'. He must also be able to disconnect the printed "fi" and "fl" as in "fish" and "fly."

Comprehension: Association of Ideas

Emphasis at second grade level should be upon teaching the child how to read silently with good comprehension. The same factors are also true of oral reading, but the emphasis should be primarily upon the child's ability to read to himself and understand. He should be able to draw conclusions from facts given in the story and predict the outcome. He should be able to find proof for his statements and associate the text with the pictures.

Comprehension: Organization of Ideas

It is particularly important for a child to be able to read silently and follow printed directions. He needs to be able to locate the main idea in a paragraph or story. One technique which is frequently used with a great deal of success for finding the main idea of the entire story is to have the child make up a name for the story. It is important that the child be able to follow the plot sequence if he is to have good comprehension.

Comprehension: Locating Information

At second grade level, the child needs to learn to use the table of contents, page number, paragraph and chapter headings. He also needs to be able to find specific information in the material which is read.

Comprehension: Appreciation

At second grade level, children enjoy being able to dramatize stories which they have read. The teacher in the personalized reading program, which is stressing silent reading at an earlier level than in the basal program, will find that dramatization of

BARBE READING SKILLS CHECK LIST
SECOND GRADE LEVEL

Copyright 1960, Walter B. Barbe

(Last Name) _____ (First Name) _____ (Name of School) _____

(Age) _____ (Grade Placement) _____ (Name of Teacher) _____

I. Vocabulary:

A. Word Recognition

1. Recognizes 220 Dolch Basic Sight Words (by end of year)

a	as	again	about	any
all	away	ate	after	better
am	be	black	always	both
an	black	but	around	bring
and	brown	cold	ask	carry
are	by	cut	because	clean
at	came	fast	been	could
big	did	first	before	done
blue	eat	five	best	don't
call	fall	fly	buy	draw
can	find	four	does	drink
come	for	give	for	eight
do	get	goes	found	every
down	going	got	full	hurt
funny	have	green	gave	know
go	her	had	grow	light
good	him	has	hold	myself
he	his	hot	how	never
help	if	its	just	own
here	into	just	keep	pick
I	laugh	keep	kind	right
in	let	kind	much	seven
is	live	long	must	shall
it	may	made	now	show
jump	my	many	off	their
like	no	new	once	them
little	old	not	only	then
look	on	of	round	there
make	one	open	sleep	these
me	put	please	small	think
out	saw	or	take	those
play	said	our	tell	together
pretty	she	pull	thank	use
ran	sit	read	that	very
		saw		
		say		

oi as in oil _____   eck as in neck _____

oy as in boy _____   ick as in sick _____

oo as in balloon _____   ack as in back _____
and book _____   uck as in duck _____

aw as in straw _____   ing as in sing _____

ew as in new _____   ike as in like _____

ight as in night _____

ind as in find _____

4. Short vowel sounds (a, o, i, u, e) (taught in this order)
5. Long vowel sounds
6. Understands function of "y" as a consonant at beginning of word (yard) and vowel (bicycle) anywhere else
7. Knows two sounds of c and g:
   C followed by i, e or y makes s sound
   C followed by a, o or u makes k sound (examples: city, cent and cat, cot)
   G followed by i, e or y makes j sound
   G followed by a, o or u makes guh sound (examples: ginger, gym and game, gun)
8. Knows initial consonant sound includes all consonants up to first vowel
9. Knows three letter initial blends
   spr _____   str _____
   spl _____   sch _____
   chr _____   thr _____
10. Phonics rules:
    a. A single vowel in a word or syllable is usually short (hat)
    b. A single e at the end of a word makes the preceding vowel long (hate)
    c. A single vowel at the end of a word is usually long (she)
    d. When there are two vowels together, the first is long and the second silent (rail, train)

I. (Sight Vocabulary)

ride, run, see, so, the, to, up, we, you

stop, three, today, two, was, will, work, yes, yellow, your

six, soon, ten, upon, us, who, why, wish, your

this, too, try, under, walk, well, were, white, with

wash, went, what, when, where, which, would, write

2. Use word form clues
   a. Configuration
   b. Visual similarity of rhyming words (call, fall, ball)
3. Is familiar with structural analysis
   a. Little words in big words (many)
   b. Compound words (barnyard)
   c. Possessives and word endings:
      's
      d   er
      ed   est
      ing   y
      t   ly
   d. Contractions:
      I'm   don't
      I'll   won't
      can't

B. Word Meaning
   1. Multiple meanings of words
   2. Synonymous meanings (jolly-happy)
   3. Opposites (up—down)
   4. Words pronounced the same (rode—road)

II. Word Analysis:

A. Phonics
   1. Knows consonant sounds taught in first grade (b, d, f, h, j, k, l, m, n, p, q, r, s, t, v, w, x, y, z and st, tr, fr, sm, sn, sw, bl, gl, fl, pl, cl, sh, ch, wh, th)
   2. Applies these sounds and blends to:
      a. initial position in words (let)
      b. final position in words (bank)
      c. medial position in words (little)
   3. Knows word families:
      ou as in out   er as in her
      ow as in show and ur as in fur
      cow   ir as in bird

followed by "r," "w," and "l"?
      star
      saw
      all

B. Structural Analysis
   1. Recognizes root or base words (mines, mined, miner)
   2. Recognizes word endings en as in waken, ful as in careful
   3. Knows contractions:
      isn't   you're
      I've   let's
      I'm   it's
      he's   we've
   4. Knows possessives (Bill's)
   5. Can disconnect printed fl and fl (fish and fly)

III. Comprehension:

A. Association of ideas of material read
   1. Can draw conclusions
   2. Can predict outcomes
   3. Can find proof
   4. Can associate text with pictures
B. Organization of ideas
   1. Can follow printed directions
   2. Can find main idea
   3. Can follow plot sequence
C. Locating information
   1. Can use:
      table of contents
      page number
      titles
   2. Can find specific information
D. Appreciation
   1. Able to dramatize stories read
   2. Able to illustrate stories read
   3. Able to tell a story which has been read previously
   4. Owns at least several books which he particularly likes

IV. Oral Reading:

A. Reads clearly and distinctly
B. Reads with expression
C. Reads fluently
D. Reads so that listeners enjoy the story

the story will frequently provide for that release which the children receive to a much more limited extent than in the oral reading situations of the traditional three group basal programs. Incorporating art work and illustrating stories read is another way of developing an appreciation for literature. Since it is not unusual to find each child in the room reading a different story, there would be more reason for having children tell stories to the rest of the class which they have read. Since the goal of the personalized reading program is to provide permanent interest in reading material, any devices which the teacher may develop to encourage this appreciation of literature should be used as much as possible.

Oral Reading

In the personalized reading program, there will be absolutely none of the traditional oral reading, going around the group with each child reading several lines or paragraphs. The children will be called upon to read aloud before the students only for a distinct purpose, but not as a check on how well the child can read. This will mean that in the personalized reading program there will be no situation when the teacher will ask the child to read aloud, before either a small group or the entire class, material which he has not first read silently. The only time the child will be asked to read aloud without first having read the material would be at the time of the individual conference and there is no reason to think that this would happen very often.

Following silent reading, the child can be expected to read the material aloud clearly and distinctly. He should be able to read it with expression and fluency, so that listeners enjoy the story. His purpose for reading aloud is not a check to see how well he is reading, but rather to read material in such a way that he will interest other students in wanting to enjoy the same material. This will relieve much of the pressure from oral reading when the child knows that he is not being asked to read merely to check how well he can read.

The second grade level reading skills are designed to lead the child into independent reading of a wide variety of materials. The personalized reading program offers the teacher the opportunity to bring the child to the type of independent reading at a much earlier stage than would have been possible had the child been in basal readers. A true love of reading can more easily be developed in this type of program with certainly earlier introduction to a wide variety of the wonderful materials in childrens' literature. Because of the abundance of books now appearing at the beginning reading level, the child should, as he has mastered these second grade reading skills, become well acquainted with many different children's authors. In so doing, he will have learned to appreciate reading as an enjoyable activity, rather than something which is a required subject in school to be ploddingly dragged through.

THIRD GRADE READING LEVEL SKILLS

The third grade is a period of thorough review of the skills of reading learned in the first and second grade, plus the addition of a rapidly increasing verbal and reading vocabulary and new reading skills.

Vocabulary: Word Recognition

Before beginning on third grade reading level skills, the teacher should once again check the child's ability to recognize Dolch's 220 basic sight words. Although this has been done before, a regular check on the child's ability to recognize these words at sight will indicate the extent to which the teacher will need to work with the child. The child actually needs to review the following skills:

A. Compound Words
B. Prefixes and Suffixes
C. Initial Consonants and Blends
D. Base Words
E. Contractions

Vocabulary: Word Meaning

Throughout the third grade reading level the child is both reading widely and experiencing many new activities. All of these things add to his speaking vocabulary so that both his reading vocabulary and spelling ability should rapidly increase. At this level he should be able to detect descriptive and figurative words and phrases. Synonyms which have been taught before should be reviewed, with the word "antonyms" being added to his vocabulary. He has already learned the opposites of words, but at the third grade level, the word "antonyms" is introduced for the first time. Homonyms are introduced for the first time but emphasis is not placed upon them until fourth grade level.

Vocabulary: Word Attack Skills

The following word attack skills need to be reviewed, retaught or introduced for the first time:
A. Consonant Blends
B. Long and Short Vowels
C. Root Words and Derived Words
D. Variance of known words formed by
   1. adding *s, es, d, ed, ing, er, est*
   2. dropping final *e* before endings (example: whaling)
   3. doubling the consonant before endings (fitting)
   4. change *y* to *i* before endings (berries)
E. Compound Words
F. Contractions
G. Variant vowel sounds
   1. Vowel and one syllable words followed by final *e*
   2. Short sound of vowel in medial position of one syllable words
   3. Silent vowels
H. Possessive Forms
 I. Variant Sounds of *c* and *g*
 J. Silent letters in *kn, wr,* and *gn*
The child must learn to form plurals by adding "s," "es," and "ies." He knows to change "f" to "v" and add "es" in making plurals out of words which end in "f," and he needs to learn the similarity of sounds such as "x" and "cks" (box, locks).

Syllabication has been mentioned before, but is introduced at third grade reading level to a much greater extent. The child is taught that there are usually as many syllables in a word as there are single vowels. When there is a single consonant between two vowels, the vowel usually goes with the first syllable. (Example: pu–pil.) When there is a double consonant between two vowels, the syllable break is between the double consonant. (Example: hap–py.)

The child learns at third grade reading level how to hyphenate words. This is part of his training in syllabication, although syllabication needs to be pointed out as the rule to follow in hyphenating words at the end of sentences.

At third grade reading level, the child should learn how to make an accent mark and how to accent the syllable which has the mark over it. This can easily be taught by actually moving the accent mark to different syllables to show how the accent changes the way a word sounds, and in some cases its actual meaning. Children love to play games doing this type of thing and it should under no conditions be made a difficult skill to be learned. In order that the child will know something about how to pronounce a word which he has been able successfully to break into syllables, he should be taught always to try the accent on the first syllable except when the first syllable is a prefix. When the first syllable is a prefix, the accent usually goes on the second syllable. This will not always work, but the child can have some guide to follow. When he has no other choice but to guess, he has a much better chance of pronouncing the word correctly if he follows the rule.

Comprehension Skills

The following comprehension skills must either be reviewed, relearned or introduced for the first time:
  A. Apply new ideas
  B. Follow sequence of events or ideas
  C. Draw conclusions
  D. See relationships
  E. Predict outcomes
  F. Follow directions
  G. Read for definite purpose
  H. Interpret oral reading

    I. Classify items
    J. Use index
    K. Alphabetize words
    L. Find proof

Little attention has been given to alphabetizing new words other than by their initial letter before the third grade reading level. By the time the child has completed third grade reading level, however, he should be able to alphabetize words completely. This may need to be a formal lesson for the entire class, since it frequently is not even fully understood by even the bright students. Those who encounter difficulty in learning how to alphabetize should be placed in smaller groups and presented simpler words on which to work.

At third grade level, the child is taught to locate the main idea in a story. This sometimes necessitates the child's using a new reading skill—skimming. He needs to broaden his knowledge of the source from which material can be obtained. This means introduction of the dictionary, encyclopedias, periodicals, other resource books, and textbooks. He also needs to learn at this level to use maps and charts.

Oral Reading

The same oral reading skills which have been stressed in the second grade are again repeated at the third grade level. Of course, reading material will be more difficult, but essentially the child must have pleasing voice quality, adequate volume, proper phrasing, clear and distinct enunciation, accuracy in pronunciation, and the ability to convey meaning to the listener.

It is of the utmost importance that the child has mastered skills at the readiness, first, second, and third grade reading level, before he progresses into fourth grade reading skills. The primary school program is much more flexible than that of the upper elementary grades, and there is more time for the teacher to work on reading skills as such. After the primary grades, a great deal of attention is given to content subjects such as history, geography, science, and arithmetic, with a decreasing amount of attention to the learning-to-read process. If the child has not adequately mastered the primary grade basic reading skills before he enters into the fourth grade, serious thought should be given to the advisability of his being retained in the third grade. Rather than repeating any of the skills which he has already learned, his program should begin where he is in terms of reading skills and be continued from there.

The personalized reading program is easily adaptable to the child who has been found in need of a longer period for learning particular grade level skills. There is no need to take the child back to the beginning of the same basal book through which he went the year before. He can merely continue reading books of his own choice, working at the time of the individual conference with the teacher and in the groups to which he may be assigned as the year progresses on those skills which he is ready to learn. The logical sequential development of skills is more easily applicable in the personalized reading program than it is in a traditional three group basal reader approach where the teacher must keep all of the children in the group at somewhat the same level.

When the child has mastered the basic reading skills of the first three grades, he is ready to move into content subjects of fourth grade level. He should be able to read silently with both speed and comprehension. His attitude toward reading should be one that encourages him to read widely, both during the school year and during the summer, so that his reading experiences will have him ready for content subject learning. While there are certainly many new reading skills which need to be presented at the upper elementary grade levels, essentially the foundation has been laid for the child's being an effective reader. If this foundation is a solid one, there is every reason to expect the child to be a good reader. If it is not, there is little likelihood that the child will meet success at the upper elementary levels.

BARBE READING SKILLS CHECK LIST
THIRD GRADE LEVEL

_____ (Last Name)

_____ (First Name)

_____ (Name of School)

_____ (Age)

_____ (Grade Placement)

_____ (Name of Teacher)

I. Vocabulary:

A. Word Recognition

1. Recognizes Dolch 220 Basic Sight Words

a	as	again	about	any
all	away	ate	after	better
am	be	black	always	both
an	black	but	around	bring
and	brown	cold	ask	carry
are	by	cut	because	clean
at	came	fast	been	could
big	did	first	before	done
blue	eat	five	best	don't
call	fall	fly	buy	draw
can	find	four	does	drink
come	for	give	for	eight
do	get	goes	found	every
down	going	going	full	hurt
funny	have	got	gave	know
go	her	green	grow	light
good	him	had	hold	myself
he	his	has	how	never
help	if	hot	just	own
here	into	its	keep	pick
I	laugh	long	kind	right
in	let	made	much	seven
is	live	many	must	shall
it	may	new	now	show
jump	my	not	off	their
like	no	of	once	them
little	old	open	only	then
look	on	please	round	there

II. Word Analysis:

A. Review and refine previously taught skills:

1. All initial consonant sounds
2. Short and long vowel sounds
3. Changes in words by:
   - a. adding s, es, d, ed, ing, er, est
   - b. dropping final e and adding ing
   - c. doubling the consonant before adding ing
   - d. changing y to i before adding es
4. Compound words
5. Contractions
6. Vowel rules
   - a. vowel in one syllable word is short
   - b. vowel in syllable or word ending in e is long
   - c. two vowels together, first is long and second is silent
7. Possessive forms
8. C followed by i, e, y makes s sound
   C followed by a, o, u makes k sound
9. G followed by i, e, y makes j sound
   G followed by a, o, u makes guh sound
10. Silent letters in kn, wr, gn

B. Learns new skills of:

1. Forming plurals
   - by adding s, es, ies
   - by changing f to v and adding es
2. Similarities of sound such as **x** and cks (box—blocks)

__play	__said	__read	__tell	__together
__pretty	__she	__saw	__thank	__use
__ran	__sit	__say	__that	__very
__red	__some	__sing	__they	__want
__ride	__stop	__six	__this	__warm
__run	__three	__soon	__too	__wash
__see	__today	__ten	__try	__went
__so	__two	__upon	__under	__what
__the	__was	__us	__walk	__when
__to	__will	__who	__well	__where
__up	__work	__why	__were	__which
__we	__yes	__wish	__white	__would
__you	__yellow	__your	__with	__write

2. Refinement of skills previously taught __

   a. Compound words __

   b. Prefixes and suffixes:

a	__ dis	__ ful __
un	__ in	__ less __
ex	__ th	__ ness __
be	__ ty	__

   c. Identification of root words __

   d. Knows all initial consonant sounds (single sounds and blends—up to first vowel in word) __

   e. Can read all contractions __

B. Word Meaning

   1. Provided many experiences to increase speaking and reading vocabulary __

   2. Able to select descriptive and figurative words and phrases __

   3. Able to supply synonyms, antonyms and homonyms __

   4. Understands use of elementary school dictionary to find word meaning __

2. Where there is a single consonant between two vowels, the vowel goes with the first syllable (pu/pil)

3. When there is a double consonant, the syllable break is between the two consonants and one is silent (example: lit/tle)

D. **Can hyphenate words using syllable rules**

E. Understands use of primary accent mark

F. Knows to accent first syllable, unless it is a prefix, otherwise accent second syllable

III. **Comprehension:**

A. Can find main idea in story

B. Can keep events in proper sequence

C. Can draw logical conclusions

D. Is able to see relationships

E. Can predict outcomes

F. Can follow printed directions

G. Can read for a definite purpose:

   1. for pleasure

   2. to obtain answer to question

   3. to obtain general idea of content

H. Classify items

I. Use index

J. Alphabetize words by first two letters

K. Knows technique of skimming

L. Can determine what source to obtain information (dictionary, encyclopedia, index, glossary, etc.)

M. Use maps and charts

IV. **Oral Reading:**

A. Reads with a **pleasing voice quality**

B. Reads with **adequate volume**

C. Reads with **clear and distinct enunciation**

D. Accuracy in pronunciation

E. Ability to **convey meaning to listeners**

Chapter Eight

Upper Elementary Grade Level Reading Skills

Reading has too often been overlooked as a subject which needs to be taught in the upper elementary grades. Even though the basal reader has attempted to provide teachers with a teachers' manual, too frequently the upper elementary teacher has been so overburdened with the wide variety of subjects to be taught that reading suffered. In too many situations, reading has not actually been taught as a skill subject. The grades in reading which were put on the report card were only a reflection on how well the child was able to read when he arrived at the upper elementary grade level. It in no way indicated the progress which he had made in reading. This was not a fault of the basal reader approach, but is a problem which must be faced regardless of the type of reading program.

Reading skills which are introduced at the upper elementary grade level are, to a large part, a review and refinement of skills already presented in the primary grades. But because of a variety of factors, not least among these is the lack of readiness on the part of many of the children for the skills which were presented earlier, some children arrive at the fourth grade not knowing primary grade skills. There are new reading skills to be presented at the upper elementary level also. If a child can only learn primary grade skills or upper elementary grade level skills, he certainly should know the primary skills first. But learning reading skills should not be an either-or proposition, but rather should be a continuous development of sequential skills, designed to provide the child with the highest possible degree of independence in reading. Merely the development of a higher reading level score because of an ever-increasing reading vocabulary does not promote the maximum amount of reading improvement.

A formal reading period should continue throughout the upper elementary grades. The personalized reading program, which allows children to select the material which they wish to read, can most easily be worked into the reading required in the content subjects. For those teachers doing unit teaching, the personalized reading program offers the opportunity for the child to do independent reading to meet special needs in content areas.

FOURTH GRADE READING LEVEL SKILLS

The fourth grade is distinctive in American public education in that emphasis moves away from instruction for the purpose of learning skills to use of the skills to learn content material. This transition is fraught with dangers. Among the more important ones are:

1. It is too often assumed that all children have mastered basic reading skills of the primary grades so that these skills are not reviewed or retaught.

2. The overcrowded schedule, in which the teacher is expected to cover a great number of different subjects, results in reading being left out of the formal teaching curriculum.

3. Some children, particularly those with better than average abilities, have relied upon their superior memories to learn new words. With the introduction of content subjects, the student is unable to remember all of the new words and sometimes develops a dislike for what seems to him to be a new type of reading.

4. Fewer upper elementary teachers than primary teachers know the "what" and "how" of teaching reading.

5. The shifting away of the great desire within each child

to please his parents and the teacher, into a stronger desire to gain the approval of his peer group, means that the attitude of the child's peer group toward reading must be good. If the children do not like reading, there is a growing attitude at this age which will increasingly influence adversely the attitude of other children toward reading.

The review of first, second, and third grade reading skills comes as well as the introduction of new reading skills at fourth grade. The personalized reading program offers the teacher the best opportunity for going back to the level at which each child needs instruction, and moving him as rapidly as possible to fourth grade skills. Since there is no goal of "getting through the book," the personalized reading program will actually take less of the fourth grade teacher's time than the traditional basal reader approach.

Vocabulary: Development

The child will need to acquire a new vocabulary for each of the many content areas taught at fourth grade level. The teacher must be constantly aware of the rapidly increasing speaking and reading vocabulary of the child. Before the child encounters difficulty with new words in the content areas, the teacher should present these words to the child, both in their form to be found in the content material and the alternate meanings which they will have. The child must be encouraged to use those word attack skills which he has previously learned to unlock new words. He needs to review and be thoroughly familiar with the following concepts:

a. compound words
b. root words
c. suffixes and prefixes
d. plurals
e. hyphenated words
f. contractions

At the fourth grade level the teacher must be concerned with the child's ability to recognize and to form plurals. The simple addition of "s" and, possibly "es," has already been developed.

The changes of form need to be pointed out in such words as: man–men; sheep–sheep; church–churches; bush–bushes; fly–flies; valley–valleys; and wife–wives.

New emphasis should be attached to obtaining meaning from context. Because of the wide variety of subjects being studied, it is important that the child learn that some words have the same meaning even in different content subjects, while on other occasions, the same word will have entirely different meaning. Examples of words with more than one meaning would be "ground," which could mean either land around a house, first floor of a building, the act of pulverizing, or a ship becoming grounded on a rock. Another example would be the word "fast" which could mean a fast runner, fast in the sense of not eating, fast to the floor, and several others. Children will particularly enjoy this type of activity if it can be treated more as a game, rather than some difficult task which may appear hopeless.

The children at this level need to develop their ability to use new words in sentences to demonstrate clearly their understanding of the meaning. A refinement of this technique is to require that they use homonyms and synonyms for the word in the sentence.

Particularly important to the fourth grade children is to learn how to choose the "right word." Too frequently the children are satisfied with a word because it means generally about what they want to say. If the children can learn at this level to select exactly the right word, there will be less difficulty at later levels in developing both writing and speaking ability. An appreciation for exactly the right word should be developed early so that the children will not fall into "sloppy" patterns of speech. This would include teaching the children at this level to use the first choice pronunciation in the dictionary rather than saying words which, although they may be correct, are not preferred. Teaching poetry sometimes develops an appreciation for exactly the right word, when it is more difficult to show the real value of exactly the right word in prose.

Punctuation needs to be reviewed and taught both as a means of writing better and a means of understanding reading material. The child must have a thorough understanding of how to use and understand the meaning of italics, quotation marks, parentheses, and exclamation marks.

The problem of change of tense of verbs should be taught at the fourth grade level. Both the pronunciation and form of many verbs change as the tense changes. Fourth grade children need to learn this difference, both for their speaking ability and their reading ability. They need to be able to read and tell in what tense the material was written. They should also be able to change the tense when directed to do so.

At the fourth grade level, the use of maps is greatly increased. It is therefore important that the children learn how to read maps accurately. Many skills involved in doing this can best be measured by how well the child can use maps.

Word Attack Skills: Structural Analysis

It is important that children at this level learn all of the basic elements of breaking words into syllables. This should result both in better word attack skills, as well as better spelling ability. The readiness for work with syllables should have begun at the pre-first grade level when the child had practice in learning to hear the number of sounds in a word. It has continued on until the fourth grade level when the teaching of syllables is a major assignment of reading instruction. The following rules should be understood by every child at the fourth grade level, although it is not necessary that he be able to state these rules from memory. It would be more important that the child be able to use these rules when he comes to a word which involves any of them, rather than be required to list the rules.

1. Each syllable must contain a vowel and a single vowel can be a syllable.
2. Suffixes and prefixes are syllables with meanings of their own.
3. The root word is not divided.
4. If the first vowel in a word is followed by two consonants, the first syllable usually ends with the first of the two consonants. (Example: pen–cil, fun–ny)
5. If the first vowel in a word is followed by a single con-

sonant, that consonant usually begins the second syllable. (Example: ba–con, a–maze)

6. If a word ends in "le" preceded by a consonant, that consonant begins the last syllable. (Example: fa–ble, fu–tile)
7. When "r" follows a vowel, the vowel and the "r" go together to make the "er" sound.
8. The letter "x" always goes with the preceding vowel to form a syllable. (Example: ex–it, ax–le)
9. The letters "ck" go with the preceding vowel and end the syllable. (Example: chick–en)

But merely breaking words down into syllables accomplishes little if the child is unaware of the use of accent. Unfortunately, English is not like some foreign languages which place the same amount of stress upon each syllable. There are certain guiding rules of accent which are helpful if children are to use what they know in pronunciation concerning syllabication.

The following rules of accent should be thoroughly understood by fourth grade level reading students:

1. In a word of two or more syllables, the first syllable is usually accented unless it is a prefix. (Example: o–ver, a–ble)
2. Two like consonant letters following the first vowel are a clue to an accented first syllable and to a short vowel sound in that syllable. (Example: rib–bon, col–lar)
3. In most two syllable words that end in a consonant followed by "y," the first syllable is accented and the last is unaccented. (Example: ti–ny, ug–ly)
4. Beginning syllables "de," "re," "be," "ex," "in," and "a," are usually unaccented. (Example: re–main, be–fore)
5. When a final syllable ends in "le" that syllable is usually unaccented. (Example: bot–tle, mar–ble)
6. Endings that form syllables are usually unaccented. (Example: run–ning)
7. The letters "ck" following a single vowel letter are a clue to an accented syllable. (Example: chick–en, jack–et)
8. Two vowel letters together or two vowel letters, one of which is the final e, in the last syllable of a word are usually a clue to an accented final syllable. (They also in-

dicate a long vowel sound for the previously learned vowel rules. Example: com–plain, a–muse)

Children at this level should learn the meaning of the following list of suffixes and prefixes. This is the best method by which vocabulary can be increased rapidly. To the extent that children learn the meaning of prefixes and suffixes, the size of their vocabulary can actually be predicted. It is not necessary that suffixes and prefixes always be learned in isolation, but the student should be able to recall the meaning of the prefix and suffix when he comes across it in a particular word.

Prefixes

dis	(not, a part)	dismiss
in	(not)	invade
mis	(wrong)	mistake
anti	(against)	anti-climax
non	(not)	nonsense
com	(with)	combine
con	(with)	connect
pre	(before)	prepare
super	(over)	superior
tri	(three)	tricycle
sub	(under)	submarine
post	(after)	postscript
ab	(from)	abnormal
trans	(across)	translate
em	(in)	embark
de	(from)	depart
inter	(between)	inter-urban
pro	(in front of)	promote
ex	(out of or out)	explain
en	(in)	enter
ob	(against)	object
per	(fully)	perfect

Suffixes

ness	(being)	sickness
ment	(result of)	movement
ward	(in direction of)	backward
ous	(full of)	joyous
ious	(abounding in)	gracious
eous	(of the nature of)	aqueous
et	(little)	leaflet
able	(capable of being)	capable
ible	(capable of being)	credible

ic	(like, made of)	magic
ish	(like)	foolish
ant	(being)	vacant
ent	(one who)	president
age	(collection of)	baggage
ance	(state of being)	disturbance
ence	(state or quality)	violence
wise	(ways)	crosswise
ling	(little)	duckling
ty	(state)	unity
ity	(state)	vicinity
ure	(denoting action)	pleasure
ion	(condition or quality)	action

Word Attack Skills: Phonic Analysis

It is necessary at this level to review, and whenever necessary, reteach, any word elements or principles assigned to the primary grades as follows: single consonants, consonant blends, and short and long vowels. Vowel teams should be learned. (For example: ee, ea, ai, ay, oa, oo, oi, oy) The vowel and consonant teams should also be learned such as: aw, au, ou, ow, er, ir, ur, or, ar.

At the fourth grade level, children should review the following generalizations which apply to vowels:

1. In attacking a vowel sound, try first the short sound; if the word then doesn't make sense, try the long sound.
2. Vowels are usually short when they appear as single vowels and are followed by a consonant.
3. Vowels are usually given the long sound when they appear alone, and are the last letters of a word.
4. When two vowels appear together in a word, the first vowel is usually given the long sound, while the second is silent.
5. In a short word containing two vowels, where one of the vowels is a final "e," the first vowel will have a long sound while the final "e" is silent.

Word Attack Skills: Training in the Use of Dictionary and Glossary

Although the use of the dictionary has been introduced at third grade level, not until the fourth grade level will the child come to depend greatly upon his ability to use reference material. One of the major skills learned in the fourth grade level will be the proper use of reference material. In order for the child to do this the teacher should review him in the order of letters in the alphabet. If he has not learned the alphabet in sequence by this time, he should be taught it before any time is wasted on dictionary or reference skills. The teacher should give the child practice in arranging words in alphabetical order, by using all of the letters in the word.

The child should be taught how to look up words in the dictionary. He should be directed to know the major breaks in the alphabet, learning first which letters are in the middle of the alphabet, which ones are toward the first, and which letters are toward the last. After this has been learned, the child should be able to open the dictionary in that general area in which he is to find the word for which he is looking.

The child needs to learn the meaning and the use of phonetic spelling that follows in parenthesis each word in the dictionary. He needs to develop an understanding of how the dictionary shows the syllabication of a word so that he will know how to pronounce it. The meaning and use of the pronunciation key at the bottom of each page should be explained. He should be given a great deal of practice in determining how to pronounce words according to the accent mark as given in the dictionary.

Fourth grade children need to learn how to select the meaning of the word which best applies to the context in which the word is used. They should also learn the use and meaning of guide words. In addition to use of the primary accent mark, the child should also learn the meaning and use of the secondary accent mark.

Comprehension: Finding the Main Idea

One of the best techniques for finding the main idea of material read is to make up titles for this material. Whether the title is for the entire story, or for only a small section of the story, it needs to be short as well as informative. Children will need definite training in being able to do this. When they are successful it will greatly aid them in better comprehension.

Another technique requiring the student to find the main idea which will improve his comprehension is having him summarize material which he has read. If the child has difficulty in doing this, the summary should at first be longer than actually desired. As the child progresses in his ability to summarize, the material should be cut down more and more. It is important that the child's summary always be carefully checked to see that it is in his own words. Merely lifting verbatim a few sentences is not the goal of teaching the child to summarize.

In order for a child to improve his comprehension, he must be able to reorganize the thoughts and material which he has read, using his own words, and be able to discuss this material with others. If he is not able to put the material into his own words, then he is actually unable to comprehend the material and it is too difficult for him.

Comprehension: Finding Details

It is not enough, however, that the child merely be able to select main ideas and condense the total story. He must also be able to find specific information, regardless of how minute the point of information may be. He must be able to interpret descriptive words and phrases and use the vocabulary which is in the new context. The student will need training in knowing which facts to pick out to remember for each of a variety of reading purposes. Reading in the social studies area will mean that the child should probably retain specific dates, percentages and figures, while when reading for pleasure it is not necessary to remember dates and quantities.

Children at fourth grade level need to learn what the main ideas are in the story as well as those ideas which support the main idea. In addition to actually being able to remember what went on in the story, they should have practice in recalling. This is a type of memory resulting from leading questions which the teacher or other children might ask. The child should be able to use study guides, charts, outlines, and encyclopedias. Throughout the child's reading, he must always be aware of the location of specific information so that when necessary he will be able to verify his answers.

Comprehension: Arranging Ideas in Sequence

It is essential that children learn to arrange ideas in proper sequence. An outstanding characteristic of the child with poor reading comprehension is that he usually repeats the thing which he has read last. He is then unable to remember a great number of the individual items which happened in the story, and feels that he has both a poor memory and the teacher feels he has poor comprehension of the material read. Actually none of us could remember fifteen unrelated facts. By recalling what happens first, the child immediately has a clue as to what happened next, then next, etc. Rather than requiring phenomenal memory, this makes use of recall which requires much less actual rote memory.

Comprehension: Creative Reading

At fourth grade level, the children need to learn to make inferences, draw conclusions, and form judgments based on context and experiences. They must be able to form judgments, evaluations and opinions based on story facts. The child should be able to interpret the story idea so that he can generalize about the story.

Seeing relationships and making comparisons are also a part of this developing of a mental ability necessary for good reading comprehension. The child needs to be able to identify and react to the mood of a passage, understanding the author's purpose. Rather than merely remembering the names of the characters, he should learn to know character traits about the characters in the story as well as the general physical description of them.

Comprehension: Formal Outlining

There is perhaps no technique better for developing comprehension than learning proper outlining procedures. The mechanics of the outline forces a child to give titles to the major sections, select topic sentences, and select key words. The very organization of the outline itself requires careful attention to sequence of events.

The mechanics of preparing the outline itself needs to be developed logically. The use of Roman numerals as the main ideas, followed by capital letters for supporting ideas should be presented first. Once the student has understood the use of Roman numerals and capital letters, he should then be introduced to the use of Arabic numbers for supporting ideas under the capital letters and then the use of small letters for supporting ideas under the heading of Arabic numbers. The very obvious fact that there can never be only one number or one letter needs to be explained carefully. If there is a time when a student feels that in no way can there be two supporting ideas under a major heading, it should be pointed out that the single idea should be the name of the heading, rather than whatever heading is there at the present time.

The outline should be used at fourth grade level to precede the child's actual reading of a lesson and his giving a talk from this outline. The great difficulty which teachers have at the upper grade levels in getting students to outline their material results primarily from the lack of proper training in outlining techniques at earlier grade levels. Once the student has convinced himself that an outline is of no help to him, he frequently will wait until after he has written the material to try to prepare the outline. Materials written without an outline are readily discernible. Giving talks or using an outline as a guide demonstrates as effectively as anything else the real value in preparing a good outline.

Oral Reading Skills: Choral Reading

Choral reading has been used most successfully beginning at about the fourth grade level to help children improve both their expression and their appreciation for a variety of types of literature. The choral reading does not have to be merely a group of children reading with expression, but can include a variety of situations which are acted out and sounds which contribute to the general mood of the material being read.

The teacher should introduce the concept of being aware of one's eye-voice span. In oral reading it is essential that the child's eye actually be ahead of the point where he is reading.

BARBE READING SKILLS CHECK LIST
FOURTH LEVEL READING SKILLS

(Last Name)   (First Name)

(Age)   (Grade Placement)   (Name of Teacher)   (Name of School)

I. Vocabulary:
A. Word Recognition
1. Introduce new words in content fields ___
2. Recognizes similarities of known words ___
   a. compound words ___   d. plurals ___
   b. root words ___   e. hyphenated words ___
   c. suffixes, prefixes ___   f. contractions ___
3. Recognizes unusual characteristics of words ___

B. Word Meaning
1. Develop ability in getting meaning from context ___
2. Use new words in sentences to show meaning ___
3. Knows punctuation
   a. italics ___   c. parenthesis ___
   b. quotation marks ___   d. exclamation marks ___
4. Use of map skills ___

C. Review Dolch Words

II. Word Attack Skills:
A. Structural analysis
1. Knows rules for syllables
   a. Each syllable must contain a vowel and a single vowel can be a syllable ___
   b. Suffixes and prefixes are syllables with meanings of their own ___
   c. The root word is not divided ___
   d. If the first vowel is followed by two consonants, the first syllable usually ends with the first consonant (example: pen cil) ___
   e. If the first vowel is followed by a single consonant, the consonant usually begins the second syllable (example: a maze, am ple) ___
   f. If a word ends in le preceded by

con	(with)	connect
pre	(before)	prepare
super	(over)	superior
tri	(three)	tricycle
sub	(under)	submarine
post	(after)	postscript
ab	(from)	abnormal
trans	(across)	translate
em	(in)	embark
de	(from)	depart
inter	(between)	interurban
pro	(in front of)	promote
ex	(out of or out)	explain
en	(in)	enter
ob	(against)	object
per	(fully, through)	perfect

B. Phonic analysis
1. Review phonic skills
   a. Single consonants and blends ___
   b. Short and long vowels ___
   c. Vowel teams:
      ee ___   au ___   oi ___
      ea ___   aw ___   oy ___
      ai ___   oa ___   ou ___
      ay ___   oo ___   ow ___
2. Review Vowel rules
   a. In attacking a vowel sound try first the short sound; if the word then doesn't make sense try the long sound.
   b. Vowels are usually short when they appear as single vowels and are followed by a consonant.
   c. Vowels are usually given the long sound when they appear alone and are the last letters of a word.
   d. When two vowels appear together in a word, the first vowel is long and the second is silent.

C. Training in use of dictionary and glossary
1. As taught on third grade level.
   a. Review order of letters in alphabet.
   b. Review the alphabetical arrangement of words.
2. Teach the division of dictionary to determine in which 1/3 or 1/4 the word may be found.
3. Teach the meaning and use of the phonetic spelling that follows in parenthesis each word in the dictionary.
4. Teach the meaning and use of the pronunciation key given at the bottom of every page.
5. Teach the selecting of the meaning which fits best according to the context in which the word is used.
6. Teach the meaning and use of guide words.
7. Teach the meaning and use of the secondary accent mark.

III. Comprehension:
A. Finding the main idea
1. Choosing titles for material read
2. Summarizing
3. Can identify key words and topic sentences
B. Finding details
1. Finding specific information
2. Interpreting descriptive words and phrases
3. Selecting facts to remember
4. Selecting facts to support main idea
5. Using study guides, charts, outlines
6. Verifying answers
7. Arranging ideas in sequence
C. Creative reading
1. Able to interpret story ideas (generalize)
2. Able to see relationships
3. Able to identify the mood of a reading selection
4. Able to identify author's purpose
5. Able to identify character traits
D. Formal outlining
1. Form
   a. Main ideas (I, II, III)
   b. Subordinate ideas (A, B, C)
2. Talking from an outline

IV. Oral Reading:
A. Review previously taught skills
B. Eye-voice span of three words

---

the preceding vowel to form a syllable (example: ex it)

h. The letters ck go with the preceding vowel and end the syllable (example: chick en)

2. Knows accent clues
a. The first syllable is usually accented, unless it is a prefix
b. Beginning syllables de, re, be, in and a are usually unaccented
c. Endings that form syllables are usually unaccented (run ning)
d. ck following a single vowel is accented (example: jack et)

3. Teach these suffixes and prefixes:
a. Suffixes:

Suffix	Meaning	Example
ness	(being)	sickness
ment	(result of)	movement
ward	(in direction of)	backward
ous	(full of)	joyous
ious	(abounding in)	gracious
eous		
et	(little)	leaflet
able	(capable of being)	capable
ible		credible
ic	(like, made of)	magic
ish	(like)	foolish
ant	(being)	vacant
ent	(one who)	president
age	(collection of)	baggage
ance	(state of being)	disturbance
ence	(state or quality)	violence
wise	(ways)	crosswise
ling	(little)	duckling
ty	(state)	unity
ity		vicinity
ure	(denoting action)	pleasure
ion	(condition or quality)	action

b. Prefixes:

dis	(not, apart)	dismiss
in	(not)	invade
mis	(wrong)	mistake
anti	(against)	anticlimax
non	(not)	nonsense
com	(with)	combine

If an individual's eye is on the word which he is reading, he is a word-by-word reader and cannot possibly read with any expression. By having his eyes several words ahead of his voice, he knows what is coming and is able to regulate his voice either by dropping it for a question or changing the pitch for whatever the punctuation calls for.

The greatly increased amount of reading in the content areas of the fourth grade level will bring to light many reading difficulties which have been heretofore unrecognized. The fourth grade teacher therefore must devote a great deal of attention to correcting any difficulties which may exist, as well as encouraging the child to read widely and to learn the new skills at fourth grade level. Greatly increased interest in reading, both in a variety of types of reading material and in actual number of books read, should be observed. Widened horizons of reading in the many content areas should be a major characteristic of this grade reading level.

FIFTH GRADE READING LEVEL SKILLS

Many of the reading skills which are learned at fifth grade level are actually only a refinement and extension of those skills learned at the earliest levels. For this reason, it is necessary for these skills to be repeated on the check list at each grade level, but there is little reason for repeating them in the listing of skills at this level. The conscientious teacher will know all of the reading skills of the grades before the one in which she is teaching so that she may frequently refer to skills learned at an earlier level and encourage students at fifth grade level to use all of those things which have been taught to them earlier.

The personalized reading program offers the teacher innumerable opportunities for expanding the reading interests of every child. By the time the child has reached fifth grade reading level, he should be able to read independently on almost any subject which he may choose. Because freedom of choice of reading material is an essential part of the personalized reading program, there is both more time for this child to read independently and more time for the teacher to devote to expanding the reading interests of the children.

Vocabulary Skills: Word Recognition

The continued development of the child's ever-increasing reading vocabulary is an essential part of fifth grade reading level skill instruction. In the personalized reading program, the child is keeping a record of those words which he encounters which either offer difficulty for him to read, or are new to him. The teacher should frequently collect these words and use them at the time the child has the individual conference to check to make certain he is learning them. The children may actually use these new words in their group activities so that they will assist one another in developing larger vocabularies, and will not be limited by vocabulary in only those books that they have read. They can in this way benefit from learning the new words that the other children have encountered.

There is some argument in favor of keeping the words on cards so that the teacher may collect them at any time she wishes. They could even be collected daily, rather than be allowed to pile up to such a great number they would seem overwhelming to the child. The idea of keeping the words in a notebook appeals to some teachers, even though it presents some difficulties when the teacher chooses to collect the material to check.

Vocabulary Skills: Meaning of Words

Interpreting word meanings is an essential part of fifth grade reading level instruction. The child is beyond the stage when he can learn just one meaning for each word, and expect it to apply in all situations. He must learn the various meanings of words, both in context and out. He learns at this level some of the elementary principles of semantics dealing with word meaning such as the emotional tone of certain words, the confusing of the "either-or" type of categorization, and the need for qualifying statements.

Children in the fifth grade level learn to read more complex maps, paying particular attention to the specialized vocabulary which is associated with map reading. They learn at fifth grade level how to read diagrams and charts. This is essentially a new skill which has not been presented earlier.

Synonyms are constantly being reviewed, of course. Antonyms are discussed, as are homonyms. The concept of heteronyms is introduced for the first time. A heteronym is a word which has different meanings and sounds, even though it is still spelled the same way. (Example: lead—the metal; lead—the verb)

Attention is given at fifth grade level to interpreting figurative and colorful expressions. These are distinguished from the colloquial expressions, which are also colorful, but which are regional in nature. There could well be an entire class unit in which each student selected reading material at his own level which included examples of colorful sectional speech.

Word Attack Skills: Phonic Skills

Rules of syllabication need to be reviewed thoroughly again in the fifth grade both as an aid to better spelling and as a word attack skill technique. The vowel sounds, both long and short, need to be reviewed also, as well as rules of accent and syllabication.

Word Attack Skills: Dictionary

Alphabetization needs to be reviewed and expanded. The ability to divide the dictionary into thirds to knew approximately where a certain word will appear needs to be learned, as well as being able to alphabetize words by as many letters as is necessary to make the best alphabetization.

The child learns at the fifth grade reading level to recognize and learn the abbreviated parts of speech as: n.—noun; v.—verb; adj.—adjective; and adv.—adverb. Children must also learn to use the preferred pronunciation found in the dictionary.

It is important that the children learn at fifth grade reading level to understand the use of diacritical markings at the bottom of the page. It is not likely that all of the students will need, or even be able to learn the names of each of the marks. Every child, however, should be able to follow the diacritical markings at the bottom of the page of the dictionary and then be able to use this as a key to pronunciation.

The children need to know how to interpret the phonetic re-spellings of the word and to be able to make cross references. They should understand the use of the dictionary in explaining plurals, both regular and irregular.

Of particular fun is the technique of changing the accent to determine the effect both on pronunciation and meaning of words. For example, the word "present," when accented on the second syllable, means to *introduce a speaker* but when the ac-cent is shifted to the first syllable, the word means *gift*. Fifth grade students will delight in finding words which can change their meaning by changing the accent. At the same time this is being learned, the importance of the secondary accent can also be introduced. The parts of a verb, present and past, are pre-sented at this level. Adverbs that are derived from adjectives can be explained, pointing out that frequently the addition of "ly" at the ending changes the adjective to the adverb.

Word Attack Skills: Glossary

The children learn at this level that the glossary is actually a dictionary of words for one particular book. They need to learn how to look for the glossary, use guide words, and find meanings to understand what is being read.

Word Attack Skills: Context Clues

The use of context clues is probably the most widely used method of word attack among adult readers. It should not be blindly guessing what the word should be, without using those other means of word attack which have already been learned. Instead it is taking from context the approximate meaning of the word, and after applying word attack skills to the word, attempting to determine if the word is one which is in one's speaking vocabulary. Quite frequently it will turn out to be a familiar word. If the word is not in one's speaking vocabulary, however, the use of context clues is used only to obtain meaning. A better technique in this instance would be to use a dic-tionary. The use of context clues does not mean blind guessing without checking in the dictionary.

The child needs to review associating ideas with words, associating ideas with characters and using the sentence structure to indicate what the word might be. In poetry, the rhyme scheme can sometimes help with word attack. Capitalization, which would indicate the word was a proper noun, is a most effective means of using context clues. The use of pictures, maps and diagrams often provides the association with the meaning of the word.

Comprehension Skills: Locating Information

The table of contents is of particular importance if the students are to know the way in which the materials in the book are organized. They will need instruction in using the table of contents, for adults rarely set an example of using this section of the book which students should be encouraged to follow. Techniques to encourage doing this would include listing titles and having pupils use the table of contents in various books to locate on what page the material could be found.

The students also need to examine books to find where the title page appears, who the publisher is, what the copyright year is, the difference between the table of contents and the index, and if the book has pictures, where they appear.

Comprehension: Reference Materials

Since more and more of the work of the fifth grade level reader is being done independently, a thorough knowledge of a wide variety of reference materials is essential. The student will need to be taught the alphabetical arrangement of encyclopedias, and how the material is divided between one book and another. This can be done by showing the student the meaning of the characters on the back of each volume. The distinctive characteristics of the encyclopedias need to be pointed out. This can perhaps best be done by comparing several different encyclopedias, both one with another, and with dictionaries. The pupil should know the names of the more important children's encyclopedias such as *World Book Encyclopedia, Compton's, Encyclopedia Britanica, Jr.,* etc.

Atlas and maps must not be overlooked as valuable reference

materials. All students can examine the atlas to find answers for questions on location, relative size, direction, and distance. The particular vocabulary of an atlas and a map needs to be explained. Methods by which latitude and longitude are derived need to be taught. The division of the globe made by the equator needs to be explained.

Magazines and newspapers should be widely accepted in the classroom as valuable reference material. Their particular value is their ability to supply more recent information than textbooks could possibly contain.

The use of the dictionary as reference material should constantly be emphasized. Each fifth grade child should have his own dictionary which is with him in the classroom at all times. If this necessitates his having a dictionary for school and another for home, this should be encouraged. Use of the very small pocket type of dictionaries, while they would certainly be a valuable supplement to the regular type child's dictionary, should only be used in addition to a regular dictionary. They should not be a substitute for a more complete dictionary. In each classroom the teacher should have available at some convenient spot in the room, an unabridged dictionary of recent publication.

Learning how to read timetables is a skill which fifth grade reading level children can master. Rather than use unrelated timetables as listed in textbooks, the teacher should collect local train timetables, bus schedules and plane schedules. The students should be able to read schedules accurately and follow their directions.

The card catalog in the library should be thoroughly explained. The students should know that every book has its own particular place on the shelf in the library, and the numbers on the back of the books have a variety of meanings. The call number for each book should be explained. The children should learn to use the card catalog, noting what information is given on it, and should be given practice in locating titles of books and obtaining books by use of call numbers.

The proper use of the telephone book, both the alphabetical listing of names and the yellow pages should be taught. Students enjoy doing this type of activity and it trains them in using those skills which are applicable to the use of all reference materials.

Other types of catalogs can be used to give children practice in using reference skills. Catalogs from mail order houses can be obtained by writing to the company and provide an enjoyable type of reading and combination of reading-arithmetic activity for many children. Catalogs of cars, guns, antiques, and many other subjects will serve to develop more interest in learning about reference materials.

Comprehension: Reading to Organize

The organization of material is what improves one's comprehension of it. Trying to remember a large number of unrelated facts is both very difficult and meaningless. Relating the material in a systematic fashion provides the student with a better chance of remembering the material as well as better understanding of it. The techniques of outlining described in the skill instruction of Grade 4 should be put into practice frequently at this grade reading level.

Comprehension: Note Taking

Children at fifth grade level should be given an introduction to note taking. This should be done both by note taking from reading material and by note taking from a lecture. At the beginning stage, the children will have some difficulty doing this for they will want either to write down everything or only those things which interest them. This is best handled by insisting that the student clearly state his purpose for reading a particular selection of material, and then judging about how much material he will be expected to remember from it. This will determine how carefully his note taking should be.

Note taking is actually only an application of outlining techniques. The child listens or reads for main ideas, including as many subordinate or supporting ideas as he feels he will have need for. The outlining skills should be mastered first, but the note taking technique actually only provides another medium in which he can practice this technique.

Comprehension: Reading to Evaluate

Students should learn to distinguish fact from opinion. They should be concerned both with the facts which they have actually learned from the reading material and material which they have read which is only the opinion of the author. The fact that merely because something is in print means that it is an unalienable truth needs to be disspelled.

The students need to be able to establish in their minds the concept of cause and effect. Certain selections can be worked on in which there is a cause and effect relationship in which the students are asked if such and such a thing happened. If they do not remember that it did, they should re-read that section of the story. Then the teacher can ask what would have happened had a certain thing not occurred. The essential idea here is to indicate that a sequence of events is established with a likely occurrence following it. The teacher might well introduce some of O. Henry's or Saki's short stories where the ending does not always follow some logical sequence of events.

Comprehension: Reading for Appreciation

In order for material to be read with full appreciation, the student must have enough fluency with the process of reading so that he can enjoy the results. The student who reads silently a humorous story and finds nothing funny in it, is actually not comprehending the material. He may actually be reading all of the words but the concepts are not being comprehended. Frequently, the extent to which a student is comprehending and appreciating a story can be judged by his reaction to it even at the time he is reading it.

Pupils at the fifth grade level should have so mastered the reading skills that they are able to form sensory impressions about the materials being read. If they need to be directed along these lines, the teacher might very well ask them what types of sounds they heard as a particular scene is being described, how the food might taste which the people were eating, or what they saw or felt about certain things taking place in the story. Some teachers require that the children actually write down the feelings which they have as they read certain parts of the

BARBE READING SKILLS CHECK LIST
FIFTH LEVEL READING SKILLS

Copyright 1960, Walter B. Barbe

(Last Name)   (First Name)   (Name of School)

(Age)   (Grade Placement)   (Name of Teacher)

I. Vocabulary:
A. Word recognition of vocabulary in content areas

Social Studies—English—Arithmetic—Science—Miscellaneous

_____
_____
_____
_____
_____

B. Meaning of words
1. Interpreting word meanings
2. Semantics
3. Synonyms, antonyms, homonyms, heteronyms
4. Knows abstract meanings of words
5. Understands figurative and colorful expressions
6. Understands colloquial speech

II. Word Attack Skills:
A. Phonics skills
1. Syllabication
  a. Each syllable must contain a vowel and a single vowel can be a syllable.
  b. The root or base word is a syllable and is not divided.
  c. Blends are not divided. (th str)
  d. Suffixes and prefixes are syllables. (dusty in come)
  e. If the vowel in a syllable is followed by two consonants, the syllable usually ends with the first consonant.
  f. If a vowel in a syllable is followed by only one consonant, the syllable usually ends with a vowel.
  g. If a word ends in le, the consonant just before the l begins the last syllable.
  h. When there is an r after a vowel, the r goes with the vowel to make the "er" sound. (er ir ur)

III. Comprehension:
A. Locating information
1. Table of contents.
  a. Examine tables of contents of several books.
  b. List titles and have pupils use table of contents to locate pages.
2. Examine books to find: title page, pictures, key, guide words, publisher, copyright year.

B. Reference materials
1. The encyclopedia
  a. Topics arranged alphabetically.
  b. Show meaning of characters on back of each volume.
  c. Compare dictionaries and encyclopedias for differences of materials.
  d. Pupils should know names of important children's encyclopedias.
2. The atlas and maps.
  a. Examine atlas to find answers for questions on location, relative size, direction and distance.
  b. Use maps to explain latitude and longitude. Compare with known facts about streets and highways.
3. Magazines and newspapers. Use to supply more recent information than textbook could contain.
4. Knows proper use of dictionary.
5. Time tables.
  a. Reading and interpreting.
  b. Following directions.
6. Card catalogue.
  a. Explain that every book has its place on the shelf.
  b. Each class of books has its own call number.
  c. Examine cards.
    Author, title, subject
  d. Give practice in location of titles and call numbers.
7. Using (telephone luh...

a. When there is only one vowel in a word or syllable, the vowel is short.

b. When there are two vowels in a word or syllable, the first vowel is long and the second is silent.

3. Accent.

   a. In a word of 2 or more syllables, the first syllable is usually accented unless it is a prefix.

B. Dictionary

1. Alphabetization.
   a. Division into quarters and thirds.
   b. Classifying words by second, third, and fourth letters.
2. Using a dictionary.
   a. Recognize and learn abbreviated parts of speech as n. = noun; v. = verb; adj. = adjective; adv. = adverb.
   b. Learning the preferred pronunciation.
3. Use of guide words.
4. Syllabication and accent.
5. Interpreting diacritical markings. (bottom of page)
6. Interpreting key to pronunciations. (bottom of page)
7. Interpreting phonetic re-spellings.
8. Cross references.
9. Plurals—irregular. (deer, deer shelf, shelves)
10. Comparative and superlative adjectives. (many, more, most)
11. Change in accent and its effect on pronunciation and meaning of words. (pre'sent, present')
12. Secondary accent.
13. Parts of a verb. Tenses—present and past.
14. Adverbs derived from adjectives. (ly ending as a clue or help.)

C. Glossary

1. Dictionary of words for one particular book.
2. Use guide words.
3. Find meanings to understand what is being read.

D. Context clues

1. Review using context clues.
2. Review associating ideas with words.
3. Review associating ideas with characters.
4. Sentence structure. (Noun, verb)
5. In poetry. Rhythm scheme can sometimes help.

C. Outlining.

1. Use roman numerals and letters.
2. Establish a sequence.
3. Pupils list sentences in order of event.
4. Summarize.

D. Note taking

1. From reading
2. From lectures

E. Reading for appreciation

1. To derive pleasure
2. To form sensory impressions
3. To develop imagery
4. To understand characters
   a. physical appearance
   b. emotional make-up

IV. Oral Reading:

A. Recognize and pronounce words with speed and accuracy.
B. Group words into meaningful phrases.
C. Interpret marks of punctuation accurately.
D. Re-express to an audience the meaning and feelings expressed by an author.
E. Express emotion sincerely.
F. Read in a pleasant, well-modulated voice.
G. Read with poise and self-confidence.
H. Dramatize portions of the story.
I. "Televise" or give radio version of story incidents.
J. Take part in a stage version of a story.
K. Verify answers to questions.
L. Interpret characterizations.
M. Interpret word pictures.
N. Interpret-general mood of text. e.g. humor—suspense.
O. Interpret sensations given by words.
P. Interpret the organization of text.
   1. Main thought in the paragraph.
   2. Main events in sequence.
   3. Main heads and sub-heads in outline.
   4. Directions for carrying out an activity.

story. The students can do this as one part of their group activity, and are usually delighted when they can come up with some new feeling themselves or when someone else has a feeling which they shared also but which they had never actually identified before.

The developing of the ability to form visual imagery as one reads is an acquired skill which greatly enhances one's appreciation for reading. This would mean visually seeing what was described by the author, actually filling in those details which the author did not complete. Art work is sometimes used to draw pictures which the author has described. The many additions which the student makes himself actually only increases his appreciation of the story.

Understanding characters in the story is another technique for developing appreciation and also comprehension of stories read. One technique is to have children describe physical appearance of different characters in the stories from what they have been told by the author himself. They need to know when they are using what the author has said, however, and when they are adding details which they have only imagined themselves. There is certainly nothing wrong with this adding to what the author has said, although it is important that the students realize at which point the author leaves off and they themselves begin. In addition to physical appearance, they should also form a picture of the emotional makeup of the characters about whom they are reading.

Oral Reading Skills

Students at the fifth grade reading level should be able to recognize and pronounce words with speed and accuracy. They should be able to group words into meaningful phrases, and interpret marks of punctuation accurately.

They should be able to re-express to an audience the meaning and feelings expressed by an author. The emotions which they describe should be expressed with sincerity. They should be able to read in a pleasant, well modulated voice, indicating poise and self confidence on their own part.

They should be able to dramatize portions of the story. Putting on television or radio productions of incidents which occurred in the story should be a regular part of the reading lesson. Re-writing certain parts of the reading material into play form, which is then produced by the class, serves the purpose both of developing better oral reading skills and developing interest in the material which has been prepared in this fashion.

Oral reading can be used to verify answers to questions. The students can be asked to locate the answers to questions in their silent reading and can then read the answers aloud when they have found them.

Oral reading is more than just word-calling with expression. The students should be able to interpret material which they have read orally. They should be able to interpret word pictures in the general mood of the text. They should also be able to interpret sensations given by certain words and the organization of the text.

SIXTH GRADE READING LEVEL SKILLS

It has been stated that, other than added experience and additional reading vocabulary, there are no new reading skills above sixth grade level. This is not entirely true, although it is true that most of the reading skills have been presented by this level. Essentially, at the sixth grade reading level, the student is able to read at the average adult level. Popular current magazines are written at about this level, although it is somewhat questionable if adults reading at this level really comprehend to the fullest extent and appreciate reading material.

Vocabulary: Word Recognition

Refinement of the use of context clues at the sixth grade level is dependent, of course, to a large extent upon both experiences and vocabulary. How the word is used in the sentence begins to have meaning more than just its relative place in the sentence, and can now actually be attacked as to whether or not it is a verb, adjective, or adverb, etc. This is a refinement of the earlier use of context clues which had to rely only upon the possible meaning of the word. With the addition of parts of speech in the upper elementary grades, the student is able to apply other aspects of the language parts to his reading program.

He is also able to remember some words merely by the visual impression which he has of those words. It is not unusual in writing, or even in material that is printed, to notice that something is incorrect in the word. Students will sometimes say that they know they have made a mistake after writing a word that isn't correct, purely on the basis that it either looks too long or too short or the configuration is in some other way broken. As adults we also use this technique.

Because students in the personalized reading program have been reading to a much greater extent than they would have in the basal reading program, they are able at the sixth grade reading level to develop an appreciation for the sound of the words as they occur in the sentence. The writing found in most children's literature is of the very highest type. When a student is reading a book that is not well written he will frequently, without exactly knowing why, say the book is not particularly well written. He is not implying that the sentences are incomplete, or there is a grammatical error in them. It is merely the general rhythm of well expressed ideas for which a feeling can be developed only by wide reading of well written material.

The following prefixes, suffixes, and root words are ones with which the student should become familiar at the sixth grade level.

USEFUL INFORMATION ABOUT COMMON PREFIXES, SUFFIXES, AND ROOTS

PREFIXES

Prefix	Meaning	Examples
a (ab)	from, away	abnormal, abdicate, avert
a (an)	without, not	aseptic, anesthetic
ad	to, toward	adjust, adjourn, administer
ambi (amphi)	around, both	ambidextrous, ambiguous, amphibious
ante	before	anteroom, antedate
anti	against, opposite	antithesis, antagonist
bi	two, twice	bisect, bicycle, biscuit
circum	around	circumscribe, circumvent

Prefix	Meaning	Examples
con (co, col, com)	together, with	concur, connect, contend, combine, collect
contra (counter)	against	contradict, contraband
de	from, down from	dejected, delegate, degrade
dis (di)	apart, not	dispatch, dismiss, dishonor
dia	through, around	diameter, dialogue
epi	upon	epitaph, epiphenomenon
eu	well	euphemism, euphony
ex	out of, from	expel, exodus, exhume
hetero	different	heterodox, heterogeneous
hypo, hyph	under, below	hypothesis, hypocrite
in (il, un, ir)	into, not	inconsistent, inelegant, illegible, irreverent
in, en	in, into, among	invade, include, entice
inter	between	interpose, interurban
intro	within, against	introspective, introduce
mono	single, one	monograph, monorail
non	not	nonalcoholic, nonentity
ob	against	obtrude, obstruct, object
pan	whole, all	Pan-American, pantheist
per	fully, through	peruse, perturb
peri	around, about	perimeter, peristyle
post	after, behind	postpone, post-mortem
pre	before	precede, prelude
pro	for, forward, in front of	propose, program
re	back, again	renew, reiterate, repress
retro	backward	retrospect, retrograde
se	aside	seclude, secede, segregate
semi	half, partly	semicircular, semiannual
sub	under	subway, subnormal, subject
super	over, above	supercilious, superfine
syn (sym)	together, with	synthesis, syntax, sympathy
trans	beyond, across	transgress, transatlantic
tri	three, thrice	trisect, triangle, triplets
ultra	beyond	ultramontane, ultramarine
un	not	unkind, unnecessary

Reprinted with the permission of the author, Dr. Ruth Strang, from *Problems in the Improvement of Reading*, Science Press, 1941.

SUFFIXES

Suffix	Meaning	Examples
-able, -ible	capable of being	serviceable, credible
-ace, -acy, -ance, -ancy	state of being	disturbance, intimacy
-age	act or condition	dotage, marriage, bondage
-al, -eal, -ial	relation to, that which, on account of	judicial, credentials, elemental
-an, -ean, -ian	one who, relating to	American, statistician

Suffix	Meaning	Examples
-ant	adj.: being	resonant, vacant
	noun: one who	attendant, servant
-ar, -er	relating to, like	lunar, vulgar, solar
-ary	adj.: relating to	residuary, contrary
	noun: one who	dignitary
	place where	sanctuary
-ate	adj.: having quality	fortunate, desolate
	noun: one who	prelate, advocate
	verb: to make	celebrate, agitate
-cle, -acle	little	pinnacle
-icle, -cule	little	molecule, particle
-ee	one who is	trustee, employee
	(object of action)	devotee
-eer	one who does	pamphleteer, auctioneer
-en	(1) little	maiden, kitten
	(2) made of	earthen, olden
-ence	state or quality	independence, violence
-ency	state or quality	dependency
-ent	adj.: being	dependent, patient
	noun: one who	resident, student
-et, -let	little	lancet, leaflet
-fic	causing, producing	soporific, terrific
-fy, -ify	to make	magnify, simplify
-hood	state, condition	motherhood, manhood
-ic	like, made of	plastic, magic
-ice	that which, quality or	artifice
	state of being	
-id	pertaining to, being in	squalid, placid
	a condition of	
-ile	relating to	puerile, imbecile
-ion	act, or state of being	coercion, fusion
-ise, -ize	to make	colonize, memorize
-ist, -ite	one who	optimist, theist
-ity, -ty	state	unity, vicinity
-ive	relating to	legislative, decorative
-kin	little	napkin, lambkin
-less	without	hopeless, worthless
-ment	state of being, act	amendment, development
-or, -ar, -er	one who, that which	elector, engraver
-ory	that which pertains to	commendatory, ex-
	place of serving for	planatory
-ose, -ous	abounding in	verbose, grandiose, gracious
-some	full of	troublesome
-tude, -itude	condition	beatitude, aptitude
-ule	little	capsule, globule
-ward	turning to, in direction	heavenward, forward
-wright	doer, worker	cartwright, shipwright

SOME COMMON LATIN ROOTS

Root	Meaning	Root	Meaning
acer	sharp	lego, legere, legi, lectum	to read, pick
agre	field	leo, leonis	lion
ago, agere, egri, actum	rouse, stimulate	lex, legis	law
albus	white	liber	book
alter	other	liber	free
amare	to love	lingua	tongue
ambulare	to walk	locus	place
amicus	friend	lux, lucis	light
amor	love	magister	master
annus	ring or year	mater	mother
aqua	water	manus	hand
arare	to plow	mare, maris	sea
audio, audire, audivi, auditum	to hear	medium	middle
aurum	gold	mirare	to wonder
avis	bird	miser	wretched
bene	good or well	mitto, mittere, misi, missum	to send
bonus	good	mors, mortis	death, mortal
bos, bovis	ox	navis	ship
brevis	short	niger	black
cado, cadere, cededicasum	to fall	nihil	nothing
canis	dog	novus	new
cantare	to sing	nox, noctis	night
capio, capere, cepi, captum	to take	omnis	all entire
cedo, cedere, cessi, cessum	to go	pater	father
celer	quick	pendon, pendere, pependi, pensum	to hand
centum	a hundred	pes, pedis	foot
cor, cordis	heart	plicare	to fold
crux, crucis	cross	pono, ponere, posui, positum	to place
dexter	right	scribo, scribere, scripsi, scriptum	to write
deus	god		
dominus	master	senex	old
domus	house	solus	alone
dormire	to sleep	soror	sister
duo	two	spirare	to breathe
dux, ducis	leader	sto, stare, steti, statum	to stand

Root	Meaning	Root	Meaning
ego	I	terra	earth or land
eo, ire, ivi, itum	to go	traho, trahere, traxi, tractum	to draw
facio, facere, feci, factum	to do or make	umbra	shadow
felix	happy	unus	one
fero, ferre, tuli, latum	to carry	uros, urbis	city
fidus	faithful	utilis	useful
finis	end	velox	swift
fortis	strong	venio, venire, veni, ventum	to come
frater	brother	veritas	truth
habeo, habere, habui, habitum	to have or hold	verto, vertere, verti, versum	to turn
homo, hominis	man	via	way
jungo, junctum	join	video, videre, vidi, visum	to see
juvenis	young	vir	man
lac, lactis	milk	virtus	strong
		vivo, vivere, vixi, victum	to live

Not every student will have to have memorized every one of these prefixes, suffixes, and root words, but a general familiarity with these ideas, approaching them sometimes from familiar words and leading back then into the meaning of the prefix, suffix, or root word, will help the student in learning them.

A student in the sixth grade must learn to listen carefully for beginning and ending sounds of words. Words in which syllables have been left out, or endings have either been dropped or added (such as *libary* for *library, acrosst* for *across*), should be given particular attention.

Vocabulary: Word Meaning

The use of prefixes, suffixes, and root words should greatly add both to the ability of the student to unlock new words, as well as to his over-all vocabulary. The fastest way to increase one's vocabulary is certainly through the study of prefixes, suffixes, and root words, and is far better than using the technique of memorizing a number of new words each week.

The multiple meanings of words should be given a great deal of attention in the sixth grade. Such words as mars, which has a variety of meanings ranging from the verb form which means to mark upon something all the way to the planet Mars, should lead students at the sixth grade level to become very conscious of the various meanings of words. Actually keeping a collection of these meanings of very common words which they can then share in the group, perhaps even at a regular scheduled time each week, will add to their vocabulary and develop their ability to discriminate between finer shades of meaning. Words which have emotional feeling such as house, home, love, should also be included in this type of practice.

Children learn in the sixth grade about levels of language usage. This is most easily introduced through dialogue in their reading but can also be introduced by the general language usage of the class itself. The students need to be taught that in formal language usage, only the highest level of usage is acceptable. Books of a formal or literary level will present only the highest level of usage except when it is used to quote a particular character. In these cases, the level of usage is often on the colloquial level. The actual acceptance of these different levels of usage, providing one knows in which situation it is appropriate, is the goal of teaching language usage.

Sixth grade children should have demonstrated to them the value of aided and unaided recall. Unaided recall relies entirely upon one's memory to recreate what has been read. Aided recall depends upon one's ability to remember what has been read when the general outline or pattern is provided for the student to follow. Obviously, aided recall is far more easily accomplished than unaided recall. This should demonstrate to the student the value of note taking as they read, outlining material that has been read and developing an outline before material is written.

The use of synonyms, which mean the same and nearly the same, homonyms which are pronounced the same but have different meanings and perhaps spelling, antonyms which are opposite or nearly opposite, and heteronyms, which are words which have different sounds and meanings but the same spelling, should be reviewed.

Interpreting colloquial and figurative expressions, particularly those well known in the locality in which one is teaching, is a major goal of teachers at the sixth grade level. Developing an awareness on the part of the student of colloquial speech, and the fact that it is a very informal level of usage, although it is colorful and not to be eliminated entirely, is a major responsibility of sixth grade teachers.

Enriching children's imagery, without the idea that this is something that has no meaning, should be done at the sixth grade level. Associational reading, broadening one's experience in reading ability about similar topics, is one way of doing this. A textbook's illustrations are another device for assuring accurate concepts.

Word Attack Skills:
Finding Constructural Characteristics of Words

All of the basic phonic elements of words have been presented before the sixth grade, but they must be constantly practiced if they are to be meaningful to the student. Initial consonants, word families, and simple endings should be reviewed, as should consonant blends and short and long vowels. Syllabication and prefixes and suffixes should constantly be reviewed.

Word Attack Skills: Vowel Sounds

The vowel rules should be reviewed, applying them to new words which the student is encountering in his reading. The rules of syllabication should be reviewed, also applying them to words in the reading situation. Blended sounds of vowel forms should be reviewed such as "au," "aw," "ou," "ow," "oy," and "oi."

The rules of syllabication should be learned thoroughly in reading at sixth grade level, with sufficient practice in their use so that they will not merely be a busy work activity. Accent rules should also be learned at this level.

The teacher should review forming of possessives and contractions and silent letters. Dictionary skills should be reviewed, as well as the use of the glossary.

Comprehension: Outlining

The basic principles of outlining learned at the fifth grade level should be thoroughly reviewed, before the teacher extends this into sixth grade level. Earlier the student is dependent mainly upon main ideas with perhaps only two supporting ideas to each main idea, but the student must now be able to develop in complete outline form the material which he has read. This involves not only stating the material in his own words, but evaluating that material which is important enough to be included in the outline.

Constant use should be required of those reference skills which have been learned earlier, constantly adding to them those new skills which are necessary to find the needed material. Understanding the use of footnotes is one of the major new skills introduced in reference work at the sixth grade level.

Comprehension: Rate of Reading

The sixth grade student is introduced to the concept that he must adjust his reading rate to his purpose for reading. This begins, of course, with the student's developing the ability to state exactly for what reason he is reading certain material. If it is entirely for pleasure, and the material is of a fiction type, with neither complicated phraseology or new vocabulary, he should be able to adjust his reading rate to a very rapid pace. On the other hand, if the material is of a scientific nature, which the student wants to understand thoroughly and in which he must ponder over many of the new words, he should adjust his rate to a very slow pace. Of primary importance is that the student understands he must know his purpose for reading particular material.

Use of the newspaper will enable the teacher to point out the value of rapid reading of certain materials with more careful attention to other sections. Actual practice in using the newspaper, first reading perhaps only headings to determine which articles want to be pursued further, will give the idea of skimming.

Skimming is a perfectly good type of reading, but it is important that the student know when he is skimming. Too often, students skim material and feel they have read it. They then do not understand why their comprehension is at such a low level.

BARBE READING SKILLS CHECK LIST
SIXTH LEVEL READING SKILLS

(Last Name) (First Name) (Name of School)

(Age) (Grade Placement) (Name of Teacher)

I. Vocabulary:

A. Word recognition.
1. Context clues.
   a. How the word is used in a sentence.
   b. Function of word.
2. Picture clues.
   a. Visual impressions of words.
   b. Configuration.
3. Language rhythms.
   a. Rhyming clues.
   b. Appreciation for general rhythm of well-expressed ideas.

B. Prefixes.

Prefix	Meaning
ab	from, away
an	without, not
ad	to, toward
ante	before
bi	two, twice
circum	around
de	from, down from
dis	apart, not
dia	through, around
ex	out of, from
im	not, in
il, un, in, ir	into, not
inter	between
in, en	in, into, among
intro	within, against
mis	wrong, wrongly
non	not
pan	whole, all
per	fully, through
peri	around, about
post	after, behind
pre	before
pro	for, in front of
re	back, again
se	aside
semi	half, partly
sub	under
super	over, above
trans	beyond, across
tri	three, thrice
un	not

Suffixes.

Suffix	Meaning
able, ible	capable of being
acy, ace, ancy, ance	state of being
an, ean, ian	one who, relating to act or condition
age	state of being
ant	relating to, like
er, ar	n.—one who, adj. being
ary	n.—one who—(Place where) adj.—relating to
ante	
en	one who is little, made
ence	state of quality
ent	adj.—being, n.—one who
full	full of
fy, ify	to make
hood	state, condition
ic	like, made of
ice	that which, quality or state of being
id	being in a condition of
ion	act or state of being
ize, ise	to make
ist, ite	one who
ity, ty	state
ive	relating to
less	without
ly	in a way
ment	act or state of being
ness	state of being
or, ar, er	one who, that which
ory	

5. Blended sounds of vowel forms. The combination of au and aw makes a sound like awe. Ou and ow make the sound "ow" like when you are hurt. Oy and oi make sound like boy.

C. Syllabication.
1. Rules for syllables.
   a. Each syllable must have a vowel and a single vowel can be a syllable.
   b. The root word is a syllable and not divided.
   c. Blends are not divided (th, str, wh, etc.)
   d. Suffixes and prefixes are syllables.
   e. Suffix—ed if preceded by a single d or t usually forms separate syllable. (rest ed)
   f. If vowel in a syllable is followed by two consonants, the syllable ends with the first consonant.
   g. If vowel in a syllable is followed by only one consonant, the syllable ends with a vowel.
   h. If a word ends in le, the consonant just before the l begins the last syllable. (ta-ble han-dle)
   i. When there is an r after a vowel, the r goes with the vowel to make the "er" sound.

D. Accents. (Rules)
1. In a word of two or more syllables, the first syllable is usually accented unless it is a prefix.
2. In most two syllable words that end in a consonant followed by y, the first syllable is accented and the last is unaccented.
3. Beginning syllables de, re, be, er, in, and a are usually not accented.
4. When a suffix is added, the accent falls on or within the root word.
5. Endings that form syllables are usually unaccented.
6. When a final syllable ends in le, that syllable is usually not accented.

E. Possessives.
F. Contractions.
G. Silent letters.
H. Dictionary skills.

ward   turning to, in direction
y   like or full of

Prefixes and suffixes list prepared by Ruth Strang.

4. Initial and ending sounds.
   a. Listening for beginning sounds.
   b. Completing sounds of words.

C. **Word Meaning.**
   1. Multiple meanings.
   2. Associating words and feelings.
   3. Formal and informal language.
      a. Speech pattern.
      b. Level of language usage.
   4. Recall.
      a. Aided.
      b. Unaided.
   5. Hyphenated words.
   6. Synonyms—same or nearly same.
   7. Homonyms—pronounced same—different meaning and spelling.
   8. Antonyms—opposites.
   9. Heteronym (pronounced differently—same spelling)
   10. Interpreting colloquial and figurative expressions.
   11. Enriching imagery.

II. **Word Attack Skills:**

A. **Phonic and structural characteristics of words.**
   Initial consonants—word families—simple endings.
   2. Consonant blends and short and long vowels.
   3. Syllabication, prefixes, suffixes.
   4. Teams—oi, oy, aw, au.

B. **Vowel sounds.**
   1. Vowel rules.
      a. When there is only one vowel in a word or syllable, the vowel is short.
      b. When there are two vowels in a word or syllable, the first vowel is long and the second is silent.
      c. When there are two vowels together, the first vowel is long and the second is silent.
   2. Rule I—Every syllable has at least one vowel in it. eg. ever—never—children.
   3. Rule II—Two vowels in a word or syllable—first is long, second is silent. kit—kite; at—ate.
   4. Rule III—When 2 vowels are together, the first is long and the second is silent. ("ou" an exception) mail, meat, pie, boat.

III. **Comprehension:**

A. **Outlining.**
   1. Note taking.
   2. Sequence of ideas or events.
   3. Skimming.
      a. Locating facts and details.
      b. Selecting and rejecting materials to fit a certain purpose.
   4. Main ideas of paragraphs.
   5. Interpreting characters' feelings.
   6. Topic sentences.
B. **Following directions.**
C. **Drawing conclusions.**
D. **Reading for verification.**
E. **Locating information.**
   1. Reference Materials in reading.
      a. Graphs.
      b. Maps—Reading and interpreting in detail.
      c. Encyclopedias—Locating materials or research.
      d. Headings and other typographical aids.
   2. Library skills.
      a. Card catalogs, use of. (Cross reference)
      b. Book classifications.
      c. Care of books and other materials.
      d. Index—use of.
      e. Glossary.
   3. Periodicals or sources of information.
      a. Authors.   f. Title page.
      b. Introductions—author's.   g. Copyright.
      c. Table of Contents.   h. Date of publication.
      d. Index—use of.   i. Footnotes.
      e. Glossary.   j. Tables.
   4. Resource materials.
      a. Packets and pictures.
      b. Charts—detail.
   5. Resource people.
F. **Rate or Reading.**
   1. Different rate for different purpose.
   2. Comprehension at high level.
G. **Critical reading.**

IV. **Oral Reading:**

A. **Choral reading and poetry.**
   1. Pronunciation.
   2. Phrasing.
   3. Rhymes.
   4. **Interpretations.**
B. **Listening appreciation.**

As with all other types of reading, if the student can first be certain in his own mind of his purpose for reading particular material, there is no reason in certain instances why he will not want to skim the material. If he is reading material to maintain a high level of comprehension, however, skimming is not an effective procedure.

The purpose of reading is, of course, to obtain meaning from the printed word. If there is no comprehension, he is not reading. A statement by a critic of the teaching of reading that he was able to call the words off the headline of a foreign newspaper but did not know what they meant was certainly erroneous. He was word calling but not reading. Students must be made to realize that comprehension is the primary goal of reading. If his rate can be increased without sacrificing comprehension, then it certainly should be increased. If comprehension suffers when rate is increased, however, then the student should not read so rapidly. It can be proved, however, that more rapid reading usually results in better comprehension. This is because more rapid reading requires more careful attention to the reading process, with actually a deeper degree of concentration, so that the student obtains through units rather than the meanings of individual words and is better able to obtain the meaning of the author from the material. It would not be expecting too much for students at this level to be able to read silently twice as fast as they could read orally.

Oral Reading

Choral reading and poetry are an important part of the reading skills learned in the sixth grade. Pronunciation, phrasing, rhymes, and interpretations are all a part of both better comprehension and appreciation of reading.

Throughout the first six grades, the teacher should have been developing the student's ability to listen with both understanding and appreciation. At the sixth grade level, the teacher should actually have listening periods, at which time students learn to enjoy even the sound of words.

Critical reading should be taught as a formal reading skill. Merely accepting something because it is in print is a very unwise practice, and should he stopped. The use of numerous newspaper accounts of the same story, often indicating exactly opposite points of views, is a technique used successfully by many teachers in teaching critical reading. Such questions as: Who wrote the material? Is he an authority on this subject, and therefore qualified to give his opinions? Is this an actual news report or only an editorial or opinion? When was it written? What was the author's bias to begin with? Did he include all of the facts? Are his conclusions logical? These and many other things make up critical reading. Of particular importance to the sixth grade teacher is to demonstrate to the students that "critical" does not necessarily mean "negative." Too often students have the feeling that when they are expected to criticize something, they must say what is bad about it. More than merely getting them to say whether they like or don't like something, or agree or disagree with it, they should be required to answer the question, "Why do you like or dislike it?" or, "Why do you agree or disagree with it?"

SUMMARY

The teaching of reading skills is not an end in itself. Not all children will need to learn all of those skills which have been presented in the preceding two chapters. The presentation of these skills, however, without requiring a great amount of repetition or drill on them should make the student better able to read. Only to the extent that the teacher incorporates these skills in the actual reading process itself will they be successful, however.

The personalized reading program offers the teacher a great opportunity to combine teaching of reading skills along with reading itself in material of the child's own selection. This should develop both better reading abilities as well as a greater appreciation for literature. To the extent that the student is able to enjoy both "the process and the results," the reading teacher has been successful.

Chapter Nine

Personalized Reading Instruction —Looking Ahead

Personalized reading instruction is a new method of teaching reading. Any new program inherently has both advantages and disadvantages. It has an advantage in the support of those people who want to try something different. This very same support may also be a disadvantage. It has the advantage of not having to "live down" bad interpretations and poor procedures, but it also has the disadvantage of not being so clearly defined as the older method. It has the advantage of the enthusiasm engendered by change of pace, but at the same time it has the disadvantage of not being so clearly defined. And so on and on, both advantages and disadvantages seem to be balanced one against the other.

The great plea in public education, however, is for flexibility. Only if teachers know of different methods, whether or not they incorporate them entirely into their program, can we be said to have a truly flexible curriculum. Whether or not the teacher uses personalized reading instruction, she owes it to her students and to herself to know more about this latest innovation in teaching reading. That it is the best method in all situations is certainly doubtful, but it is equally doubtful that the basal reader approach is the best method in all situations. To the extent that teachers know about and understand the techniques of personalized reading instruction, and use them wherever applicable, more effective reading instruction will take place.

Individual differences among children have been the major concern in reading instruction since the appearance of the twenty-fourth year book of the National Society for the Study of Education in 1925. The basal reading program has attempted to provide for individual differences by the use of ability or achievement grouping. To some extent, this has been highly successful, and is certainly an essential first step toward individualizing or personalizing reading instruction. Whether or not ability grouping in the basal series is the final level of grouping to which teachers can attain, however, is highly questionable. Just as children differ themselves, teachers also differ. The methods by which they can best teach reading are also likely to differ.

IMPLICATIONS OF PERSONALIZED READING INSTRUCTION

There are many problems confronting the teacher or school which considers shifting to personalized reading instruction. Whether or not the benefits of the personalized reading program outweigh the difficulties which must be overcome can only be answered at the local level. Any attempt to dictate that the personalized reading instruction method is better in all situations would only be an indication of the same degree of rigidity as that held by the proponents of the basal reader.

Within the classroom itself there are a number of implications of adopting personalized reading instruction which need to be carefully examined.

1. What effect will changing radically the procedure of teaching reading have upon children?
2. What effect will personalized reading instruction have upon the teacher's ability to teach reading?
3. How will personalized reading instruction affect the relationships between the teacher and her pupils?
4. How will personalized reading instruction affect the relationships between the children within the room?
5. How will personalized reading instruction affect the students' attitudes toward reading?
6. What effect will personalized reading instruction have upon the reading level, interest and habits of the pupils?

These implications must be considered both within the classroom and without. Changing the method by which reading is taught in such a manner is bound to have repercussions throughout the school, school system, and community itself. If the teacher, principal and administration are not prepared for the necessary adjustments of a new method of teaching reading, it should not be undertaken. If the program can be entered into both with confidence of success and clear evidence of the teacher's ability to handle adequately the techniques of this method, there is virtually no chance of failure.

Effect of Change on Children

While it is very true that children are quite adaptable themselves, change merely for the sake of change is not good. In changing over from the basal reader, to which children and teachers both have attached such importance in the years past, it is possible that the child might feel less secure in the learning to read process. If this is true, and it would most likely be truer for those children who have already been through a number of the basal readers than for those who are just beginning, then a change-over to personalized reading instruction would not be advisable.

If the change-over to personalized reading instruction can be an advancement in methodology which will aid children to read better and more, then there should be no hesitancy in adopting it. The effect of this change-over within the classroom will in no small way be determined by the attitude of the teacher, the administration and the child's parents. Approached with intelligence and careful planning, personalized reading instruction should provide no major problems for the children themselves within the classroom. Actually, the learning to read process should appear much less formidable when it is so closely connected with reading itself, rather than remove so many steps by the unrealistic type of story found in so many basal readers.

Effect on Teacher's Ability to Teach Reading

The implications of the Personalized Reading Program's

effect on the teacher's ability to teach reading are perhaps of the greatest importance. Personalized reading instruction is, of course, no panacea which will eliminate all problems. It will not make up for deficiency within the teacher's training, mental ability, or personality. It should provide a means, however, by which good teachers can do even a better job of teaching reading. There will, of course, still be some children who have difficulty learning to read, but the personalized reading program provides a means by which the classroom teacher will have both the time and the materials to aid those students at their level, rather than expecting them to fit in any one of several groups within the classroom.

Personalized reading instruction, by providing the teacher with a guide for skill instruction, as well as freedom in selection of materials which is so essential if children are going to develop a true appreciation for good reading, offers an administrative plan through which the creative teacher can best employ her skills. To the extent that the resourceful teacher accepts personalized reading as a plan in which she must use her own initiative in determining when certain skills are taught and how they can best be taught, following the reading skills guide sheets only as a means of assuring herself that certain skill instruction is not being skipped entirely, she can be successful. It is true that the program does provide a somewhat rigid skills presentation program, not in sequence nor in methodology of presentation, but in the actual listing of which skills are to be taught. It is not unlikely that skilled teachers will want to add to the skills taught at each grade level, or even possibly change some of the skills from one level to another with the understanding that this is being done by the teachers both above and below that particular grade level. For beginning teachers, however, it would seem advisable for them to teach the reading skills at the level in which they are presented in the charts discussed in Chapters 7 and 8.

As has been said before, the teacher's manual is unquestionably the greatest contribution of the basal reading series. The degree of quality of the activities outlined in these manuals could not be surpassed. It is not unlikely that even in the

personalized reading program, the classroom teacher would frequently refer to the basal reading manuals of different publishing companies to understand better how to present certain skills which the children are to learn. It is not even impossible that the teacher may wish to bring together at different times certain basal readers for groups of children to use when they are learning a particular skill. There would be no going from story to story within the basal reader, however, for this would be denying the very basis of the personalized reading program. If the classroom teacher found this happening, she would need to understand that the routine, habit forming pattern of three reading groups, with each child reading one story each day, was threatening her efforts to teach the children to love reading.

A measure of the effectiveness of good teaching of reading in the basal reading program can be determined to a large extent by the use the teacher makes of the teacher's manual. The poor teacher either has no teacher's manual, or can rarely find it. The good teacher, while she has been resourceful enough to deviate from the manual whenever it was necessary, has nevertheless utilized those activities which were developed by reading specialists along with the stories in the basal readers. It is asking a great deal to expect teachers to now give up this valuable aid. But for the goal of development of greater appreciation of reading itself, as good a crutch as the teacher's manual should not be discarded entirely, but put to one side to be used only when needed.

Effect of Personalized Reading Instruction on
Relationships Between Teacher and Pupil

One of the greatest arguments in favor of personalized reading instruction is the positive relationship which it allows between the pupil and the teacher in a person-to-person relationship. There can be no question but that individual instruction provides for the greatest exchange of information between the pupil and the teacher, as well as the greatest depth of understanding and appreciation of one another's points of view. In mass education, such one-to-one relationships are frequently impossible, but in the personalized reading instruction program, limited in time as it may be, one-to-one relationships are an essential factor of the program.

The individual conference which the teacher has with the child about once every three days is not just a checking period to determine the child's progress, but is also an extension of the sharing period which is so successful in the primary grades. The child has this opportunity to "catch" from the teacher those good attitudes toward reading which are so desirable. The child has the opportunity to express to the teacher his likes and dislikes, fears and confidences, and joy and unhappiness toward reading. By such a means, it is hardly conceivable that all children would not learn to love their teacher better and to appreciate learning for its own sake rather than for the sake of a particular grade on a report card.

In such a close relationship between the teacher and each individual child in the personalized reading program, the teacher is placed in a more difficult position. Attitudes which are actually "caught" and not "taught" are spread from the teacher to each of the children individually. The appreciation of good literature comes first of all from the teacher herself. It is, of course, hoped that the child will gain this appreciation from the enjoyment he finds from reading material which he has selected himself. But the process of self selection alone does not develop an appreciation for reading if the child does not feel this appreciation from the teacher herself. More than in any other type of program, the teacher's attitude toward reading will affect the attitude of the children in the classroom. If the teacher is one who is too busy to find time to read herself, then it is not likely that she will take full advantage of the individual conference and develop good attitudes toward reading. Only if the teacher herself truly appreciates literature, including adult literature as well as children's literature, can it be expected that the child will "catch" the joy of reading. This may well mean that a requirement of teacher training programs should be a literature appreciation course, just as a music appreciation course has been such a great aid for so many years.

In the personalized reading program, the teacher is offered the opportunity to develop within each child those intangible attitudes toward reading which are considered desirable. The program can only offer the opportunity to do this. It depends upon the teacher herself to love reading in such a way that the children themselves cannot help but know of the teacher's attitude. If there is a teacher who does not love reading, then there is little likelihood that she will be anything more than a technician, mechanically introducing reading skills for some distant goal, unknown both to her and her pupils. The personalized reading program, however, offers freedom of expression for the children and the teacher, as well as the freedom of selection of materials, so that it is not unlikely such a teacher could quickly develop this love of reading along with the children if she did not previously have it.

Effect of Personalized Reading Instruction on Relationships Between Children

The personalized reading program is likely to have a great effect upon the attitudes of children within the classroom toward one another, as well as toward themselves in relationship to others. Since a major part of the personalized reading program is the individual conference itself, this eliminates the child's attitude that he belongs to a particular reading group. It has long been known by classroom teachers that children themselves are not fooled by such labels as "bluebirds," "airplane group," or the name of the leader in each of the groups. The children know that such a group is either the "dumb" group, "average" group, or "smart" group, and frequently refer to it by these labels in spite of the teacher's efforts to call it something else. Not only have children known into which group they fell, but they have also been rather good judges of the group into which other children fall. Such categorization, which occurs frequently even at the first grade level, creates an attitude in the children, both toward themselves and toward others, which is certainly not desirable. Attempts at flexible grouping, as desirable as they may be, have not been highly successful within the basal reading type of program because the ability or reading level grouping has been so dominant that the children themselves have not been able to escape their label.

Personalized reading instruction offers an effective means of, first of all, breaking down the traditional three group system, and secondly, maintaining the values of group instruction for a specific purpose. It is not feasible to say in the modern mass education program that all children should receive only individual instruction. Such instruction would be prohibitive in cost and many other features would make it undesirable. But combining the individual approach in the personalized reading program with group instruction to learn a particular skill means that the group itself might possibly be maintained for a period of several days, but absolutely no longer. As soon as a single skill or purpose itself is accomplished, the group would be broken. If it appears that some children are regularly falling into certain groups, it would mean that the teacher was falling back into the basal reading pattern and should artificially break this pattern by placing the child in other groups for other purposes.

One of the truly great values of the personalized reading program would be its aid in teaching children that the goal of education is for them to improve themselves. The traditional three-group type program sets as a goal, first of all, getting ahead of the other children in the group. As unlikely as the next goal may be, it does somehow hold out the idea that to be in the next higher group is desirable. No provision is made in such grouping for ever bridging the gap between the two groups, however. If the child ever does succeed in reaching the level of the next higher group, that group has already moved on ahead and he is somewhere between the two and not a part of either. In the personalized program, in which the child is never a part of a reading level group for any prolonged period, his goal is not to get ahead of the other children in the group or to catch up with the next higher group. The goal is, instead, to improve his own reading for the single goal of enjoying reading better. By selecting his own material and pacing himself, the child is able to progress, not at the teacher's rate or at the rate of the other children, but at his own rate toward the final goal of successful reading and reading appreciation. The teacher's attempt to develop within each child a desire to be a better reader, not for the goal of surpassing someone else, but instead to improve himself. This change in the basic goal of the program should provide for better attitudes within the classroom between the children themselves. Whether the child is slower or brighter, he will have his own place in the total reading program and need not be ashamed of that place. He should better be able to accept other children in the classroom for themselves, rather than for some artificial group into which they have been placed. He will not in any way be labeled as either a particularly good reader or a poor reader, but rather identify himself with the books which he is reading. This does not mean to imply that the rest of the children will not know which ones read better than others, but it means that the emphasis will be placed upon reading and not upon reading level.

Effect of Personalized Reading Instruction on Children's Attitude Toward Reading

The greatest contribution which the personalized reading program makes is the attitude of the children toward reading. By being introduced to children's literature from the very beginning, so that they understand that the goal of reading instruction is to read, it is not necessary to, somewhere along at the junior high school level, hope the children will transfer the skills they have learned in the basal reader into the reading process itself. Children are introduced to good literature early, taught how to select materials which they can read and enjoy, and urged to read both quantitatively and qualitatively more than would ever have been thought possible in the basal program. Upon this single point rests the success or failure of the personalized reading program. An improved attitude toward reading itself is, of course, the goal of the personalized program.

Effect of Personalized Reading Instruction on Reading Level, Interests, and Habits of Pupils

It is not the purpose of the personalized reading program to push children through reading skills at any faster pace so they will make higher scores on reading achievement tests. In this present "craze" for being above national norms, more emphasis is being placed upon getting through faster than upon quality. The personalized reading program is in itself more concerned with quality reading than with merely scoring at a higher level on an achievement test whether or not the child is able to read at this higher level. Therefore, it is neither the goal nor is it likely that the children under the personalized program will score higher on reading achievement tests than did those children who were in the basal reader program. It can certainly be expected, however, that they will score at least as well as children in the traditional program. To compare the reading levels of children in the personalized program with those in the basal reader would be misleading. The achievement tests are measuring essentially those skills which are taught in the basal reading program only, omitting the more important skills such as ability to select appropriate materials, the frequency itself with which such materials are chosen, and attitudes and interests in reading. The personalized reading program does not provide for teaching children reading skills at the next higher grade level until the child reaches that grade level. For this reason, and it is hoped that this is also followed by those people using the basal reader program, merely seeing how many children can be above grade level on some standardized test has no meaning. It is possible in both the personalized reading program and in the basal reader program, to push children into higher reading skill instruction than their present grade level and have them score higher on achievement tests. This does not mean that they are reading any better, but merely that they have been prepared artificially for a test so that they will make a higher score. The personalized reading program provides for skill instruction as does the basal reading program. If skill instruction is overlooked in either program, then the program will be ineffective. The personalized program provides for more of an opportunity to develop those intangibles such as appreciation of literature and the joy of reading. These intangibles cannot be measured by any standardized achievement tests but are actually far more important than those items which are scored on the reading tests.

The personalized reading program teaches children how to

select materials for a variety of purposes. To the extent which the children do this on their own, outside of the personalized reading school program, the program has been effective. If they do not read on their own, then the program has been ineffective. Those programs of personalized or individualized instruction which are operating throughout the country report an amazingly high degree of success on these intangibles, with at least the same level of success in skill instruction as they obtained in the basal reading program.

Not all of the implications of personalized reading instruction concern the activities within the classroom itself. The implications of personalized reading instruction outside of the classroom should concern itself with:

1. The effect of personalized reading instruction on the total school program.
2. The effect of personalized reading instruction upon home, school, and community relationships.

At its present stage of development, personalized reading instruction is being practiced widely in individual classrooms. At this point, it has not developed into either an all-school or an all-system program. That this is coming soon, however, must be recognized. The flood of reports of individual teachers who are practicing personalized reading instruction clearly indicate that it will not be long before personalized reading is widely accepted in many schools as the method of teaching reading. So, where personalized reading is at the present time an individual teacher problem, it will soon be a total school and total school system problem which must be faced.

Just as the basal reading program has been through many years of trial, where one teacher used one basal series and another teacher used another, the personalized program is likely also to go through this period of adjustment. Of utmost importance to the child's learning to read process is sequential development of skills. When the child is taken from one basal series in one grade to another basal series in another, much time and effort is wasted bringing the child up to were he can read the vocabulary of the reader at that level. Different vocabularies are presented in different basal series so that unless the child has been exposed to the series at the preceding level, he will not be able to read the series at the next level. Of course, through the use of supplementary readers, the good readers have been exposed to this vocabulary. The poor readers have not, however, and the program is less effective than would otherwise have been possible had the school itself followed a continuous program.

The personalized reading program faces many of the same problems. The vocabulary control will not be so great in this type of program, but if the child is moved back and forth between the personalized program and the basal reading program, he is bound to encounter difficulty. The teachers themselves will encounter more difficulty for skills will have to be taught which will be applicable only to that particular reading situation in which they are engaged and others must be learned for the next reading situation. The personalized reading program must have its beginning somewhere and the logical beginning point is, of course, a single classroom. To continue personalized reading in a single classroom, however, would be a mistake. The goal must be for the expansion of the program to other grade levels throughout the school, or a return to the basal program. Personalized reading instruction is at the present time on an experimental basis in individual classrooms. To prove its total effectiveness, however, it will have to spread to entire school systems. Until this happens, many of the advantages of the personalized reading program will not actually be realized.

There are a number of problems of having personalized reading programs at only one grade level. Among these is the lack of understanding of other teachers as to what is actually happening in the personalized reading program. The prejudices and biases of all of us tend to make us critical of those programs in which we are not engaged. This negative attitude will spread to the children not in the program, and eventually reach those children who are participating in the program. On the basis of the development of that attitude by those not connected with the program, it can be urged that the personalized program should be at least school-wide, and perhaps even school-system-wide. If the program cannot be started in the total school, then it would perhaps be wise to follow it from the single grade in which it had already started into the next higher grade level, continuing to add the next higher grade each year on up through elementary school and even into junior and senior high school. If it is started in first grade level, then it would be easy to add on each year another year of personalized reading instruction so that the children would never have to go back to and relearn those techniques involved in the basal reader program type of instruction. If the program begins at fourth grade, and some authorities suggest it should, then it should be continued on after fourth grade up to fifth and sixth and even seventh and eighth grades.

The personalized reading program in the total school pattern places special duties upon the principal to be a supervisor as well as an administrator. The basal reader manuals have in themselves provided a pattern which teachers are expected to follow from grade to grade to insure systematic presentation of skill instruction. One of the greatest dangers of the personalized reading program is that it could develop into merely an independent reading period, without giving adequate attention to skill instruction. The use of the checklists discussed and reproduced in Chapters 7 and 8 would be one means of assuring sequential development of skill instruction. Whether or not these particular checklists are used, principals and supervisors must be aware of the need for sequential skill development, and provide classroom teachers with necessary guidance so there will be presentation of all necessary reading skills, without unnecessary duplication and omissions. It will mean that each teacher must know more than just her particular grade level skills, but will also need to know those things which are presented at the grades before the one in which she teaches, as well as those grades above. Careful keeping of records in the personalized reading program, in some such form as the checklist of skill development, will indicate to the next grade level teacher those skills to which the children have been exposed. The teacher will, of course, have to review many of the skills learned at the earlier level but the checklist will provide her with a guide to know which skills are new for the children and which ones are to be relearned and indicate to her those areas of difficulty which each child has individually encountered.

Always a problem to any program, but particularly to a new type of program, is the child who transfers either into or out of the program. Transferring into the personalized reading program should present little difficulty. The teacher may have to spend more time with the child in the initial periods of teaching him the pattern of the personalized program, but this should in no way impede his development of reading skills or reading interests and habits. Transferring out of the personalized reading program will present more problems. It is not thought that the problems will be any greater than those encountered in transferring from any one basal series to another basal series, however. It is not at all unlikely that those children transferring out of the program will carry to their new classroom situation such convincing evidence of the value of the personalized program that the teacher in the new situation will be encouraged to try personalized reading.

Another implication of the personalized reading program to the total school organization is its effect upon the use of library materials. More necessary than ever before is the elementary school library. In addition to libraries within each classroom, there is also a great need for a central library. The present system in many communities whereby teachers are urged to buy a certain number of books or spend a certain amount of money each fall on library books borders on sheer waste of money. The duplication of orders within a school is often ridiculous. The manner in which substitutions are made by either administrative officials or wholesalers is inexcusable. The pressure placed upon teachers to order in a very short period of time all of the books which they will possibly want for the entire year cannot be justified.

Having a central library in the elementary school means, of course, that wherever possible there should be a trained librarian. When it is not possible to have a trained librarian in each elementary school, there should be one librarian for several schools. A library supervisor for an entire system is needed even if she has to use untrained people, either volunteer parents or a single teacher within the school. Having a library supervisor is a necessary aid in providing meaningful requests for books and proper distribution of good books. In many instances there will be orders of five and six copies of single books, or even more. When there is duplication of orders, however, it is for a specific purpose and the material is worth ordering in duplication.

The permanent library within each classroom should contain at least one set of reference books, dictionaries for every child in the room, an unabridged dictionary, atlases, and other reference material. Certain other books which contain material which is specifically of concern to the content material of that particular grade level might be in the room library, but should be cross-referenced in the central library so that children from other rooms might have access to it.

In the personalized reading program, there will be a minimum of one hundred books within the classroom at each time, approximately three books which are of interest to and are at the reading level of each child, but these books will be rotating so there will be three books which each child has not read at all times. Those books could probably best come from the central library within the school, although they might also come from public libraries, other school libraries, or children's own libraries.

Another implication of the total school program which is of major concern to the administration itself is the amount of money which needs to be spent on textbook materials. If the money spent on basal readers were immediately diverted to the purchase of library type reading materials, there would be sufficient funds without any question to supply the personalized program. In the early stages of the personalized program, however, it is not likely that these funds will be immediately shifted over. Gradually, however, it can be expected that the classroom teacher and the school will build up a library of sufficient volume to adequately provide for each room's personalized reading program. Careful selection of new materials will soon become the only library ordering task, once the basic library itself has been established. Eventually the cost of library materials may be even less than that of basal readers and library materials as they are being purchased today.

Effect of Personalized Reading Instruction in the Home and Community

Any new program, particularly one involving the teaching of reading, will meet within every community both acceptance from some people eager for change and rejection by others who like the old system. There is no reason to think that the personalized reading program will be different in any way from that of other new programs. Since the teaching of reading is today so much in the public view, with every person considering himself an expert on how it should be done, it is not unlikely that the introduction of this method could cause some reactions. Merits of personalized reading instruction should not be weighed by the general lay public itself, however. The decision to use this method is primarily a professional one. Explanation of it to parents and interested people is, of course, a duty of public school administrators. The school board itself should fully understand what the program is attempting to do, the reason for changing over to it, and be in agreement with the decision to incorporate it into the school program. Community discussion of it should not be discouraged, but neither should it be attempted or abandoned on the strength of lay pressure. Careful attention to sequential skill development will avoid many of the criticisms directed at present day reading instruction.

PERSONALIZED READING INSTRUCTION VERSUS BASAL READERS

In spite of statements by many of the proponents of personalized or individualized reading instruction programs, it is not necessarily an "either-or" proposition. The two methods of teaching reading are not incompatible. For personalized reading instruction to be successful, all basal reading instruction does not have to be eliminated. There are certainly strong features of both programs and the desirable method of teaching reading is the one which works most effectively for each particular child. The wise teacher has many methods at her disposal and does not hesitate to use another method when the one being tried is unsuccessful.

It is, of course, logical to assume that the classroom teacher will have difficulty alternating between a personalized and basal reading program. The two are basically administrative decisions and allow for great flexibility within their pattern, but do not provide for great flexibility between the two. This may not be absolutely essential but in the early stages of any new program there is a tendency for it to appear as though it must either be totally accepted or rejected, with no in-between ground. There are a number of possible ways in which there can be a combination of the basal reader approach and personalized reading, many of which are being successfully tried in a number of communities. At this stage, it will be necessary to await the report of a variety of action research type situations to determine the actual effectiveness of this combination. In other situations, the combination is only the in-between step from the basal program to personalized reading instruction entirely.

It is quite important that any controversy not become a battle between the proponents of each of the two methods so that neither side can see the advantages of the other's position. For those interested in personalized reading instruction to take such an extreme position would be denying the very fact of which they have accused the basal reader proponents. Reading is very much an individual process, which is the basis of the personalized reading instruction proponent's claims, and therefore should not be so rigidly bound by an administrative procedure that a variety of methods could not be used. If the basal reader method is most effective for any particular child, even though the administrative position has been to follow personalized reading, for that particular child sequential development of skills through the basal reader series should be followed. This would, of course, under the personalized reading program, be at the child's own discretion in choosing materials. The skill instruction, however, is directed by the teacher.

Several possible combinations might well be examined, and

it would be hoped that any combination would be a bringing together of the strong features of both programs, rather than merely placating one group or the other by hanging on to the basal readers without using the teacher's manuals, or any other such impossible unperceptive solution. The proponents of either method should not be so rigid in their demands for acceptance that they lose sight of the fact that the goal of the reading program is to develop in each child the highest level of reading ability possible, along with an appreciation and understanding of literature.

One possible combination of the two programs which is being practiced in a wide number of situations, but which is gradually losing out in favor of the personalized reading program at all grade levels, is the use of basal readers at the primary grade level and movement into the personalized reading program at the upper elementary and junior high school levels. This is a procedure which meets little criticism but one factor must be watched with great care. If upper elementary teachers have not been teaching reading skills and see in the personalized program a way of avoiding formal instruction in reading skills, then this is not a wise practice. It is true that the personalized program does not force any page-by-page following of the teacher's manual, but it is also not a way of avoiding teaching reading skills. Before upper elementary teachers move from the basal reader into the personalized program, administrators must be certain that they are already doing a good job of skill presentation. If they are not, then the personalized program cannot be expected to be successful and may actually be harmful. Where upper elementary teachers are successfully teaching reading skills, but realize the need for means whereby children will be more interested in reading, movement into the personalized program, whether or not the children have been in this type of program in the primary grades, is highly desirable.

Another combination of the basal and personalized reading program approach is followed in several situations where the children go through the pre-primer and primer of the basal readers, and then move into the basal readers. The fact that they can do this successfully speaks for itself. This author feels that with proper use of experience stories and charts, use of pre-primers and primers is not absolutely necessary. If first grade teachers find a need for pre-primers and primers, however, and they can successfully make the transition from these into the personalized reading program, then there can be no criticism of their following this procedure.

Another technique combining the two methods being used in some situations, but which actually appears to be little more than trying to placate both groups, is teaching the basal reader first and then moving into the personalized program in the latter part of the year. There is great danger here that the goal will be, as it has been in the past in too many situations, merely getting through the basal reader without attention to skill instruction so they can do the more interesting activities involved in personalized reading instruction. But once again, where local conditions prevail which would make complete acceptance of personalized reading instruction more difficult, going through the basal readers first is one method of adapting the program.

Since personalized reading instruction depends so much upon the teacher's knowledge of skill instruction and her ability to teach these skills, and there is no single manual for such teachers other than the skill lists presented in Chapters 7 and 8 of this book, some schools are allowing only experienced teachers to move into the personalized program. This is recognizing correctly the great benefits of the teacher's manuals in the basal series and the need for many beginning teachers to have this guidance. Once the teacher has thoroughly learned the sequence of skill presentation, and techniques of teaching these skills, moving her into the personalized program is sensible. With adequate supervisory help from principals, other teachers, and supervisors, such a transition stage would not be necessary for all teachers and would avoid moving the child from one type of program into another.

The major argument in favor of the basal reader approach is the highly skilled development of the teacher's manual. This includes, in the readers themselves, the development of a carefully controlled reading vocabulary. Whether these advantages outweigh the advantages of the personalized reading instruction program must be decided by each teacher or principal or school system itself. That there are great advantages in each method must be recognized. Whether or not the advantages found in the basal program can be incorporated into the personalized reading program will depend upon the ability of the teacher herself. The biggest disadvantage of the basal reader is, of course, its inability to allow the child either to select materials himself or actually to progress at any kind of individual rate.

The major advantage of the personalized reading instructional program is, of course, its ability to develop and maintain an early interest in reading in a wide variety of areas. The vocabulary control advantage of the basal reader approach may be lost in the personalized program, but losing this advantage and replacing it with the wide-spread reading vocabulary possible in the personalized program may actually completely overshadow the advantage of a controlled vocabulary.

The major argument frequently heard against personalized reading instruction is its lack of any sequential skill developmental program. Indeed, the need for the teacher's guide is great. It has been the purpose of Chapters 7 and 8 in this book to discuss those skills which should be presented at each reading level. This is an attempt to provide, not an answer to the question "how" but instead an answer to the question "what" in the way of reading skills themselves. The extent to which the personalized reading program has been successful in providing teachers with a guide which they can follow in skill presentation, along with developing a high level of interest in reading itself, must be decided by teachers themselves.

Personalized reading and basal readers are not an "either-or" proposition. Local conditions will have to decide which program is the major one, although it is not unlikely that combinations of the programs may be in operation in many places. Successful teaching of reading will require, above all other factors, a sensitive and resourceful teacher. She must be trained in understanding the philosophy of teaching reading, teaching each child at his level, the need for sequential skill development, and effective classroom management. The administrative plan, either personalized instruction or basal reading, merely makes it possible for the teacher to do a more effective job utilizing those techniques which she has at her disposal. The success or failure of reading instruction depends to a large extent upon the teacher herself. Her attitude and skills are both major factors in determining the level of success which she will have. Personalized reading instruction offers another method by which teachers may wish to adapt their reading program to the needs of their children.

SUMMARY

The importance of adequately teaching the child how to read effectively cannot be emphasized enough. Throughout the child's school career his reading ability will influence his achievement level in all areas. Only mental ability itself will be a more important factor than reading ability. There is little, if anything, that the classroom teacher can do about innate mental ability, but there is a great deal that she can do toward helping the child be a better reader.

The need for using a variety of methods of teaching reading is already apparent to every experienced teacher. Critics of education like to claim that one method is being used to the exclusion of all others, where another method would be more effective. This is certainly not true in most instances, and the introduction of personalized reading instruction is not meant to be another attack upon education. The goal is, instead, to present a new method of teaching reading which will provide the teacher with another way to help children. Whether or not the teacher uses this particular method will depend a great deal upon conditions in her own community with which the author of this book could not be familiar. As another method though, it is important that teachers know of it as a possible way for instructing children in reading.

Personalized reading instruction is built on the concepts developed by Willard Olson of "seeking, pacing, and self-selection." It assumes that the child will want to read and will seek out ways of learning to read. By allowing him to select his own reading material, many of the disadvantages of the basal readers are overcome. The pacing, which the child establishes mostly on his own, will determine how fast he is able to progress. This is not entirely a self-determined type of thing, but is determined by the inherent limitations or capabilities which he has.

Personalized reading is essentially a means whereby children read from material which they have selected themselves. Once about every three days, the child comes to the teacher and she checks to see how he is progressing in his reading. If he is having difficulty in attacking certain words, or comprehending the material, the teacher then groups him with other children having the same type of difficulty and teaches them as a group. There is no three-group pattern followed day by day with regular progression through a basal reader. The child is presented the skills either at the time of the individual conference or, when there are more children who need it than just this one, at the follow-up period after the individual conference. The teacher knows which skills to present by following the check sheets provided in Chapters 7 and 8.

The typical personalized reading instruction period would last perhaps one hour and a half. The first ten or fifteen minutes would be spent with the entire group planning those group activities which would be needed (including such things as discussions on materials read, practice on certain reading skills, or silent reading on the part of the children). Approximately the next hour would be spent with the teacher seeing each child for about five minutes (this way taking about three days to see every child), during which time she checks the words which he has recorded as ones giving him difficulty, checks his comprehension of materials read, and his skills for that particular level. The rest of the class is either reading silently or working in the group activities which have been assigned at the first of the period. The remaining fifteen or twenty minutes in the hour and a half reading program are spent either in follow-up activities checking with each of the groups, or in working with certain groups on skills which they need. The groups are established by the teacher each day, with no group staying in existence for more than two or three days. A group is formed only for a specific purpose and is disbanded as soon as this purpose has been accomplished.

There are many problems connected with going into any kind of new program. One of the problems inherent to the personalized program is the difficulty in evaluating it. The basal program is built around the skill development plan as outlined for the basal text. In personalized reading, it is hoped that by use of the checklist of skills the child will do at least as well as children in the basal program. It is not the aim of the personalized program to carry him into higher grade level reading skills than the grade in which he actually is, but it is believed that through the process of self-selection the child will develop a greater appreciation for reading itself. Since the final goal of reading is actually enjoying and understanding what one reads, the personalized program appears to lend itself better toward the development of this goal than the basal reader approach.

The advantages of the personalized reading program are that it provides the child reading instruction in a natural situation, without having to resort to the unnatural reading situations found in the basal readers. The disadvantage is certainly that there is danger of no sequential skill development program when there is no teacher's manual to follow. The purpose of Chapters 7 and 8 is to discuss those skills which should be taught, and present them in such a way that a teacher could follow this skill development program.

Selecting materials for the personalized reading program is in itself a very great task. The teacher must become highly conversant with children's literature. The list of publishers in Chapter 6 should provide her with knowledge about how to obtain information about current books and resorting to such book lists as those published by the American Library Association should indicate which books are of an approved nature. It is not meant that she will buy no books except those on any list, but instead it means that the teacher is given a guide in helping her in selecting books when she is uncertain about them. The personalized program demands that the teacher be aware of how to determine reading level of materials, of vocabulary level, and of children's reading interests. The teacher in the basal program should also have these skills, although the teacher in the basal program without such skills would not be so noticeable as one attempting the personalized program would be.

In the personalized reading program, the teacher must be aware of the different reading levels. She needs to know how to determine the child's reading level in each of a variety of situations, and how to use reading achievement and reading diagnostic tests. Her ability to determine these levels will make her a better teacher of reading, whether in the basal or in the personalized program.

The absence of the teaching of reading skills in many so-called individualized reading programs sharply distinguishes them from the personalized program as described in this book. In the personalized program, there is a sequential development of reading skills. Each teacher is provided with checklists to go in each child's folder of the skills which he should learn at that level. By following these checklists, not necessarily in order but in general areas, the teacher is able to move the child from level to level without any gaps. Whether in the basal program or in the personalized program, these checklists should provide the teacher with material which can be placed in the child's folder clearly indicating which skills he has been presented, whether or not they have been learned, and where he needs to go from here.

The goal of personalized reading instruction is to help all children to learn to read better and to enjoy both the process and the results of reading. To the extent that the teacher using personalized reading instruction achieves these goals, she has been successful. When reading is more than just a school assignment, the reading program has been successful.

CONCLUSIONS

Personalized reading instruction is new. Because it is new, it faces many of the problems of any new program. It is not unlikely that it will suffer both from its proponents as well as from its opponents. Believing in it too much, its proponents will claim it is a panacea for all problems. Opposing it, others will claim that it accomplishes nothing. Its actual place is perhaps somewhere between these two extremes. Personalized reading will not cure all reading problems, but then neither will any other method. It is believed that personalized reading instruction will accomplish the goal of developing more appreciation for reading than other methods.

It would be a great mistake at this point to force personalized reading instruction into a careful word-by-word pattern which would rigidly describe the steps to be followed. Quite obviously, such a rigid step-by-step program would be easier to follow, but would be just as ineffective as any other rigid program which did not recognize that all children are different. If such a situation develops, the very claims against the basal reader approach will be directed justifiably against the personalized reading approach. Personalized reading instruction is not a rigid type program but is essentially a flexible type program including skill instruction which the teacher must adapt to her own particular situation. Because it is not held down by any graded vocabulary level or sequence of readers, it should offer the teacher a more flexible pattern to follow. It is not a laissez faire type of program, but it is developmental in the nature that it begins with each child at his level, and is sequential to the extent that skills are presented in a logical manner, progressing as a child learns one skill into a new skill which will help him read better at the next higher level.

It is important at this stage of development of personalized reading that people not memorize any rigid definition for personalized reading—nor should people be willing to follow the pattern exactly as someone else has set it. At this stage of its development, personalized reading should be considered an idea to be discussed. How it is implemented should be developed within each particular school situation. It is more important that we think about different methods of teaching reading than that we adopt any one method. The very interchange of ideas among teachers will result in the development of better methods of teaching reading.

Index